Nomad Trader

CAMERON E. WILD

Paperback Edition ISBN: 978-1-9997360-1-9

DEDICATION

To ~~the market Gods~~ Caroline

Cameron Swen

CONTENTS

1. THE FIRST WAVE OF GEN Y

Street Fighter II was my favourite arcade game growing up. I was obsessed with it. I even dreamed in SFII mode, sounds and all. Generally, you couldn't play alone for very long before someone challenged you. This was new in the video game world which had previously relied on high scores to determine the best players. Over the years I got better and eventually became the champion of the arcade. But after that no one wanted to challenge me, and that meant less playing time. So I started going to different arcades looking to hustle, not for money, just to stay on the machine and keep playing for as long as I could. Sometimes new versions of SFII were released with better graphics and faster gameplay. When the Turbo and Hyper versions came out it was like a whole new addiction was born. That's how I spent my weekends in the early 1990s.

During the week, I didn't go to the arcades. I just

hung out in the computer room after school with a bunch of kids messing around in DOS and GW-Basic. One day a kid said, *"Hey, that computer is on the Internet."* So we stood around and stared at it for a while, and finally, I sat down. The program on screen was Netscape Navigator which sounded like something from outer space. *"Type something in,"* the kid said.

"Ok, what?" I replied, and we all drew a blank. What could we possibly want to search for? Finally, someone said, *"Type in cars,"* so I did and a bunch of stuff came up on the screen. But what was displayed was boring, and there weren't any pictures, so I turned my hands over and shrugged my shoulders. *"What's the point?"* I said. *"This is stupid."* And that was the end of that.

Later that year a kid got his hands on a floppy disk, and everyone piled into the computer room to take a look. On it were two folders. The first was named XXX and contained a bunch of TIF files. One was a nude picture of Elle Macpherson, though since she'd never done a nude photo shoot before, it might have been one of the first ever fake nude celebrity pics. The second folder was named TTC and contained a text file called The Terrorist's Cookbook that showed us how to make bombs out of things we could steal from the school chemistry lab. The content was just incredible, but no one understood that it had come *from the Internet*. So we continued copying and circulating disks around school without ever realising we could have just found it online.

After high school I went to live at Emmanuel College at the University of Queensland. Again, we had our own computer room, and it wasn't long before I was introduced to Quake – the John Carmack blockbuster that was the first game ever to be considered electronic sport. In my second year of college, Emmanuel set up a local area network (LAN) with connections in everyone's room. That prompted a lot of us to buy our own PCs, and soon we had 20 to 30 guys battling it out each night. But though multiplayer Quake worked perfectly on our LAN, we couldn't play anyone out there on the Internet. Not only was the ISP speed too slow, but all our PCs had to pipe through just one gateway PC. As such, people still didn't care too much about the Internet.

But then we discovered this free thing called Hotmail. At first glance, Hotmail didn't seem to do much. I mean why would you bother emailing someone instead of just walking over and telling them? But what happened was that once you signed up you started getting all kinds of chain letters and other stuff. And even though most of it was junk, we felt compelled to log in every once in a while to check our messages. And that's really where the Internet started for a lot of people – web based email – with its strange allure of distribution lists, chain letters, pyramid schemes, scams, and spam.

To be sure, the Internet was a dodgy little world for a very long time. You had to be totally paranoid about the criminal aspect of it because it was totally their domain. Bad guys were lurking behind every link, no one ever used their real name for anything, and only an idiot would type their credit card number into a website. Hardly anyone studied Information Technology because it seemed like a waste of time that wouldn't get you a job. I know it sounds silly now but here's the thing. It wasn't just that phase of technological advance that I couldn't foresee. It was every single phase that has since occurred. Even to this day it utterly astounds me that no matter how much I have loved and lived technology, I have never been able to predict its course of evolution.

When we weren't playing Quake, we were drinking in the city and forever winding up at the Treasury Casino. Australia happened to be the most gambling addicted nation in the world, and I soon found myself part of a core group who started going during the day too. Otherwise, I studied a double degree in economics and finance since it was well known that such sensible degrees would lead to a good job.

Well, that turned out to be a bullshit sandwich with the first evidence coming when Goldman came to visit our campus. I didn't know anything about them, but after an hour of listening to their marketing pitch, I was hanging on their every word. And I'd bet that every single one of the 2000 students crammed into that lecture hall were too. But then, after a flawless presentation, something odd happened. Beaming with pride at a job well done, they proceeded to ask for questions from the audience.. My friend Gherkin piped up and asked, *"So how many jobs are you recruiting for?"* The speakers looked back and forth at each other trying to decide who should answer until, finally, one of them replied, *"Well.. umm.. for next year in Australia.. oh and New Zealand.. we will take on three graduates."*

"What?!" The room erupted in jeers and laughter as they were revealed as nothing but a marketing machine. We knew they were pitching at all the big universities across the country, with a total audience

that might have exceeded 30,000 students. And all that for a measly three jobs. *"Come on mate, let's go,"* I said to Gherkin.

"Yeah," he said. *"These guys are full of shit."*

We left in disappointment, but even so, we sent off our applications in hopes of being in the top one basis point of graduates in the country. Incredibly, a month later, Gherkin actually landed one of those jobs, and for the next 12 years he worked in various Goldman treasury departments around the world. As for me, I spent the next six months applying to every bank, broker and fund manager I could find. But somehow the thriving new concept of graduate recruitment just wasn't my thing, and though I sometimes made it to the second or third round interviews, I just couldn't nail down a job. Eventually it became clear that Australia simply had too many graduates and not enough jobs. So, with no other options in hand, a whole wave of us headed to London.

2. HSBC

When I arrived in mid-2001 my impressions were of an exciting city full of possibilities. But after a few months we realised there weren't any jobs in London either. The media was full of stories about how a new world order was upon us in which the Internet was revolutionising commerce and productivity and blah blah blah. I was getting tired of hearing that human beings were no longer needed to run the economy. Until all of a sudden *Boom!* they flipped and started complaining that technology had failed us. WTF? In actual fact, the media was just parroting what the stockmarket was doing. Up-up-up in the dot-com bubble and down-down-down in the crash now underway.

I found a job as a bartender in a pub near Embankment station. It was fun and great to get out of the house, but my salary of £4.17 per hour was hardly enough to pay for lunch and the tube home, let alone rent and living. And so, I burned through my savings and prayed for a miracle.

Three months later I found a job as junior desk assistant on the trading floor of HSBC Investment Bank. I couldn't believe my luck. I took the job and my salary rocketed up to £10 per hour. Alas, it wasn't long after joining that I learnt what a dark and dismal place the financial world had become. Every person on our trading floor, no matter how senior, was terrified of being fired, for it could happen at any moment. Stockmarkets were getting killed, and the fraud of equity research was unravelling with high profile lawsuits hitting the banks. But then the debate about whether research actually had any value was put on hold, when on September 11 the Twin Towers came down, markets were decimated, and the global economy froze in fear.

That was a great opportunity for companies to air their dirty laundry of scams that underpin the proper functioning of capitalism. But regular people might hardly have noticed, for the media focussed all their efforts on creating an endless stream of apocalyptic terrorism fear. It really was pathetic how western society was transformed into a bunch of scared shitless idiots fretting non-stop about being blown up by a suicide bomber.

It started with Enron, a stock on which 13 out of 18 analysts rated *Buy,* until the day it became the largest bankruptcy in world history. No one had a scooby-doo what was going on inside the company yet here were these charlatan analysts rating the stock as though they did. Just as Enron manipulated electricity prices by turning off power plants, equity analysts manipulated investors by pretending they understood how companies worked. Next it was WorldCom, who smashed Enron's record, and then on they came with Global Crossing, Adelphia, US Airways, Conseco, and Arthur Andersen – one of the biggest accounting firms in the world. And as they tumbled in a steady stream of corporate collapse, it did nothing but justify an ever lower stockmarket.

With so many people out of a job and the constant panic of terrorism, we soon entered the worst bear market for 30 years. Anyone still clinging to a job in the markets, particularly the stockmarket, were seen as revolting useless scum to be hurled overboard the sinking ships in the devastating wake of global recession.

As for me, I learnt that when the HR department took out the axe I had to duck and weave. As junior desk assistant, most of my job was really about keeping everyone happy, which happened to be impossible since no one was happy to begin with. So I branded myself as *that Aussie kid* who just wanted to help, and eventually I started taking breakfast orders for the greasy spoon across the street. Soon I was taking 25 orders per day, and to my amazement, I found that with a hearty breakfast in their stomachs, the attitudes of those around me started to improve. Trips to the post office, picking up dry cleaning, buying anniversary presents – nothing was too much for me as bottom rung shit-kicker.

Sometimes we had mass firing days where the HR robots – completely devoid of empathy – would terminate people's access pass to the building. The next day the turnstile would beep, flash red, and swallow their card. Then a security guard would say, *"Please sir, move to your left,"* before another guard would escort them straight back out into the street. *"You no longer work here,"* he'd explain. *"Please call your manager for more details."*

The first thing I did each morning was print, photocopy, and hand out thousands of pages of research to the stockbrokers and traders in my department. A lot of it went straight to the bin unread, and why not, it was almost always wrong. Ingrid, who sat behind me, never bothered to read it since though she was a broker, she was totally honest about having no interest in markets. Her real job was to look pretty, be cool, and entertain soft dollar clients. The way it worked was that HSBC had agreements with all the large UK pension funds, that in return for guaranteeing us a certain level of commission, we'd pay some of their bills for them. For example, we might pay their electricity bill or buy them a bunch of new computers. The rules about it were forever changing, but the point was that we knew in advance that certain clients would pay us certain levels of commission no matter how good or bad the service. As such, Ingrid would take care of them, which really meant taking them out for lunch whenever they pleased. She really was lovely though, and I wished our entire business model had been based on soft dollar agreements.

"If I were you I'd get out of this shitty business," she said to me one day in her posh Swedish accent.

"What do you mean? I've only been here for a year."

"No, not here at HSBC. I mean out of the whole brokerage business, especially the stockmarket."

I supposed she was right. The trading floor had shrunk from 600 people to 300, and I had no idea how much longer I'd survive. And even if I did, how was I ever going to get promoted? I was about to reply when suddenly we heard an announcement, and we looked around to see what was going on. Instead of regular phones, we had these ridiculous dealer-boards that were part of the must-have technology that had driven the now busted telco boom. There were so many buttons and dials on the thing that it took weeks to figure them out. One was to broadcast a message to your own department and another was to broadcast to the entire trading floor. Until then, I'd only heard it happen on 9/11.

"You have no new messages.. and.. one.. saved message," came the announcement. Someone was playing a voicemail message. *"Message received at.. two.. twenty.. seven.. am.."* Then we heard the unmistakeable voice of Sammy, one of the traders in my department, who hadn't shown up for work that day. From the morning's gossip, we'd learnt that he'd been out all night at Stringfellows – one of the city's premier strip clubs. If ever there was a stereotypical banker wanker it was Sammy.

"Oh shit man, this is serious!" The voice boomed over the trading floor. Then we heard arguing and a few things indeterminable. Then back into the phone came Sammy's pleading voice close and scared. *"Come on man. Get back here! My cards maxed out. I can't pay the bill and.. and.. the bouncer has me up against the wall and.."* Then we heard a thumping great crack as Sammy's mobile was smashed into the ground. We all laughed like crazy, and no one seemed to worry about

what might have happened to him. And then, not 20 minutes later, in came Sammy, shuffling along with his head down. When he was spotted people stood and the applause spread across the trading floor in a matter of moments. With that he stopped walking, lifted his head, and took a bow. That's when we noticed his black eye.

May 1st in London was a special day for all the unemployed people to shout about the evils of capitalism and cause a nuisance by marching through the city and disrupting traffic. It was customary that the procession of trouble makers would wind their way through the financial district and past our trading floor around lunchtime. Of course, it had to be Sammy who came up with a plan to show them what capitalism was really about.

Now known as *the photocopy-kid* he handed me a £50 note and told me to get busy. I started by colour photocopying it over and over until I had enough to cover one of those big A3 pieces of paper. Then I photocopied that twice and glued them together back-to-back. Then I double-sided photocopied that until I ran out of paper. But though the counterfeits looked pretty real, the texture just wasn't quite right. So I grabbed a bottle of window cleaner, and after a light coating, the sheets dried to a lovely crisp finish. Then I got some other assistants to help me use the guillotines to cut them out into individual banknotes. Finally, we dumped them all into these giant green recycling bins. It took us several hours, but we finished just in time for the procession of anti-capitalist protestors to reach their peak on the street below.

We opened up the windows and since our building at Thames Exchange was only three floors high, we could clearly hear the insults being hurled up at us. Sammy shouted back, *"Eh! Fook you! Get a job you fooking twat!"* Some of the protestors even carried signs that were directed squarely at us:

HSBC – GLOBAL LEADER IN TERRORIST FINANCING

Shouting went on for some time before one of the leaders took up a megaphone and addressed the crowd. *"Dis lot 'ere,"* he said pointing up at us, *"is one of the most appalling financial institutions in the world. Dey're criminals, dey is. Every last one ov 'em!"* Howling in anger, the crowd started throwing fruit and other things at us. In reply, Sammy shouted back, *"Oh you want some money huh? You want some of OUR money huh?!"* Then he gave us the signal, and we tipped our giant bins out the window, unleashing £350,000 into the fiery mob below. As I said the copies were pretty good, but there was something else working in our favour. You see for some reason £50 banknotes weren't very common. Even when you got out £400 from the ATM, it was rare to receive £50 notes. And I think what happened was the unemployed mob just weren't all that aware of what they were supposed to be like.

And so pandemonium erupted as the protestors first reached for the sky, then crawled around on their hands and knees, or else attacked each other to get their hands on the free cash. This continued for several minutes until eventually there was a collective realisation that the notes were fake. Of course, that only served to exacerbate their anger, while up on the trading floor we were rolling around in hysterics. Well, at least I can say there were one or two happy days during that shitty bear market.

When bonus season rolled around it was to our dismay that HSBC paid zero bonuses to the entire equities division. That had never happened in the history of the city, and I suppose it was a fitting example of just how bad the bear market was. Well, the next day the trading floor refused to operate in protest. Not me – I still had to get everyone breakfast and photocopy all the useless research – but the sales-traders and traders just sat there and did nothing. A rumour went around that for every day the trading floor ceased to operate the bank lost £5m. The stalemate continued for three days but then the HR robots embarked on a new round of mass firings, and those remaining got back to work.

The traders on the floor were a breed apart. And though I sometimes noted erratic behaviour, darting eyes, and fear, they typically possessed an air of invincibility about them. They were like the strike force, the defensive line, and the decision makers all rolled into one. They were the run-on team; everyone else was just there to support them.

Eventually my luck turned and I was offered a job as a junior stockbroker on the Canadian desk. My new boss, Roger, took me under his wing and things were really looking up for me. I enrolled in the Securities Institute course, and three months later I passed the exam and became a licensed broker. Roger, who was an excellent salesman, wanted me to follow in his footsteps though he soon acknowledged that I had more of a trader's temperament than a broker's. As such, he concentrated on teaching me about order flow and trading. We soon fell into a routine where he spent his days talking the talk with clients on the phone, and when he felt an order might eventuate, he'd snap his fingers to get me on the line. I'd pick up just in time to hear the client say something like, *"Ok Roger, please buy one hundred and fifty thousand Encana, careful discretion,"* and I'd write it down. Then, after we'd hung up, he'd swivel around to help me fill out an order ticket. Then I'd call the traders in Toronto and relay it to them. It wasn't long before I could (mostly) understand what the clients wanted and correctly express it to the Toronto traders.

One day Roger told me about a company called *Research in Motion* that was developing a product called a Blackberry. He said it was like a mobile phone, except you could also get your email on it. I thought about it for a moment and then told him what I thought was pretty obvious, *"Well I guess some people might want email on their phone, but most people won't want to be bothered by it all the time."*

"Hmm, yes, you might be right," he said. *"But we have an order here to buy a hundred thousand shares."*

"Ok, I'll let the traders know."

Over the next few weeks, we bought a lot more RIM for our clients. I really didn't understand all the fuss since the idea of having your work email on your person was kind of ridiculous, and anyway, what right did a company have to bother you outside of working hours? Indeed, back in my share-house, we'd always berate someone if they talked excessively about work. *"Leave your work at work man!"* Jez used to say.

Most of our clients got into RIM at around $14, but a few months later the stock had fallen to $9. That was when I got my first lesson in stop-losses. *"You got to know when to get out,"* said wise old Roger. *"You have to protect your capital above all else."* Well, he was only half right for it wasn't long after our clients exited their positions that the stock started up again. But instead of getting back in at higher prices, Roger feared another sell-off and recommended that clients wait and see. A year later the stock was up 100%. The next time I looked it was up 1000%.

Back in high school when I'd first seen that PC that was *on the Internet* I was just a kid and hadn't really thought it through. But this time I'd carefully considered a piece of revolutionary technology and yet simply could not recognise it as such. Roger had sought my advice because he was 'an old guy who didn't understand this stuff'. In fact, young or old, no one could ever predict the evolution of technology.

Each day at 1:30 pm we dialled into the morning meeting in Toronto. Alas, one day no one was there to connect our call. It was about half an hour later when one of the biotech analysts called from his mobile. *"You wouldn't believe it,"* he said, *"but they put chains around the doors and locked us all out."*

"Oh dear. You mean no one has spoken to you at all?" asked Roger.

"No, we're all just standing out here in the cold."

"Ok, well please keep us informed."

An hour later a conference call was set up. The global head of trading explained that HSBC was pulling out of the Canadian stockmarket, effective immediately. I later marvelled at how it coincided with the exact start of the great bull market in commodities in which Canadian stocks did so well.

For the rest of the day we waited patiently for direction from David, our local boss, but he never came. Days came and went, and still, we never heard from him. So we kept a low profile in our quiet little corner of the trading floor and just nodded and smiled at anyone who walked by. Meanwhile, we spent all our time searching the Internet for new jobs. It was about two weeks later when David happened to walk by, and I could literally see the realisation spread across his face. But he wasn't angry, just embarrassed that he'd forgotten about our little operation.

First, he took Roger into a meeting room and had a chat. Then Roger left, and I was invited in. *"Hi Damon. Well, obviously you know about the Canadian business being closed down."* It was clear that he'd been having a tough time. Stockmarkets were caught in a horrible choppy decline, and his traders weren't performing. I figured he didn't want to hear any complaints from me, so I said, *"Yes it's a real shame. But I want to say thanks for everything. I know you were involved in moving me over to the Canadian desk and it was a big opportunity for me even if it didn't work out."* He smiled and seemed happy to hear it and then leaned back as if to have a frank conversation. *"Look Damon, there's no future for you here. The bank is downsizing, and I don't see an end to it. But, you know, I always thought you were more of a trader or a sales-trader than a broker."*

"Yeah Roger tells me that all the time. That's why for the last month I've been relaying all the order flow between here and Toronto."

"Good. Well here's the thing. We've got a few people taking vacation at the same time, so we're a bit short-staffed. I'm not offering you a job, I just need someone to help me out for a few weeks. How would you like to trade the European markets? I'll set you up

on the retail desk, just small orders, but it will give you a feel for trading. See how you like it."

"That would be great," I said. I could barely contain my excitement.

I learnt an enormous amount on my first day of trading for HSBC. The job itself wasn't that hard if I simply did what I was supposed to do – answer the phone, buy or sell some stock, tell them the price.

"Ok, so I click here on the stock, and then I hit F4 to buy or F9 to sell," I said.

"Yep, that's pretty much it," my new boss Frank replied.

Though it sounded easy enough I must admit that the first time I faced the final dialog box asking, *"Are you sure?"* my heart skipped a beat, and I was scared to pull the trigger. But then I clicked "*Yes*" and in went my order to buy €200k worth of Unilever – the most amount of money that I'd ever spent in my life. Eventually, however, I stopped calculating the value of what I was buying or selling since it was a whole lot easier to think, *'Ok, I'm buying fifty thousand shares,'* instead of, *'Fifty thousand times 19.50 equals.. Oh my God.. It's almost a million Euros worth of stock!'*

After lunch Frank showed me how to make some extra money by taking risk. *"So Damon, it looks like you have most of the software sorted out."*

"Yeah, this GL app is pretty clunky, but I guess it does the job."

"Software is the bane of our existence pal. You just have to deal with it and move on. Ok so let me show you something." Just then the phone rang, some guy in Geneva. Frank took the call and I listened in.

"Hi Frank," the voice said.

"Hi mate. How are you?"

"Vodafone, sell a hundred k at market."

"Hold on.. ok done at 137."

"Thanks. Usual account. Bye."

After he'd hung up, Frank turned to me and said, *"Ok, did you see what I did there?"*

"Well, sort of, but I'm a bit confused. I know that k means thousand, so he wanted you to sell one hundred thousand shares. But I was watching, and you didn't actually sell anything at all."

"Exactly. You see we'll give him the price of 137p. That's done. But as you say, I didn't actually sell any yet. Now if I wait ten minutes and sell it at a higher price then we get to keep the difference. Otherwise, if the price goes down and we sell it lower, then we'll lose the difference. Got it?"

"Yeah, I get it."

"Right, just so you understand, we are not screwing the client here. 137p was a good price. It was the best bid in the market at the time, and he could see that, so he's happy. But now I'm running risk on the position, and any profit we make comes back as a year-end bonus."

"Sounds good."

An hour later things got very busy. The phones were ringing non-stop, and I was left to fend for myself. This was in late 2002 and Western markets were acting all crazy-like. Not a day went by that the media didn't assure us, *"You're all gonna die because of the evil terrorists!"* or, *"Accounting is just a scam! You can't trust anything these companies say!"*

I picked up the phone and took an order from a screaming client to sell Roche Pharmaceuticals. I looked up and down the screen, but I couldn't find the stock. I tried to ask Frank for help, but he was busy on a call. *"Did you get that? Have you sold the stock yet? What's going on?!"* the client demanded.

"Oh yes, just a second sorry." Finally, I found Roche listed under Switzerland, not Germany as I'd thought. *"Ok sir, you sold twenty thousand Roche at 104.50,"* I blurted out while staring at the best bid on Virt-X.

"104.50 for the whole size?"

"Yes, sir."

"Ok, done."

Actually, I hadn't sold it yet and proceeded to offer the stock on the market at 104.60. But as soon as I did the market collapsed. So I grabbed Frank by the arm and pointed at my screen. Eventually, he got off the phone and said, *"What's up mate?"*

"I'm long twenty thousand Roche at 104.50, it's now trading 102.50."

"Oh for fuck's sake Damon. What happened?"

"I don't know. It just collapsed."

"Did you check the news?"

"No, how do I do that?"

He right-clicked the stock and brought up a Marketwatch newswire, and there, right at the top of the news panel, was the offending headline:

14:27 HORMONE REPLACEMENT THERAPY INCREASES RISK OF CANCER – New Study

12:14 MERRILL'S MOVES TO OVERWEIGHT FOLLOWS THE HERD – European Pharma

10:14 ANALYSTS ARE IDIOTS – Poll Results

10:04 EU BACKBITING COULD PUT TRADE DEAL AT RISK – CSSH

09:55 SWITZERLAND POISED FOR GROWTH REFRACTION – SNB

"Oh shit!" he said. "Roche is one of the biggest makers of HRT drugs in the world! Ok, dump that stock right now. Market order."

"*Ok,*" I said and hit the bid and three more below it in one click. Then we calculated the loss. It was almost £20,000. "*Look don't worry about it man,*" Frank said. "*Perhaps you should take a break.*"

I nodded, got up from the desk, and wandered around the trading floor in a daze. I couldn't believe that I'd just lost the equivalent of my annual salary in less than 30 seconds. And on my first ever risk trade. '*This is not a fucking video game!*' I scolded myself.

Eventually, I put on a brave face and returned to the desk, but I felt sick and didn't take risk again. Frank explained that a screaming client was often trying to get you to take risk at exactly the wrong time. "*Is it done yet? Is it done yet?!*" they'd shout hoping that you'd cave and say, "*Ok fine, yes, yes, it's done,*" even when it wasn't. So I learnt to tolerate their aggression and make them wait until I'd actually filled their orders before telling them the price.

The people I worked with were really great. They were true speculators who might just as well have taken that Roche trade the same way I did. Two weeks later I thanked everyone and said goodbye. Then I went to see David in his office. He said I'd done a good job, thanked me for helping out, and wished me luck in the future. I wondered if Frank had told him about the Roche trade. I wondered if I'd blown my one chance of being a trader.

I spent the next three months looking for a job, but the city was too scared of terrorists to hire anyone. Then I gave Roger a call, who was himself still out of work, but surprisingly, I found him quite upbeat. *"Look Damon, every couple of years there's some sort of crisis. But then something will happen and all of a sudden the economy will be booming and there'll be jobs everywhere."*

With all five of us at home now unemployed, we started playing monster sessions of a board game called *Risk*. The purpose was to take over the world by pitting your armies against one another with battle success determined by rolling dice. But the math was chaotic and you'd often see armies march onto incredible winning streaks against larger more powerful armies.

Well, after a few weeks Risk became very serious in our house and tempers started to fray. A loss could disgrace a person for days, and if someone double-crossed a supposed ally, the loser would erupt in fury at the deception. In what turned out to be our last game ever I gave Euan free access to the Ukrainian border even though I'd promised Jez I wouldn't. He didn't speak to me for a week after that. Plus, on the very next move, I was destroyed by Harvey's army who went on to take the entire continent. With only two players left in the game tensions were running high, and Euan was confident of a win. An attack was launched, and the dice started rolling. But just as it became apparent who the winner would be, Harvey picked up the board and threw it against the wall, sending cards and cavalry all over the living room. He'd ruined a five-hour game that was two minutes from completion. With that, Euan flew into a rage screaming, *"Typical Aussie! Such a sore loser!! Hey, I think it's time you ran into your room and had a good cry wank!"*

"*Well at least Australia's on the map, you bloody sheep rooter!*" Harvey replied.

The truth was that we loved our little house, but we were nearing the limits of unemployed despondency. But then, just a few weeks later in March 2003, America bombed Iraq. The media explained that it was fantastic news and they named it *Iraq War II* as though it were a sequel to a Hollywood movie. Implicit in the message was that it was payback for 9/11 and terrorism, though it wasn't long before people realised that Iraq had nothing to do with either. So we went along to the *Stop The War* protest in Hyde Park and it turned out to be the largest in London's history. No wonder why – half the city was unemployed.

A week later I was playing Frisbee in the garden with Jez when my phone rang. It was someone from Amrobas Bank asking if I could come in for an interview. Now that the war in Iraq had been declared *over and won* London surged into a frenzy of hiring and corporate deals and a month later everyone in the house had a shiny new job.

3. AMROBAS BANK

My eyes widened as I was ushered onto the Amrobas trading floor for the first time. All over the place were TVs and multi-screen grids, double decker Bloombergs and dealer-boards. Standing at a podium was a line of analysts and strategists presenting live to the floor, their voices straining over the ever-louder traders and sales-traders throwing risk at each other like verbal hot potatoes. The chaos reflected the markets and the markets reflected our chaotic world of economics, earnings, politics, wars, and of course, buying and selling. It was an altogether different experience to the ailing giant of HSBC.

At one end of the floor was the back and middle office. They were a long way from the action, and I never went down their end. Next was the IT department, the research department, the equity derivatives department (EQD), the equity sales-trading department (where I sat), and finally, the trading department. My role was unique in that I worked for both EQD and equity sales-trading at the same time. Indeed, I was the link between the two worlds and had to keep them each informed of what the other was up to.

Tanner, my EQD boss, had called the night before to explain that on my first day we'd be launching a new deal. *"EMI Music,"* he said. *"Three hundred million dollar convertible bond. This is inside information so keep it quiet."* I had felt so excited at the prospect, but as I sat down at my desk for the first time, I realised I was way out of my league.

"102 bid for 20. What's the axe?! Chris – update – what's the axe!"

"Just a second. Who is it?"

"Highbridge. They need it now!"

"Ok done 20 at 102, leaves me 2 at 3."

This was known as the grey market – a 10-minute period following the allocation of a new convertible bond issue when clients bought and sold excess positions to get what they really wanted, not just what they asked for. It was pretty intense, and I honestly didn't understand what they were talking about. Indeed, despite my experience at HSBC, it took me months to become proficient in the language of trading. That is, to utilise the semantic and perspective idiosyncrasies to convey positions and needs in a concise and unambiguous manner at high speed. And until that day came, I got burned many times.

For the first few hours neither of my bosses came over to say hello. Instead, I had a stream of IT people help set up my systems and software. They gave me one mouse to control four screens and another to control two more. It was the coolest technology I'd ever seen, and I couldn't help thinking, *'Imagine playing Quake with this setup!'*

Finally, Tanner came over to have a chat. I'd learnt during the interviews that he'd been a Blackhawk pilot in the first Iraq War, and I must say, his style was about as military as they come. For him it was all about the battle, though nowadays, the battle was the money.

"Listen up Damon," he said. *"So long as you can maintain the right attitude this job will be the most challenging and rewarding thing you've ever been a part of. I hired you for two reasons: First, because you love technology, and I can tell you you're gonna find more of it in here than you ever dreamed of. And second, because of your Army background. You should view this as warfare because a lot of guys will try to screw you over. Not just the clients – I mean, of course they will – but our own traders too. So just be careful and don't get screwed by anyone."* He paused for a moment and then went on. *"Four hundred thousand Euros. That's how much it's costing me to keep your ass in that seat. So I expect results. I'm giving you my best clients, all of them, so don't screw it up. Got it!"*

"Yes sir," I said promptly. I knew that writing TSS Army Cadet School on my CV had been one of the key factors in getting the job. I later learnt that Tanner had trouble dealing with non-military people without screaming or abusing them. Indeed, he'd been sued twice by former employees of the bank.

For the next half-hour he talked enthusiastically about the hedge funds I'd be trading for in the world of convertible bond arbitrage (CBArb) – Highbridge, UBS O'Connor, Tribeca, KBC AIM and Harvard Endowment

Fund. Then he handed me a raggedy old pile of photocopies. *"First thing's first,"* he said. *"You need to understand what our clients are doing. Study this, take it home tonight, but bring it back to me first thing in the morning. And don't make any copies of it, you hear!"* He glared at me like death. I'd have sooner swallowed broken glass than defy him.

After he'd gone, I set about carefully studying the document. It was written like a thesis, but it bore no university emblem or author. It was the kind of thing you could never have found on the Internet. When I came to the section describing the mechanics of CBArb I found it so compelling that I thought, *'This is the smartest thing I've ever read. If you trade like this, you couldn't possibly lose.'* It also seemed like the state of the world was just perfect for the strategy to make money. That's because running CBArb was said to be the equivalent of betting on fear, which seemed like the smart thing to do in a world so gripped by terrorism propaganda.

"Where is Saddam Hussein hiding?" the neurotic media screamed at us repeatedly.

"He's in an underground bunker plotting to kill us!" they assured.

To put the strategy into practice our clients bought convertible bonds and shorted the company's stock against them. Together that package was known to be *long volatility* and it worked like this. If the price of the company's stock went up they made money on the convertible bond since it contained an embedded call option. However, they also lost some money because they were short the stock. But here's the thing – the mathematics of it worked out such that they made more money on the convertible bond than they lost on the short stock. And it also worked in reverse – if the stock price went down they made more profit from the short stock than they lost on the convertible bond. Try as I might, I couldn't argue with the proofs I held before me. All that was needed was for financial markets to be volatile. Then they could gain the sure profits contained in every fluctuation.

Typically, a client would send me a Bloomberg message instructing me to buy or sell some stock. I'd execute it as fast as possible then reply back to them with the price it was done at. So I spent my days buying stocks if they went down and shorting stocks if they went up. The lower they went, the more I'd buy. The higher they went, the more I'd short. I also traded currency since around half my orders related to *quanto* convertible bonds which was when the currency of the bond was different to the currency of the stock. That meant I had to execute a currency trade along with each stock trade in order to hedge the FX exposure.

Well one day, a few weeks into the job, I found myself in a sticky situation. A real scumbag client called Seth phoned up and started quizzing me about the new convertible bonds we were launching that day in Swiss Re. Then he sort of hesitated as though he was unsure of something. Finally, he asked, "*Ok, can you trade Swiss Re stock?*"

"*Yes, of course,*" I replied. "*Why not?*"

"*Oh, I thought you'd be restricted since you're leading the deal.*"

"*No, I'm not restricted. I can trade whatever you want me to.*"

"*Ok then. Go ahead and short fifty thousand shares*

around these levels."

"Ok will do," I said and hung up. It took about five minutes to work it on the market, and when it was finished I sent Seth a Bloomberg message to confirm his fill. But three hours later he replied, *"What? Not for me."* I immediately called and said, *"Yes, this is your fill."* He replied, *"What fill?"* and I said, *"What are you talking about? You told me to short fifty thousand Swiss Re!"* and he replied, *"No, you said you were restricted in the stock. Oh look, I have to go. Bye,"* and hung up.

I couldn't believe it. I'd been very clear that I wasn't restricted and was certain he'd passed me the order. Then I looked at the chart. Swiss Re was trading way higher which meant he was facing a big intraday loss on the trade. Clearly, that was why he was trying to weasel out of it. I was too scared to tell Tanner what happened, so I explained it all to Andy who sat on my left.

"Oh, he DK'd you huh," he said.

"DK? What is DK?"

"DK means 'Don't Know'. As in, he's saying he 'don't know' the trade."

"Yeah but it's bullshit. He gave me the order."

"Oh, I'm sure he did. But that's the shitty thing about DK'ing someone. It's your word against theirs."

"Not these days. We got tapes. I'll just play it back."

"Sure, you could do that," Andy said. *"But it will take you an hour to go upstairs and talk to compliance and then find the right file and then sit down and verify it and then come back to the trading floor and then tell the client you have the evidence and then maybe he'll take it. But do you really have time to do that on deal*

day? And if you do force him to take it, do you think you'll ever get another order from him? And do you think he won't go and bad mouth you to the rest of the buy-side?"

Eventually, I summoned up the courage and went and told Tanner what happened. He glared at me and then shouted, *"Damn it, Damon! What are you doing over there? Do your job! Get on the phone and make him take it!"* He shouted so loud that everyone paused for a moment and everyone stared at me. That was the worst thing about the trading floor – if you made a mistake everyone knew about it.

"Ok, I'll call him again," I said and went back to my desk. But then a weird thing happened – I started to doubt myself. 'Wait,' I thought. 'Did he even give me an order to sell fifty thousand shares? Or did he pull it? Maybe we were just talking about it but he never actually said to go ahead. Maybe this is my mistake. Oh, shit..' I argued with myself for about two minutes, but then I put the doubts aside and picked up the phone and dialled. *"Hey, what the fuck Seth! Is everything okay with that trade or not?"* He replied immediately, *"Oh yeah. Everything's cool. No problem man. I'll take it."*

I never traded with Seth again, but I learnt my lesson real good. That moment of doubt where I wasn't sure if it was my mistake or not was the key. If I'd been of weaker character or had a lapse in memory, he would have gotten away with it. And that's really the essence of the concept known as *taking an option* on someone. You see there were two sides to the financial markets industry. The *sell-side* were the brokerage firms that were mostly owned by investment banks. So firms like Lehman Brothers, Amrobas, Goldman, Bear Stearns, Morgan Stanley and Deutsche Bank, were all sell-side firms. The clients of the sell-side were called the *buy-side*. It comprised of hedge funds, pension funds, and mutual funds. The relationship existed because to trade something the buy-side always had to send their orders through a sell-side firm.

What you wound up with were guys like Seth on the buy-side who actually sought out young guys on the sell-side in the hope that they'd screw something up so they could exploit it for profit. For example, let's say Seth told me to sell 50k shares of Swiss Re, but I made a mistake and thought he said 15k. So I sell 15k and then send him a message (called a fill) to that effect. When he sees that I only sold 15k he ought to tell me about the mistake, whereupon I'd make it right by selling another 35k. But if he waits and does nothing for an hour, one of two things can happen – the stock could go up, in which case he wouldn't mention the error, and just sell an additional 35k shares at the new higher price (Seth wins); or the stock could go down, in which case he'd call up in an angry tone and say, *"Hey, what's this fifteen thousand share fill you sent me? I told you to sell fifty thousand, you idiot!"* The sales-trader then has no choice but to agree that he made a mistake and fill Seth for the entire 50k at the original higher price (Seth wins again). I'm not exaggerating when I say I met buy-side traders who made their entire living out of screwing over young sell-side guys in that way.

The Swiss Re convertible bonds we launched made a lot of money for us and so too did the eight other deals we launched that year. What surprised me was just how consistently we could screw over the corporates whose bonds we sold. What I mean is we'd sell them too cheap and give our best clients the bulk of the allocation. In turn, they'd immediately sell half of them for a higher price in the grey market to a desperate small client who got no allocation from us. I can tell you that those shenanigans amounted to a meaningful chunk of the annual performance of the *best* clients. Which is to say that being the best had little to do with being the smartest or the hardest working. It's not what you know, it's who you know.

4. SALES

By now the Internet had evolved substantially, though it still lacked in the trust department. Bloomberg, on the other hand, was like an entire other Internet, and having a login was like having the keys to a secret world of trustworthy information that regular people weren't allowed to see. Yet, with all that information at my disposal, I had to make a choice about what to use it for. Did I want to be a sales-trader or a trader? That is, did I want to talk other people into trading so I could make commission, or did I want to predict the market to make trading profits.

Andy was the best salesman I ever met. Unlike a broker, whose job it was to talk people into long-term trades, Andy was a master at talking clients into short-term trading. In fact, though we were both sales-traders, whose role was to facilitate trading between the client on the phone and the trader sitting nearby, our styles could not have been more different. *"Look!"*

he said to me one day. *"You need to get on the phone more. You seem to just sit there and wait for the orders to come to you."*

"Yes," I said. *"That's exactly what I do. My order flow doesn't come from telling stories. If the market moves up or down by a certain percentage my client's CBArb strategy will generate orders that need to be filled."*

"Ok, but you could make ten times the commission if put some effort into generating trade ideas."

"But that's my point, Andy. My clients aren't interested in that stuff. They only want to stick to their CBArb strategy, and that's it."

"Bullshit. I bet every one of your clients would put on a trade outside their immediate mandate. Everyone's a sucker for market action."

"Ok, but what if my idea doesn't work. I could lose all their CBArb flow just because of one stupid idea that lost them money."

"I doubt it. Just remember that people have terrible memories. You can be wrong seventy percent of the time, and yet some clients would still think you're really good at predicting the market simply because they like your personality. How else do you think weather forecasters keep their jobs? Selling is everything. Always Be Selling!"

A few hours later I came up with what I thought was a neat little plan. It was 1:15 pm, and in 15 minutes the US Non-Farm Payroll Report (NFPR) was due for release. The headline number of new jobs created each month was the most watched economic figure in the world. My plan was to talk a client into buying a Swiss stock called Adecco, then the largest recruitment firm in the world, if the NFPR figure came out higher than expected.

"Ok, but how are you going to convince a client that you know the figure will beat the estimate? It's just as likely to disappoint," Andy countered.

"I'm not going to. I'm gonna get the client to agree that if it's a good number, he should buy the stock."

"So you think you can be faster than everyone else at buying it in the split second after the figure comes out?"

"Yeah, why not?"

"Come on Damon, it's not a computer game. You can't just win money by clicking the mouse faster than other people."

"Well, that's the best I can come up with Andy. I'm just no good at making up bullshit stories."

"See that's your problem. You have to believe it's not bullshit and that you're really adding value. Talk to me about what's going on today."

"What do you mean?"

"I mean from all the crap you read what do you think is going on in the financial world."

I recounted the major news stories, but the boredom in my voice was apparent. *"Good, ok, but how can we spin that?"* I shrugged my shoulders and drew a blank. *"Well, what trading are we doing on the desk in the stocks that you mentioned?"*

"Jimmy's a seller of four million Arcelor. Nick's buying some Infineon and STM. Karl's still a buyer of Munich Re from yesterday."

"Ok yes, but what name really stands out. What stock do we have a lot of flow in that also has news out today?"

"Arcelor. We're selling lots of Arcelor."

"Good, so we need to find buyers to take the other side, right? What's the news about Arcelor?"

"Oh it's earnings.. bad earnings out today.. actually they're not that bad. I'd say it's a mixed bag."

"Wrong, it's always a mixed bag. No matter how good or bad the headline numbers are you can always find something to spin in your direction. Plus, you know they just make that shit up so it really doesn't matter anyway. My advice is to stop spending so much time reading stories made up by other people, and instead, start making up your own stories. Ideally, you want the client to say, 'Oh that's interesting. I haven't heard that from anyone else.' Then they'll give you the order instead of some other guy regurgitating the same shit as everyone else. Anyway, we're a seller, so we need to make up a story about why someone needs to buy the stock. So get to work."

An hour later Andy had three compelling reasons why someone just had to buy the stock *right now!* while I only had one lame idea about wind turbines that no one would ever believe. Of course, we went with Andy's idea. He typed out a Bloomberg (they were never more than three lines long) and sent it out to his client base. Then, probably 30 seconds later, his phone rang. He pulled the lever on his chair to lower it all the way down. Then he squeezed himself under his desk to have a private conversation with his client. Even me, his protégé, wasn't privy to the strong-arm techniques he used to force them to pull the trigger. Suddenly he jumped up, turned around to face the traders and yelled, *"Arcelor! Where can I buy a million shares?!"*

"Touch!" replied Steve, the steel trader.

The word *touch* meant Steve had filled the full million share order at the market's best offer price. For the client that was of considerable value because if they tried to buy that sort of size on the stock exchange they'd wind up pushing the price and paying a lot more for it. Then Andy stuck his head back under his desk and continued mumbling into his phone. Then he stood again and said, *"Reload. Where can I buy another million Arcelor?"*

"Touch! Hey, stop jerking me around Andy. Just give me the full size!" said Steve but Andy ignored him and kept mumbling into his headset. Finally, he replied, *"Ok that's me done. Thanks matey."*

A moment later his phone rang again, and Andy repeated the process. *"Arcelor, where can I buy two million shares? New client!"*

"Touch," said Steve hesitantly.

Andy worked it so that the total size of his client's orders exceeded the size of Steve's original sell order. That meant Steve's book was now short and he had to turn and start buying in the market to get flat. But despite buying everything in sight, he could never keep up. In essence, whichever of Andy's clients got in first would make an easy profit, while Steve would struggle just to break even. Andy did this to all our traders but not quite often enough that they'd refuse to deal. Plus, he had such charisma that he could always talk them into stepping up to the plate and taking one for the team.

"What are you saying down there under your desk?" I asked.

"Remember, if you're ever struggling to come up with something creative, you can always fall back on

merger rumours. Nothing scares the shit out of a client more than missing out on a hot merger rally. But anyway, it doesn't really matter what you tell them. If I can convince enough clients to trade, and therefore push enough volume to move the market, then that'll be all the confirmation they need."

He went on to explain that the best salesmen did anything and everything to gain their client's trust and affection. For instance, years earlier Andy had learnt to play croquet and then organised to accidentally run into one of his big clients at the Roehampton Croquet Club. Thereafter they became genuinely close friends. "For the rest of my life I'm going to get a lot of orders from him, and he knows that our friendship is more important than whether my ideas make money," he explained.

"So you like croquet?" I asked.

"You must be joking. Only a halfwit with more pence than sense would engage in such an imbecilic waste of time. I do it for the business, period."

A few hours later he grabbed me by the arm excitedly. "Look here," he said. He had a browser open with porsche.com in one tab and autotrader.com in another. "Any moment now Porsche is gonna unveil their new car design. No one's supposed to know what it looks like, but there's a rumour going around that it's as ugly as a bus."

The rumour turned out to be true for at first glance, at least, the Porsche Cayenne was a shocker. Andy was quick to send out the Bloomberg message he'd prepared earlier saying, "Oh my God Porsche! What are you thinking?!" with two links – the first to porsche.com showing the images, and the second to autotrader.com where you generally went to buy second-hand cars. More recently, however, autotrader.com had become the go-to place for brand new cars in high demand. So if you'd got in early and managed to secure one of these hot models straight from the dealer, you could usually sell it on autotrader.com for an immediate profit. But on this occasion if you'd pre-booked a new Cayenne you were in for a nasty surprise. Up on autotrader.com went the offers. At first, they were roughly around the listed price, but then they fell until brand new Cayenne's were offered for €10k less than the listed price. That was when Andy received a barrage of sell orders from his event-driven hedge fund clients who promptly knocked the stock down 6%.

"See Damon," Andy said. *"It's not all bullshit. I added real value for these guys today. You just got to use your imagination."*

Though most of my clients were based out of the US, I had a few in London whom I was obliged to take out from time to time. One day Tanner explained that my expense account wasn't going to expense itself and that I should, *"Damn well use it soldier!"* Some clients had no interest in meeting me at all. It was clear that they only passed me stock orders (and therefore paid us commission) so that Tanner would give them a larger allocation in the next convertible bond we launched. On the other hand, KBC AIM was relatively new in the world of CBArb, and with €5bn under management, had become one of the biggest hedge funds in Europe. The team was mostly made up of young guys, and I seemed to get along with them pretty well. So eventually, I asked if they wanted to meet up. *"Hey Mike, let's go out for dinner tomorrow night. I owe you for all the nice orders you've been giving me."*

"Sure, ok," he said. *"What do you want to eat?"*

"I don't know, you're the client, and I'm paying, so you decide. But if it were up to me I'd say steak."

"Really? Steak?

"Yeah man, I'm from Australia. We eat steak for breakfast."

"Fine. We'll go to Gaucho Grill then. There's one near Liverpool Street. Actually, why don't you swing by the office first and I'll show you around. Be here at 6:30pm."

"Ok. See you tomorrow."

Mike was standing outside when I arrived and after a quick chat to make sure I was worthy he took me upstairs. What shocked me was how small the operation was. I mean these guys were running so much money and all they needed was three rows of desks and about 12 staff. It was such an incredible concentration of capital in the hands of so few, and I started to wonder what it all meant. Was it dangerous? I never got the chance to meet their legendary boss who spent the whole time staring at his screens and mumbling into his headset. But I sure heard all about him during the dinner that followed.

We jumped in a cab and got out again at a bar next to Gaucho where we downed a few pints. There were four of us in total – Mike and Tony, the clients, and Ryan and I, the sales-traders. At the restaurant, Mike and Tony ordered lobster salads, two bottles of red, and four KBC Specials. But upon hearing it, the waiter replied apologetically, *"I'm sorry sir, we do not have the KBC Special today."*

"Ok, what can you do?" asked Mike.

"We can do 55 ounces, sir, about 1.5kg."

"Yes, that will be fine."

"Four?"

"Four."

I sat there for a moment and then, for reasons unknown, I got mixed up between thoughts and speech. So, accidentally, I said out loud, *"You're ordering six kilos of steak for the table."*

"Well done Damon," said Tony. *"I'm glad you can add."*

"Actually, I used this other thing," I replied. *"It's called multiplication. You probably haven't heard of it."*

"Yeah because brokers are so much smarter than hedge fund traders."

"You know," Ryan interjected, *"Damon really hates being called a broker."*

"That's right," I confirmed. *"I'll have you know I'm not a broker. I'm a sales-trader."*

"Yeah because sales-traders are so much smarter than brokers."

"Anyway," I said changing the subject, *"so this is the KBC Special."*

"It is," said Mike, *"though it's usually a 2kg steak."*

"And how often do you eat these things?"

"Probably a few times per week," he said proudly.

"Well no wonder you're so fat then," I said before I could stop myself. Insulting the client wasn't in the game plan, and I thought of how disappointed Andy would be if I messed it all up. There was a moment's pause, but then everyone started laughing. Then Tony said, *"That's a low blow pal. Mike's very self-conscious*

about his weight."

"*Mmm,*" said Mike, "*let's just wait and see if the young broker can finish his dinner.*"

When the steaks arrived I was already pretty full from the beers and starters. But as I devoured that first cut, from the exquisite cylinder of eye fillet sitting on my plate, it was like eating the food of the gods, and I was the god of eating. Unfortunately, though I was glad to have started from the thicker end, I hit a wall about half way along and found that I wasn't really in the conversation anymore. "*Earth to Damon,*" someone said.

"*Huh,*" I said looking up in a daze, my forehead covered in sweat, and mouth in bloody juices.

"*You know, if you can't eat the KBC Special then we can't give you any more stock orders.*"

"*Sure,*" I said sitting back to take a break. "*But in that case, you might find yourself getting zeroed in the next deal.*"

"*Yeah right, keep dreaming. We're your best client.*"

"*You think so? Or maybe you'll wind up paying 102 in the grey with all the other chumps.*"

"*Let's cross that bridge when we come to it,*" said Tony. "*For now, I'd like to know why you've stopped eating? Is there something wrong with the food?*"

"*No,*" I said. "*I'm just having a break is all.*"

"*No. No break,*" said Mike. "*We don't take breaks. In fact, young broker, you're way behind.*"

It was true. The other guys were about two-thirds done, but I was only at 55%. So I picked up the pace and by 80% it was anyone's race. But then the clients pulled ahead and finished up one and two. Ten minutes later a food coma engulfed the lot of us, and we called it a night.

I felt fine, no different to any other drunken night out, but as the tube approached Notting Hill station, I suddenly had to do a shit real bad. So I waddled out of the station and headed into Mooks Bar where I waited in line for my turn to use the only toilet. Finally, I got inside and let rip the biggest baddest shit I ever did in my life. Damn, it felt good. Then I took two swipes, stood, and turned to flush. But what I saw in the bowl wasn't shit. It was blood.

My first thought, being in such a drunken state and not feeling sick, bad, or sore, was that it wasn't my blood, it was the cow's blood. And so I went home and didn't worry about it. Indeed, the next day at work I felt fantastic. I was screaming out orders and kicking ass all over the shop. I possessed an energy like never before, and it continued well into the following day. So enlivened was I that Andy asked what was up. I explained what I'd since discovered, that steak in high doses, with all that blood and haemoglobin, can push a person into an energy super-state. *"Oh yes,"* he said, *"I heard about that. The ancient Greeks used to eat enormous amounts of red meat before the Olympic Games. Apparently, it made them perform better."*

A few weeks later I was out with Jimbo and his girlfriend, Quack, who was a doctor. I told her proudly about how I'd eaten a 55-ounce steak, and perhaps a little less proudly, of how I'd shat blood. She looked at me in horror. *"That wasn't the cow's blood you idiot – that was your blood! You stretched your stomach lining so badly that you probably came close to tearing it. And do you know what would have happened if you'd torn it? You'd have been dead. Yep, dead. Your stomach acid would have gone into your bloodstream and you would've died in two minutes flat."*

"Oh shit," I said feeling pretty dumb about it.

"You mean no shit!" she replied. *"Look, just promise me you'll go and get a colonoscopy. And don't ever do that again."*

5. TRADING

My friend Sacha took care of filling my currency orders, and since he sat a long way from me, I preferred to walk over to his desk instead of yelling at him across the floor. One day his phone rang just as I got there and since he looked busy, I wrote out my order on a piece of paper and left it in front of him: BUY 7MM EURUSD. The convention we used was that in the currency and bond markets "MM" meant million, while in the stockmarket little "m" meant million. But though I thought my order couldn't have been any clearer I was to learn that a 7 in Australia looks exactly like a 1 in Switzerland, where Sacha came from. So he only bought 1MM EURUSD, and neither of us knew about it until two days later when the middle office gave me a call. Immediately, I went over to talk to Sacha.

"No Damon, no. Look I keep ze ticket see. Zhis is what you tell me before," he said pointing to the scrap of paper I'd left him.

"Yes, exactly!" I said. *"It says to buy seven million."*

"No, Zhat is a one!"

"How can that be a one? It's clearly a seven!"

"No, no, cannot be. Seven has ze line like zhis." With that, he drew a horizontal line through the middle of my seven.

Well, it didn't really matter because on that occasion we dodged a bullet. EURUSD had fallen in the meantime so when Sacha bought the additional 6MM he made a tidy profit on the difference. Still to this day I can't help but cross my 7's every time. Better safe than sorry.

Later, while I was waiting for another fill, I looked down at his desk and saw a scatterplot on a piece of paper. *"Hey Sacha,"* I said, *"What's that?"*

"Oh, zhis is ze client stop loss orders."

"Ok, but why have you drawn them out like that on paper?"

"Ah Damon, you know I am ze very old trader from Basel. Zhis is ze way we have always done it, and now I am still doing ze same."

"Oh, ok," I said slowly.

"Well, let me show you how is ze currency market working. You see ze clients zhey like to give me ze big orders away from ze market. You know, for stop ze loss. Zen zhis clients, zhey is happy because zhey know zhey can only lose zhis much money when zhey is wrong and ze market is move against zem. So zhey buy here, and zhey give me anozher order to sell here," he said pointing to different levels on his hand-drawn chart.

"Ok so why are there so many stop loss orders

down here at this level?" I asked.

"Exactly!" he said. *"Zhere is no reason why. It is just coincidence. Every day ze clients put out ze stop loss orders, and I draw zem on ze paper. Sometimes zhey are all over ze page. Sometimes zhey are all togezher in ze, ze.."*

"Cluster?" I offered.

"Yes, yes, ze cluster like zhis. Oh, suppose ze analyst say somezhing, and it make all ze client put ze orders in ze same place. I don't know why and I don't care. Tiz just anozher day."

"So what now?" I asked.

"Now we wait for ze right moment, and we take ze market down."

"What do you mean down?" I asked not understanding how one man could move a such a large market at will.

"Well look, if we wait until ze television say somezhing bad about ze Euro, zhen I can sell a few millions, and a few more millions, and see what will happen. And maybe zhere is some ozher traders like me, and we all have ze client stop loss orders coming ze same level. So zhere is maybe big cluster here. And when I sell many millions, and zhey sell many millions, we can see ze market is very weak and we know we are all togezher, pushing togezher. So if we can be very strong and push very hard zhen we can take ze Euro down to ze cluster. And when it get zhere I know already ze client stop loss is triggered, and now I am getting everyzhing I am shorting on ze way down. And now I am flat again. You can see I sold here, all ze way down at zhis prices, and zen I buy from ze client at zhis prices here, so I make ze profit here zhis much."

"So you're basically screwing the client out of their position. You're moving the market down to the level where you know they'll give up and exit the trade."

"Yes, but tiz zheir own fault, no?"

"How's that?"

"Well, ze smart client, zhey never give ze working stop loss order to ze broker."

Whereas Tanner was my EQD boss, Jimmy was my equity sales-trading boss. I suppose it was the result of exaggerating on my CV that Jimmy assumed I knew what I was doing and didn't need any help from him. At any rate, I found a distinct advantage in having two bosses in that each considered the other to be my primary boss, which meant they left me alone to do what I pleased. Or perhaps they were just too busy thinking about money, first, last and always, to worry about me.

Well, one day Jimmy gave me some random overseas client that no one else wanted, and soon enough, a guy called up from Hong Kong. *"I'm Zing Blah from Blah Blah Capital,"* he said. *"I wanna sell figh hundred tousan' Xstrata."* I said ok and had Rob, the resources trader, work it over the rest of the day. When he'd finished, I sent Zing his fill and went home. The next day, however, Zing asked for his fill in AstraZeneca. I explained that he'd told me to sell Xstrata, not AstraZeneca. Apparently, it had been lost in translation.

Ten minutes before the open Jimmy stood glaring at me. *"Come on Jimmy, it's not my fault,"* I said. *"This guy Zing Blah can barely speak English. Plus, I made sure to repeat the order back to him, and he agreed with what I said!"*

"Then in future, you use the stock ticker as well as the company name!" he fired back.

"Ok, I'm sorry. Look the markets were weak in the US overnight and this morning in Asia too. I think we should keep the Xstrata short and fill Zing Blah in AstraZeneca at yesterday's price. Then Rob can cover Xstrata and Pete can sell AstraZeneca. I reckon net-net it'll be profitable for us."

"I agree," said Rob, though Pete, the pharmaceuticals trader, looked a little dubious since I was effectively asking him to take one for the team. Jimmy pondered it for a moment and then agreed, and a few minutes later I was back on the phone with Zing. *"Ok no problem,"* I said. *"You sold five hundred thousand AZN LN at 511."*

"Fank you vewy much," he replied. An hour later Rob had made £40k in Xstrata and Pete had only lost £5k in AstraZeneca. Of course, the buck stopped with the traders, and had my error produced a big loss, they'd have hated me for it. As they say, it's better to be lucky than good.

I dearly loved the technology and resources I had at my disposal and often stayed late into the night analysing markets and studying the financial system. That was nearly impossible to do during the day since it was a mad rush from 6:15 am to 5:30 pm with my entire concentration focussed on not screwing anything up. And believe me, there were a million ways to screw up. My goal was to understand the entire financial system from the macroeconomic down to the thousands of stocks I traded. But after more than a year of reading, learning, analysing and predicting, I found myself repeatedly bamboozled by the markets. When I thought EURUSD would go up, it went down. When I thought mining stocks would go down, they went up. I predicted all sorts of things, but mostly stocks and currency, and I'd write them all down in a little notebook. But more often than not I was wrong in my predictions. Indeed, being more wrong than I would have been by chance alone was distressing because I worked so hard to understand it.

In fact, I used to dazzle people with my knowledge. When I met someone socially and they told me where they worked I could launch into a detailed description of their company and industry. People loved it because they didn't often get the chance to talk about what they did for a living with someone who genuinely cared. Sometimes they'd even exclaim, *"That's amazing! How do you know that? Are you friends with the CEO or something?"* And I'd lie and say I used to work there. At other times, I'd just pick a random company, say Burberry, and then talk about it for a while. I could pretend I was a construction manager, a telco provider, a medical equipment manufacturer, an oil and gas engineer. It was easy for me, and fun too.

Now if I were a different person I might have ascribed my terrible market predictions to simply not being smart enough, or not studying hard enough, or not having the right information. But I was confident in my intelligence, my hard work, and my sources and that meant there were only two possibilities: 1. Information without direct experience doesn't lead to real knowledge; or 2. Real knowledge doesn't lead to accurate predictions in financial markets.

There were no electronic exchanges for convertible bonds, so all that business was done over the phone. As

I explained, the usual process was for clients to trade them in a package along with a short stock position. So when a client bought from us they'd actually execute two trades simultaneously – they'd buy convertible bonds, and they'd short the stock. But because the stock was traded over the phone someone had to manually report it to the stock exchange for record keeping purposes. Reporting this *off-market* trade was one of the jobs that fell to me.

In the UK, there were a whole lot of silly rules about reporting, and the problem I ran into was that they required all trades to reported in pence sterling. Unfortunately, in the case of quanto convertible bonds, the stock was actually traded in a different currency, and if I simply used the current FX rate to convert it back into pence sterling, it would mean reporting trades that were nowhere near the current market price. So I called up the compliance department, but they really weren't very helpful. *"You have to tell the stock exchange about the trade within three minutes of dealing,"* the compliance man said.

"Yes, I know that."

"And you must tell them how many shares were traded and at what price."

"Yes, yes, but the reporting system doesn't allow me to enter it in US dollars."

"What price was it traded at?"

"Seven dollars fifty."

"How can that be? You just told me you traded the stock of a UK company. What price did you trade it in pence sterling?"

"That's what I'm trying to tell you – we never traded it in pence sterling!"

Of course, his instructions were to convert the dollar price into pence sterling at the current FX rate, which in essence, forced me to report real trades at silly prices.

I explained all this to Pete one day and together we came up with a sneaky plan to make some money. Half an hour later the EQD team traded some decent size in Shire convertible bonds, and I was asked to report the stock trade. I rushed over to Pete's desk and said, *"Hey Pete, I got some OTC Shire to report. I'm gonna do it just above market. Big size. Get ready."*

"Ok, just give me a few minutes," he said.

I stared at a three-minute candle chart and Shire had been trading down all day. But then I saw the downtrend halt and the price begin to rise. That was Pete buying up the stock. After a few minutes he yelled out, *"Ok Damon,"* and I hit *[Enter]*. With that my trade report flowed through to the exchange and then out to the world as part of the official time-and-sales feed. Suddenly the stock's bearish looking chart pattern became a mighty strong one, and technical indicators flashed buy signals. It didn't matter that the trade I reported was outside the possible range it could have been in that moment. It was considered a legitimate print, and so it flowed through to the screens of thousands of traders around the world. I could just imagine their excitement. *"What the hell was that?"* they'd scream. *"Something's going on in Shire. Reversal here on big volume!"*

Sure enough, we saw real buying materialise as speculators jumped on the bandwagon, their heads spinning at what important news would follow. And into the buying frenzy Pete sold out his line as quick as he could, and with that, we had our first easy profit. Alas for the poor speculative sods, probably retail day traders no less, there never was any impending news, and the volume was just a hedge and meant nothing. In fact, they should have known better. I clearly marked it as an OTC report and any trader worth their salt would have considered that before leaping into action. Indeed, the problem may have stemmed from the fact that when you first subscribed to Bloomberg or Reuters (the two dominant data vendors at the time), the default last_trade feed was set to show everything including OTC, block trades, special trades and other weird stuff. It was imperative to filter out all that junk, yet clearly, a lot of young traders never did.

I was able to manipulate many stocks like that, and I made sure that all the traders on the floor profited from the loot. That gave me a pretty good reputation since no one else had figured out how to make easy money without hurting our own clients. Not once did I consider it to be bad or wrong or unfair. I was required by law to enter those trades, and the only front running we did was against the anonymous market itself. It was trading, simple as that.

6. THE FIRST ALGOS

One day I was staring at the screen and one of my favourite stocks, Parmalat, got hammered. It was the biggest milk company in the world and a stock I traded every day. *"Parmalat!"* I yelled. *"Something's going on. Stock's down eight percent."* No one replied so I jumped on Bloomberg and typed PRF IM Equity CN <GO> to show me the news. Alas, there was nothing that explained the move. Then I did the same on Reuters. But again, nothing.

"Damon, figure out what's going on!" yelled Tanner.

"Yes sir!"

I went to talk to the trader, but he knew nothing. I went to talk to the food & beverage analyst, but he knew nothing. Then I called the fixed income trading floor downstairs. *"Hey mate, what's going on in Parmalat bonds?"*

"We're looking at a possible default. One hundred

and fifty million Euro payment due yesterday. Not paid."

"No one knows why?" I asked.

"No one."

I couldn't believe it. This was a company I thought I knew intimately. I jumped off the phone and shouted the news over to the EQD department, before turning around and repeating it for the equity department. Then I got back on the phone with our food and beverage analyst. He was astonished to hear it since, as he explained, Parmalat claimed to have over €4bn in cash. *"I can't imagine why they'd miss a measly one hundred and fifty million Euro payment,"* he said.

The stock stayed lower for most of the day, but then it rallied after the company said there'd been a mix-up due to the Thanksgiving holiday. *"Everything's fine,"* they said. *"Some staff were away and we couldn't process the payment in time. We'll sort it out on Monday morning."*

'What the hell has Thanksgiving got to do with anything?' I thought to myself. *'This is an Italian company. They don't celebrate Thanksgiving. This is a big fat bullshit sandwich!'*

I got stuck in and called everyone that might have some idea what was going on. Finally, Luca, who was one of our traders in the Milan office, said he'd heard something about a Cayman hedge fund that had blown up. Apparently, the fund had been seeded by Parmalat.

"So they owned a hedge fund that lost all its money?" I asked.

"Yes, pretty much."

"What kind of fund was it?"

"Currency trading."

"How much money was in it?"
"Around half a billion dollars."

That was when algorithmic trading was first being developed. I'm referring to execution algorithms that saved us from having to repeatedly send out small clips of a large order. The years that followed saw an incredible surge in the use of *algos*, but at that stage most of the street still didn't have working products. Our team in Paris had been leading the charge in this exciting new field, and for many months I'd been helping them test out beta versions in live trading. The first one they gave me was called *with-volume* which was a common order type that clients liked to pass us. Previously, to execute such an order, I had to stare for hours at the order book and the time-and-sales feed, and then trade certain amounts to keep up with what the stock was printing. But if I used the with-volume algo, I only had to enter one order, an algo order, and it would automatically trade a percentage of the volume for me. The birth of financial Skynet? Probably.

Next, they gave me a *VWAP* algo which worked great over longer timeframes but what I really wanted was a short-term algo that could aggressively hammer a stock. It might seem as though a market order would do just that, but in fact, it was a little more complicated. You see every stock exchange had different rules (what we called microstructure) that were often designed to limit a trader's ability to smash a stock. Some exchanges didn't even allow market orders, so you had to enter everything as a limit order. And then they might reject your limit order because it fell outside some band, say 5% from last_trade or 10 ticks from last_trade. And since I traded on eight different exchanges it got to be frustrating when my orders got rejected because of some silly rule in that country. Of course, Murphy's law always applied such that by the time I re-entered the order, I'd miss the bid, and the client would scream at me for being too slow.

So I came up with the *DoubleSlash* algo that was designed to get all the volume in an aggressive move without breaking the rules of each exchange. For example, if a limit order had to be within five ticks of the last print, then that's what the algo would send. But then it would immediately send another order with a limit five ticks beyond that, which, by the time it got there, wouldn't get rejected. It was like switching from a shotgun to a rocket launcher in Quake – I could fire a second rocket before the first had even hit its target. But besides being good weapons for us to use in the market, the efficiency gains that resulted from algos were truly staggering. Suddenly one trader could do the job of 10 traders, and do a better job of it too.

Well, when Monday rolled around Parmalat did indeed pay the €150m they owed to the bond holders. However, we learnt that the money had actually come from the Italian government. It simply didn't add up. How could a company with €4bn in cash, or €3.5bn if you adjusted for the hedge fund blow-up rumour, be unable to make a €150m payment?

It was around 2 pm when Tribeca called. That was unusual since they normally just Bloomberg'd their orders through. *"Hey Steven,"* I said.

"Hi Damon. Parmalat. The company is toast. Let's have some fun with it. Short fifty k at market."

"Yes sir," I said and fired a round of 50k

DoubleSlash. My secret weapon worked a treat, and he was impressed.

"What the hell?" he said. *"How'd you do that?"*

"Magic," I said proudly.

"Well, whatever it is, I like it. Go ahead and short another fifty k here."

For the rest of the day, I shorted the stock in clips of 50k which was about three times the size of the best bid. It broke badly on my selling, and it seemed like no one else had implemented a DoubleSlash equivalent for the Italian market. Finally, after I'd whacked it down 10%, the exchange halted trading. I half expected to get an angry phone call demanding to know why I was crushing one of Italy's most beloved company. But nothing happened, and five minutes later the stock was reopened for trading. It tried to rally, but then I DoubleSlashed it, and it teleported lower. Again and again I hit it until it reached -15% and was once again placed in a trading halt. Each time it happened it caused a lot of confusion because no one knew when or if it would reopen. So I stared at the order book waiting to pounce, while my Bloomberg flashed with message alerts from clients wanting to get in on the action. By now they'd all heard that I was the man for Parmalat. Without warning the stock was suddenly alive and printing once more. It put on a little rally -14% .. -13% .. -12% .. but then I smashed it back down to its lows of the day -14% .. -16% .. -19% .. -20% .. after which trading was suspended for the rest of the day.

After the close Jimmy took me into a meeting room for a chat. *"Hey Damon, that was great work today in Parmalat. You got some serious flow there Pal. Well done!"*

"Thanks. But it's really the algo team that deserves the credit. I couldn't possibly have sold that quickly without using DoubleSlash."

"Yes, that's true, though we're a little concerned about what the exchange might say."

"Well, we didn't break any rules so they really can't complain. All we did was use the freely available information about native order types and then send and modify orders at high speed. Plus, who are the stock exchange to complain? They shouldn't allow bankrupt companies to be trading at all."

"We don't know for sure that the company is bankrupt."

"Yeah, right. They've just misplaced four billion Euros. I'm sure it's gonna turn up soon."

The next day, amidst rumours of massive fraud, the CEO resigned and a turnaround expert was installed to run the company. With that, sentiment improved dramatically, and the stock traded way up. All the talk was about how ridiculous it was that such a huge company could be in trouble. But then in came the sell orders and I smashed it back down to its lows. Our clients were already short as part of their CBArb strategy, and in fact, they should have been buying stock every time it moved lower. But it was just so obvious that there was something wrong with the company that everyone kept shorting more and more of it. Finally, on Friday, Bank of America announced that Parmalat's €4bn in cash held by one of its affiliate banks didn't actually exist. And with that, the exchange finally halted trading for good.

So what happened to all the money? Well, the story I heard, which came from Luca's aunt, who lived in Palma, and knew someone who's sister had dated a guy who.. Well, it started with a guy from Bank of America who worked on the Parmalat account for many years. Then he quit being a banker and went to work for Parmalat directly, but not before grabbing a bunch of letter-headed paper on his way out. This he used to forge an official letter of credit, and once the faxes were sent and approved (yes it was literally done by fax), he launched a series of hedge funds and trading accounts in which he and his buddies could speculate. It certainly didn't help that legislation had been amended to lessen the penalties for fake accounting. Anyway, I guess they were bored of the milk business and yearned for the excitement of trading in the currency market. Their favourite trade, apparently, was to short EURUSD. Sometimes it fell, and they won, other times it didn't, and they lost. But being inexperienced in the ways of the market they did what every young trader did – they kept doubling up their losses until they won. Trading like that was called martingaling, and it was as old as the hills. The trap was that it could work just fine for a really long time. Until the day it didn't, and they lost everything. In this case, it was €14bn and the largest bankruptcy in European history.

7. MADRID TRAIN BOMBINGS

For no apparent reason I found the market acting all crazy-like one day in March 2004. By that I mean intraday volatility was amongst the highest I'd ever seen. When stocks rallied I shorted them near the highs of the day. And when they plummeted I bought them back near the lows of the day. And that happened over and over again, all day long. In fact, it was the very essence of what we called *gamma trading* and exactly what my CBArb clients hoped for in being long volatility. Of course, it wasn't just the clients who made a lot of money. I managed to rack up €20k in commission – my highest one-day total ever.

The next morning, I was at work at 6:15 am and went about my morning routine of frantically entering in the 100 or so orders I received overnight. It was a horribly arduous process but had become a *type-1* brain function that I could do accurately without really needing to think. I was about 80% done when the morning meeting began. Every trader, sales-trader and analyst throughout our network of European offices were plugged in. The global head of trading started by listing out the prop positions we needed to liquidate. The sales-traders took note as the rest of their day would be spent pitching them to clients using silly arguments about interest rates, profit projections, or whatever other nonsense they could make up.

Next Jimmy explained which clients he wanted the traders to take care of. *Taken care of* meant standing ready to buy a block of stock even if they didn't want it. Then the analysts spoke and the trading brained among us stopped listening. Those guys were so consistently wrong in their predictions of stock prices that I'd have rather listened to the idiots on CNBC. So I turned off my dealer-board feed and went on entering my orders.

I could still hear other people's dealer-boards around me, and the analysts droned on until we got to Sergio who was scheduled to talk about Spanish banks. But in an instant, my ears pricked up, and I looked away from my screens. Something was amiss. I looked over to Jimmy who was by now repeatedly calling for Sergio to speak. But from the Madrid office, all was silent. Sergio wasn't there, and neither was anyone else. And then slowly we became aware of a distant wail of sirens. For a moment, we couldn't tell if they were coming from outside our own office in London or through the dealer-board from Madrid. So I turned up the volume and it got louder. That's when I realised something terrible had happened.

Since I had my own TV, I reached out and flicked through the channels looking for some news. But no one was saying anything about Madrid. So I jumped on

Bloomberg and launched a scrolling news panel, and after a few minutes the first headline came across the wire. But it wasn't just any old headline, it was a screaming red block highlight that stayed frozen at the top of the stream:

06:57   MULTIPLE EXPLOSIONS HIT MADRID COMMUTER TRAIN
NETWORK – Policía Municipal de Madrid

The terrorists had struck again! There was a small panic and a lot of shouting, and Jimmy kept calling into his dealer-board microphone. *"Is anyone there. Are you guys all right?"* But we heard no reply from the other end, just the eerie sound of faraway sirens coming over the airwaves. We later learnt that 10 explosions on four commuter trains had killed 191 people, and it was the worst terrorist attack in Spanish history. But when the news reports spoke of no advanced warning I was suddenly overcome with guilt, for it was evident to me, that there was plenty of advanced warning in the stockmarket the previous day. I felt a lump in my throat and suddenly I had trouble breathing. So I ripped off my necktie and threw it in the bin. *"How can I do my work when something is choking me?"* I shouted at no one in particular.

'Just relax,' I thought. *'You weren't part of this.'*

'But I profited from the death of real people!'

'Yes, but you had no way of knowing what would happen. It's not your fault.'

I was desperate for an explanation so I dug out my trading records from the previous day. Alas, it was all right there in front of me – the most volatile session I'd ever seen, the most trades I'd ever done, and yes, the most profitable day I'd ever had. As a thousand scenarios whirled through my mind I struggled to come to terms with what had happened. Of course, the most palatable explanation was that it had been a total coincidence – the market just happened to act all crazy-like and then a massive terrorist attack occurred. But I just couldn't accept such a naïve view of the financial world. To me, the only thing that could explain it was active trading in big size, and that meant people knew in advance that an attack was going to happen. Of course, the terrorists knew, and their leaders, and maybe their friends and family. But could they really have traded in such size to move the market around like that? I doubted it. And in that case I had to wonder, who else knew?

8. BLOWING UP THE TRADING FLOOR

A month later I was busy playing with charts when a very unsettling headline scrolled across the wire:

15:27 **AMROBAS BANK TO SELL EQUITIES UNIT** – Sources

A simultaneous gasp was heard across the floor. It was the first any of us had heard about it, and poor old Jimmy suddenly had 60 people glaring at him. *"What the hell Jimmy? Are we all fired or what?"* But Jimmy didn't look up. He just stared at his screens like he had something important to do. Later, after the market had closed, he stood up and said, *"Ok everyone. Meeting in the conference room."*

A few minutes later we were all jammed in there like sardines and Jimmy stood on a chair to speak. *"Look, I found out almost the same time you guys did so don't look at me as the bad guy."* Then he went on as though it was just an ordinary day, asking questions about what was going on in the market and what clients were up to. Bewildered, we just stared at him and shrugged our shoulders. Finally, he addressed the elephant in the room. *"Look, there's no need to be despondent. You know what this business is like."*

"But who are we being sold to?" someone asked.

"Does it even matter?" he responded harshly. That's when I realised he was just as screwed as we were. Then he turned to the sales-traders among us and said, *"Listen up you guys. This is no time to slacken off. Our clients are the most important thing right now because we'll be taking them with us to our next jobs. We are, all of us, going to treat them very well over the next few weeks."* Then he turned to the traders and said, *"And you guys, this is your time to shine. We're raising your limits, and when there's a client order in play you need to step up and fill it on risk without question. Otherwise, you can do as you please. But you must give the sales-traders and our clients first priority. Be on the IOIs all day in every stock. Our mission now is simple – we're going to muscle our way into the top three trading firms in Europe. I'm serious guys. We can do it!"* With that, a great big smile lit up his face. It was as though he'd only just thought of it and was impressed with his own idea.

An IOI, or *indication of interest,* was effectively an advert on a bulletin board that let the buy-side know we were willing to trade in big size. And because access was by invitation only, none of our competitors could see what we were doing. A murmur went around, and people started nodding and saying, *"Yes. Yes. Let's do it. We can do it!"* It was an exciting moment to think that our little operation could compete against the mighty flow of Morgan Stanley and Deutsche Bank. And why not? Our bank didn't give a shit about us. They'd gone and sold us, and we all knew what that meant. It meant the new buyer would fire 90% of the staff and keep the brand. So why not have some fun in our final days and let the new buyer pay for the party.

The next morning one of the big bosses flew over from France to make a speech to the floor. It was all very politician-style, and he harped on about new beginnings and all that. But the thing I'll never forget was how at the end of the speech he said, *"Et voilà,"* and then walked out. Well, I happened to be learning French at the time, and as I understood it, Et voilà meant something like, *"Ok all good."* I suppose it might have been the way he said it too, since it sure felt like the most inappropriate thing you could say to a room full of people about to lose their jobs.

Not more than five minutes after the snooty Frenchman had left we got busy making a name for ourselves. Andy was particularly fired up and turned to me and said, *"Those bastards! Let's hit 'em. Let's hit 'em in big size!"* He looked mischievous.

"Hit who? What are you talking about Andy?"

"Hit our own traders, that's who. Get your clients on the phone! We're gonna make a killing!"

"That's not really what I do Andy. My clients trade CBArb remember?"

He shook his head at me in disgust and then turned to hit a number on his speed-dial. Then he pulled the lever on his chair and retreated down under his desk. A few minutes later he resurfaced and turned to me and said. *"I need a stock that has good liquidity, but almost everyone on the street is a seller."*

"Oh, that's easy," I said. *"Vodafone. Most of the street are size sellers, yet all of the analysts give it a buy rating. The stock's just waiting to bust wide open."*

"Perfect. Let's sell some." With that he stabbed the redial button for his client, and after a short pause he said, *"Vodafone,"* and waited. Then, a few seconds later, he stood tall and shouted, *"Vodafone. Where can I sell five million shares?"*

"Touch," replied Tim, the telco trader.

"Done," said Andy but kept standing and mumbling into his headset. Then he shouted again, *"Reload. Where can I sell another five million Vodas?"*

"Touch."

"Cheers matey."

I watched the VOD LN chart and it didn't do much. But then all of a sudden it just fell apart. I assumed it was Tim getting out of the position, but I wouldn't have been surprised if it was Andy's client who was selling on the screen too. Now on a typical day that kind of behaviour wouldn't have been tolerated, but it was not a typical day on the Amrobas trading floor.

"New client!" Andy yelled. *"Where can I sell ten million Vodafone? Come on matey. Now please."*

"Touch."

Andy worked his way through his client list telling the same story over and over. *"You see that Vodafone chart? Yep, that was me. You know you really should sell some here. It's due for a whopping big break my dear lad. Uh huh. Uh huh. Yes of course I can. We are the market now. I can buy any size you want matey. This is our stock. We're doing the business now. Serious size. Ok, ten million to start, hold on. 'Vodafone! Where can I sell ten million shares?'"*

"Touch," replied Tim but then added, *"Who's the client?"* He was, after all, the head of the trading desk and needed to keep tabs on such things.

"Who cares who it is!" Andy snapped. Then he walked forward as far as his phone line would reach. *"In fact,"* he said contemptuously, *"let's make it twenty million."*

With that, the trading floor stopped dead in its tracks, and you could have heard a pin drop. Never before had someone disrespected a trader in such a manner. Suddenly Tim was on his feet, his chair hurtling backwards, and outrage contorting his face. Their eyes locked like a couple of fighters in the ring, and a stifling tension hung around thick in the air. They might have been veterans in this game of risk, but we all knew that this time was different.

"Ok," said Tim. *"162.50 bid for twenty million."*

"Done," said Andy quickly.

"Total on the day is forty million shares."

"Agreed," Andy confirmed with a nod.

It didn't take long for word to hit the street that it was killing season on the Amrobas trading floor. *"Any stock in any size,"* was our new motto and clients lined up to gorge themselves on the reckless liquidity. All in all, the equities division booked more than €250m in losses over the next week. Or perhaps more accurately, we laundered €250m of the bank's money through the stockmarket and into our client's accounts at other banks. And that's how we blew up the trading floor. Et voilà, as the man had said.

9. ROGUE TRADING

On the first mass firing day about three quarters of the floor was wiped out, and after that, people just sort of disappeared from time to time. One day I looked around and thought, *'Hey, where the hell did everyone go?'* That's when Tanner came over and said, *"Ok Damon, pack your stuff. Let's have you come and join us on the EQD desk."* He went on to explain that since my local trading platform would be shutting down, he'd arrange for me to trade through another that was running out of Paris. That turned out to be the bank's highly secretive prop trading desk called Maitreya.

It didn't take long for their programmers to build me a custom GUI and pipe me into their system. In effect, I was set up as a prop trader even though I was just an execution trader. And so again, I found myself working for two departments at the same time – EQD in London and Maitreya in Paris. As far as Tanner and I were concerned, we just wanted the platform to be reliable, which it was, while my new boss from Maitreya just wanted a cut of the commissions generated. In my first month with them I racked up €100k and everyone was happy. Again, they didn't care what I did, they just wanted to make money.

In fact, the new platform was fantastic, and I was soon able to offer direct market access (DMA) to my clients. Previously, they had to call, email or Bloomberg their orders to me, after which I'd reply, *"Got it,"* and then enter them into the system. Then, after they'd been filled, I'd have to write back with the prices they traded at. But with DMA, clients could enter their orders themselves, and though they'd first flow through my screen, they'd otherwise go straight onto the market. Soon enough, most of my clients were happily trading via DMA, and I was one giant step closer to being automated out of a job. So it was, that in the months that followed, the personal nature of the business went by the wayside. There was no longer any reason for clients to call and ask for a fill, or question why I'd done something a particular way. That said, I started pulling in a lot more commission because hardly anyone else on the street was offering such a service. So, all in all, the business grew, even though I had a lot less to do.

That's when I started to think about prop trading instead of just doing what clients told me to do. I wanted to be like all the other guys in the Maitreya team. *'They're so lucky,'* I thought, *'being able to trade whatever they want, whenever they wanted.'* It sure seemed like fun.

The platform had no functionality to trade FX, which was a problem since my clients needed it as part of their CBArb strategy. So I asked the programmers to build me a simple FX book that we could bolt onto the side of it. Then I said, *"I'll just trade currency directly with the FX department. That way you don't need to worry about execution. And then I'll use the FX book to allocate currency directly into the client accounts."* They agreed since it was much easier that way. Then I spoke to the FX department and asked them to set me up a single house account instead of multiple client accounts. I explained how I would post allocate trades directly into the client accounts since they already existed in the Maitreya system. They agreed since opening just one house account was a whole lot easier than opening 20 separate client accounts. What they didn't know, however, was that with such a setup in place, I'd be able to trade FX whenever I wanted even when I didn't have a client order behind it. That's because the Maitreya back office wouldn't see the FX trades at all, while the FX back office only cared that the house account was flat by the end of the day.

So I lunged headfirst into the currency market. I stayed late after work and studied hard. I read everything from everyone and for many months I thought of nothing but Dollars, Euros, Swissies and Sterling. Well, one day it looked to me like EURUSD was about to fall, and having waited so patiently for so long, I went ahead and sold 50k EURUSD in my house account. In my mind, it was a prop trade. In truth, it was a rogue trade. But lucky for me it worked, for an hour later, with a smile on my face, I covered the short and locked in my first profit.

A few days went by, and I sat nervously wondering if the Parisian risk management people were on my case. But no one called and nothing happened. So when

I saw EURUSD form a triple MACD divergence followed by a spike in volume, I couldn't help but go for it a second time. You see the currency markets were like the wild west. There were no rules and no regulators, and because they operated as a fragmented marketplace it was impossible to measure total trading volume. Nevertheless, there was one venue, EBS, that was the go-to place for big players to fill size orders. That's because unlike the other ECNs, EBS actually published their volume feed to subscribers. And I can tell you that having that feed on my charts gave me a massive advantage over those who didn't. So, having just seen a price divergence followed by a spike in volume, I went ahead and bought 500k EURUSD, held it for 20 minutes, and then sold it for a profit. Again, I waited nervously for a few days, but again, no one said a word.

Typically, I traded about €5m worth of stocks each day for clients, and since I charged 10bps commission, it translated into €5k in profit. The way I saw it, I could risk no more than that amount in my own rogue trading so as to be sure that the total profit would still be positive at the end of the day. Of course, if I consistently lost almost all my commission every day then someone would realise something was wrong. But it would be a whole lot worse if I ever had a down day because it should have been impossible to lose money when trading stocks for commission. So I waited patiently for perfect setups and always traded with strict stop-losses in mind.

About a month later, after I'd clocked up around €30m in unauthorised trading, I received a phone call from the Maitreya middle office in Paris. I still couldn't speak French very well, but neither could the other guy speak English. *"Salut?"* he said. *"Sava, et toi?"* I replied.

"Sava. Alors.. Ahh, Damon. What iz ze client for ze five hundred tousand Oooro-dollar?"

I responded confidently. *"No, my friend, it is not for client,"* but didn't elaborate.

"Ok but Damon, why you buy ze Oooro but not for client?"

"No, no. It is not for client. I had to buy Euros to hedge the book." He ummed and arred for a moment, so I cut in and said, *"You understand, right? Hedge."*

"Ah ok," he said. *"Hedge. Hedge ze book. Ok, now I can see ze book is being very flat after ze hedge."*

"Yes, we are flat now. Thank you."

I was sure I'd outsmarted him, but the very next day Tanner escorted me into a meeting room next to the exit of the trading floor. *"Damon, I know what you're doing in the currency market,"* he said.

"Oh, ok," I replied. He glared at me like a criminal and for a moment I wondered if a security guard was about to burst into the room and drag me out of the building. But I didn't apologise, I just sat there and met his gaze. My rogue trading had made €20k in profit so far, and though it was hardly earth-shattering, it was better than nothing wasn't it? Finally, after a silence that had dragged on far too long, he said, *"Look. You're doing well, and I can see you're working really hard at it. So I'm gonna let you have some fun.. err.. what I mean is.. well not fun but.. Look, just don't fuck it up!"*

"Yes, sir! I blurted out. *"I won't let you down."*

"And another thing," he said. *"Since you're gonna be busy with it, let's hire an assistant for you. Someone*

young that you can train up to trade stocks."

"That'd be great," I said, and with that we shook hands and left the room. Nothing was signed, and there was no discussion of limits. I supposed that *Just don't fuck it up!* was a catch all mandate. And that's how it came to be that at the age of 25 I found myself managing an unlimited prop trading account for the largest bank in Europe.

Over the next six months, my position sizes went from 500k EURUSD up to 50MM. I waged a one-man war against the currency market and an even bigger one against myself. I could never have anticipated the psychological damage that prop trading would have on me, and regrettably, it was my new assistant who took the brunt of my anger when a position didn't go my way. That poor girl, she really didn't deserve it. So where did the anger come from? Well, I suppose the pressure, anxiety, and trauma of running risk led me to prioritise perfection over empathy, and success over enjoyment. I just don't think I could have beaten the market without sinking to such a state.

I consumed every analyst, strategy, and economic report I could get my hands on, and I doubt many people in the world worked as hard as I did to beat the currency market that year. So perhaps it wasn't surprising that I got angry when I lost, even though overall, I did ok. But then, like a giant spanner in the works, I got to know a guy called Brophy, who sat behind me. He repeatedly argued that much of what I thought I knew about the financial system was total bullshit. *"Come on man!"* he said one day after spinning around in his chair to face me. *"Every day I see you over there killing yourself fighting the dollar. Never* fight the market man. Never."

"But the dollars' gonna go down dude. Didn't you see the trade deficit they just reported!" I replied.

"The what? You must be joking. Man, back in the Chicago pits we used to trade straight through that shit without even looking at it."

"Ok, but surely inflation differentials suggest that.."

"Ha! You mean fakeflation. Don't you know they just make that shit up? It's like the unemployment rate where all they do is change the participation rate to goal seek whatever figure they want. Look, even if I conceded that the statisticians are honourable people doing the best they can to get it right, there's still a massive problem."

"What?"

"That it's an impossible task to begin with. It's so subjective that it's virtually meaningless. Plus, they keep changing the methodology so you can't even compare serial data."

I really liked Brophy, and he was a senior guy with a lot of experience. But cutting economic data out of my thinking was just too extreme for me to bear. So I kept on consuming it for the duration of my prop trading days. Unfortunately, those days were numbered, for the better I did, the closer I came to the day of reckoning.

It was totally out of the blue when the head of the FX department called up. He and his team of market makers (whose prices I traded against) sat on a different floor and since I always dealt via an electronic platform we almost never spoke. "Hey Damon," he said.

"Hey yourself. What's going on down there on the second floor?"

"Oh, you know, same shit, different day. But look dude you're killing us down here with these trades. I don't know how your clients are doing it, but I'm gonna have to widen you out to ten pips."

He had no idea that there weren't any clients behind the trades, that it was me prop trading directly against him. Perhaps if he'd known, he might have offered me a job, but I was too scared to tell him. I said it sucked and that my clients would be annoyed at such a wide spread. He said he understood but his decision was final.

I got off the phone and had my assistant take over trading. Then, for the first time in almost two years, I went out for lunch. But I didn't eat. I just wandered aimlessly around Regents Park considering my options. I knew that a 10-pip spread would kill my strategy and if I could no longer be a prop trader then what was the point of staying at Amrobas? But then it dawned on me that they'd only widened my spread because I'd beaten them at their own game. And for a moment, at least, all the stress and worry had been worth it.

10. CONVERTIBLE MELTDOWN

Chris sat a few chairs down from me. He was our only convertible bond market maker in London with the rest of the team based out of Paris. I never quite understood why he was there until the day I learnt that there are some things that can only be done in person.

We took a cab to a quiet little bar on the other side of the city where to my surprise we met up with one of our competitors from at Bear Stearns. After 10 minutes of chit-chat at the bar we moved into a small room in the back where no one else was sitting. That was when Chris pulled out our client holdings spreadsheet, which showed (to the best of our knowledge) what clients owned what convertible bonds. It was just about the most confidential thing we possessed, yet here he was showing it to our competitor. In turn, the Bear man slapped down his own spreadsheet, and together we cross-referenced who held what. After a while Chris asked, *"What do you think?"* and the Bear man replied,

"EMI, Accor, and STM." I desperately wanted to know what he meant, but I kept my mouth shut. *"Dresdner's on board too,"* he said. *"Same names. We start tomorrow."*

In the cab on the way home, Chris opened up. He explained that the convertible bond market was very weak and they felt it was likely to break wide open at any moment. What we'd ascertained was that there were a few convertible bonds that were tightly held by just a few hedge funds. By ourselves, we could never know for sure what funds owned what, since there was no public registry for OTC derivatives. But in colluding with a few other banks, we got a good handle on where the concentration of risk lay. For example, we'd confirmed that just two funds held a large percentage of the EMI Music convertible bonds. That meant if we marked them down those funds would probably cave and start selling. In effect, we could screw over the clients with a pretty small chance of it backfiring. And that's exactly what we did the next day.

You see the spike in volatility after the Madrid bombings was short-lived, so there wasn't much profit to be had after the initial windfall. Indeed, in the dull markets that followed, our CBArb clients did nothing but bleed money. Yet still, they refused to reduce their positions since, after all, their primary mandate was to be long volatility. What I didn't understand at the time was just how easy it would be to move the convertible bond market lower. That's because many, if not all, the large derivatives houses were massive sellers of volatility. So no matter how much of it the clients bought we always had more and more of it to sell. To our client's way of thinking, CBArb was the perfect way to make money out of fear and terror since *if bad shit happened volatility would go up*. But that wasn't true at all because no matter what occurred in the real world we remained a huge natural seller of volatility, all coming from the structured products department who manufactured it out of corporate deals and securitisation.

What it all meant was that in spite of the media hysteria that spewed forth on a daily basis, no matter the double wars in Iraq and Afghanistan, no matter how terrified were the sheeple about leaked Bin Laden tapes and Disneyland terror plots, the reality was that stockmarkets became calmer and calmer, and those who bet on rising volatility lost a hell of a lot of money. Harvard was one of the first to dump their convertible bond portfolio, and I suppose they got some decent prices. But when Derox tried to do the same the market makers sat back and refused to deal. Eventually, a few -30% subject bids floated around, and I could hardly believe it when Derox hit them. That was the beginning of the end for the convertible bond market, for after that, liquidation was the only game in town. Eventually, the downward spiral would reach its natural end, when all the inventory had been taken back onto the bank's balance sheets. That, of course, would be the start of a brand-new bull market.

When bonus day arrived we sat around like sick people waiting to see a doctor. We all knew that the media hype about how much traders got paid was total bullshit, though I for one, expected to do ok. I watched as the people before me exited their meetings, all wearing their best poker faces, until finally, my name was called. Tanner explained that it had been a really tough year and that our clients had been hurt badly by the meltdown in the convertible bond market. I argued that none of that was my fault, that I'd worked hard and grown the client base. *"And what about all the money I made in the currency market?"* I pointed out.

"What money?" he said casually before turning to stare out at the trading floor. I was so shocked by his betrayal that I couldn't even think of a response. Then, he turned back to me and said, *"Your bonus will be five thousand Euros. It will be paid to you along with your next paycheck."* I stood, put on my best poker face, and walked out the door. When I got back to my desk, I called Jez and had a good laugh about something funny we'd done on the weekend. But after I'd hung up the rage rose inside me like a volcano threatening to erupt. Despite the adverse conditions I'd expected a €50k bonus, but all I got was an insult for my hard work. I stared at my desk and tried to be calm. It was all I could do to stop from picking up my keyboard and smashing it through one of my screens.

Though we weren't supposed to talk about it, word quickly spread that everyone had been screwed. So people started turning up late and taking long lunches. What was the point of working when your boss would just steal what was rightfully yours? Eventually, the day came when our bonuses cleared into our bank accounts, and a subtle nod went around the desk. Then, without uttering a word to Tanner, half the department stood and walked out the door. We drank beers into the night and wished each other luck. Then I said goodbye to my French friends and caught the last tube home.

11. THE CHERRY BOX FUND

Since our lease was ending, and a few in the house had found love, we decided to break up our sharehouse and go our separate ways. Well, it wasn't long before I found a great little flat along Portobello Road. On one side of me was the private club atop *Electric Cinema* which, from what I heard, had a three-year waiting list for membership. But all I had to do was climb out my window, hop over a ledge, and then I'd be standing on the smoking balcony of the club. The flat on the other side was even more interesting, since it doubled as a part-time pirate radio station (drum & bass, of course) and a full-time meth lab. I used to hear dealers in the street, yelling up at all hours of the morning, and I'd hide myself behind the curtain to watch as rolls of cash were exchanged for filthy baggies of bathtub crank. That was what made Notting Hill such a unique environment – rich and poor living side by side, with me somewhere in the middle.

Each morning the Portobello market would thrive outside my window, and I soon became friends with all the stall owners. One day Cheryl gave me a couple of empty wooden cherry boxes which I took upstairs and glued together to form a solid base. I'd earlier spent my shitty bonus on buying two laptops, two extra screens, a router, a keyboard and a mouse. Upon the base I positioned the two screens, and below them, the two laptops such that their screens would perfectly overlap and form a four-screen grid. I wired it all up, subscribed to Bloomberg and Reuters, and opened spread bet trading accounts with Eiger Index and Sema Markets. And just like that, I was ready to go.

I called my little outfit the Cherry Box Fund, though I'm not sure why I gave it a name since I had no investors and a total staff of me. I traded currency according to the strategy I'd refined over my years at Amrobas, though as a retail trader, I no longer had access to the EBS volume feed. My brokers, in fact, they were bucket shops, let me trade FX on a two-pip spread, and with that, I traded along profitably for quite some time.

But eventually I started to lose myself in the boredom of working alone, and to make matters worse, most of my friends had left London at the expiration of their working holiday visas. So I spent my days working alone in the flat and the nights trying to stay out of it. You ever seen a busy restaurant with a single guy sitting alone at a table? Well, for a long time that was me. I suppose I never noticed it creeping to the fore but trading had changed my personality, and I could no longer relate to the general population. It seemed to me that the vast majority of their ideas, beliefs, and opinions were simply planted there by the media.

One day, when the market was quiet, I got to looking around on Internet dating sites. It wasn't long before I found a beautiful girl called Karina from Lithuania. When we met for the first time, I could hardly believe my eyes. I wondered if she'd come from the future, or was born in a test tube in an underground genetic engineering lab. But though she started out being utterly sweet and adorable, I soon discovered a side of her that could be emotionless and as hard as nails. Not that I minded, I actually thought it was pretty cool. She was like the trader I wanted to be.

One day, while shopping on Kensington High Street, she turned to me and said, *"You know darling, I might be looking like angel, but I am devil."* I laughed and pretended that I thought it was a joke. But inside I knew it wasn't. Later I asked about her past, which she'd always kept a tight lid on, and then I made the mistake of asking about her job.

"I tell you already. I have website," she said coldly.

"Yes, but what website? Can I see it?"

"Why you want to look? Why you want to make me so angry!"

"Ok ok, forget about it Zuikis," I said.

Zuikis was her pet name ever since she told me about her favourite children's book growing up – Zuikis Puikis. But unlike the cute little bunny from the book, Karina possessed a viciousness that started to come out more and more. Eventually, I realised that she was into some bad shit with some bad people. But I didn't care since by then I loved her and wanted to save her. I imagined us running away together and escaping the troubles in her life. But then I came to understand that she wasn't in any trouble at all. She was right where she wanted to be.

One Saturday night we were hanging out at Beach Blanket Babylon. Karina could drink vodka like water, and as usual, she matched me drink for drink. Alas by closing time she could hardly stand and I all but had to carry her back to my flat. There, for the first time, she opened up and told me her story. It turned out she wasn't born in an underground lab, just a regular hospital in Vilnius. But she had bad parents and ran away from home when she was 16. Soon enough she was kidnapped, transported, and sold to the Albanian mafia. Between Greece, Italy and Germany she was probably whored out a thousand times by the age of 18. But she wasn't angry about it or distraught. Rather she spoke of it with pride as having seen the world and knowing how things really were. *"Life is not like TV,"* she said knowingly. After that, she claimed to have risen to the top of her small Albanian gang and assumed leadership of the human trafficking operations. I believed it since her looks were off the chart, and when I said she was as hard as nails, well that was an understatement, she was the toughest person I ever met. Now 23 she'd been running that side of the business for five years already. That explained how she could throw so much money around on dinners, drinks, clothes, apartments, and a Range Rover. She hardly let me pay for anything.

We spent almost every day together for the next two months, and life was good. We talked a lot about the future, about moving to Australia, and even about starting a family. But then one day, lying on the couch watching TV, her phone rang. *"I have to go now,"* she said. *"Goodbye."*

"What do you mean?" I asked.

"I'm sorry. Must work now."

I didn't understand it, but she was in no mood to explain herself, so I walked her down to the corner of Portobello and Westbourne Park Road. Minutes later a black limousine approached from Ladbroke Grove. *"Go"*, she said. *"You not stand here. They not see you."*

"Ok," I said, but when I leaned down to kiss her, she pulled away.

The next day I discovered that my passport was missing, and all at once, dread washed over me. I called her number, but she didn't answer the phone. Nor did she for the rest of the week. Then one night, as I was walking home from *The Westbourne*, I realised that I was being followed. I turned to see a steroid-pumping Eastern European thug on my tail. I immediately grabbed the phone out of my pocket and pretended to answer it. Then I pretended to be talking to someone so the guy wouldn't attack me. *"Hi mate,"* I said loudly. *"Yes, I'm outside."* Then I stopped walking and said, *"Come outside, I'm here already,"* before staring at the front door of some random house. With that, the tail crossed to the other side of the street and continued on. My plan had worked, but I was pretty shaken up.

The next day Karina finally answered her phone, but she spoke as though I meant nothing to her. *"We cannot see anymore. Now everything is finish between us. Goodbye,"* she said.

"What the fuck Karina! I know you stole my passport! Why would you do that? I was so good to you!"

"I don't know what you say. You crazy man. You beat me."

"Huh? Did you say 'beat me'?"

"You very drunk. You say you want kill me. Now I tell my Albanian friends. You make trouble they kill you!"

The last sentence was frighteningly ambiguous. Was she saying that *if* I made trouble, they *would* kill me? Or that I'd *already* made trouble, and they were *going* to kill me? *"Zuikis,"* I said calmly. *"You know I'm a good man. Please don't do anything crazy. If you don't want to see me anymore, then that's fine. Let's just say goodbye."*

"Goodbye Zuikis," she said.

After that, I fluctuated between fear and despair – fear of the Albanian mafia and what they might be doing with my passport, and despair at having lost the most beautiful girl in the world. Of course, I kept right on trading, even though I really shouldn't have, being in such a state.

On the day it happened, I skipped breakfast and loaded up on GBPUSD instead. Cable had been weak for several days, and the news flow and economic data didn't support the move. An hour later, it fell again, and with no blood sugar and a calamitous monkey-mind, all my years of experience went out the window. *"Stupid cable!"* I yelled at the screen, and backed up the truck to buy more. Eventually I'd used every last multiple of leverage the bucket shops would give me. And then, not 10 minutes later, *Boom! .. Double Boom!! ..* That was the moment of the London 7/7 terrorist attack. GBPUSD fell in a vertical line and I was stopped out. All the longs were stopped out. I turned on the TV. *"You're all gonna die!"* it said. I turned it off and sat there in silence. There was nothing more to do. Nothing more to say. I'd blown up my account and ruined my life. If only I hadn't traded angry. If only the bucket shops hadn't given me enough rope to hang myself, for that's exactly what I did.

London was a strange place for me after that. On the one hand, I felt lucky to be alive, but on the other, I was distraught that Karina had left me, and I'd been ruined as a trader. Feeling close to my wit's end, I decided to give Jez a call. He listened calmly as I spoke, and after I'd finished he said, *"Damon, you need to snap out of this. The way you're talking it sounds like you're in a bad way. But let me tell you something – you will bounce back from this. We don't know how you do it, but you always do. That's what we love about you mate. So don't get too down about it. Just try to stay positive. Everything will be ok."*

12. THE GLASS DOOR

They say happiness comes from earned success. But what about when you earn success and then it's taken away from you? Well, that's how I felt. I had loved and lost a career, and I had loved and lost a girl. And even if I could gather a stake, I didn't think I could beat the market anymore. I'd lost my confidence, and that was no state to be in as a trader. So I took to getting drunk and playing pool in Mau Mau Bar just up the street. I'd always been pretty good at pool, but now that I was playing every night I got a lot better. But then one night I got to being all cocky about how I could beat anyone in Notting Hill. It might have been true on a good day but not in the state I was in. At any rate, it turned out to be a fateful night where I barely cheated death and learnt the hard way about some serious limitations in my personality.

So there I was, the champion of the bar and the self-proclaimed champion of Notting Hill. I was mouthing off and generally being a twat when I was kicked out and told to go home. But just as I was arguing with the bouncer along came Karina with her new boyfriend. I tried to talk to her, but I slurred my words, and she looked at me in disgust. The bouncer let them into the club but held me outside. I explained that I needed to talk to her, but he wouldn't budge. Then I flipped my lid and smashed my arm through the plate glass door, before collapsing, screaming and crying, in a pool of blood.

I awoke in St Mary's hospital to a doctor explaining that I was lucky to be alive. *"Lucky!"* I said. *"That's a matter of perspective my friend."*

"Well, the lacerations to your forearm are severe. You managed to cut clean through several nerves and tendons but you missed, I might say miraculously missed, the veins and arteries."

A few hours later I was taken into theatre where a surgeon spent four hours repairing the damage using microscopic surgical equipment to reconnect the nerves. It was cutting edge technology at the time, but as he later explained, in an oddly humorous tone, *"There were a few nerves that were just too mashed up to be repaired, so I just tucked them under the skin before sewing you up. But it's ok, they're only sensory nerves, and you don't really need them."*

A few days later I went into the bathroom, took off the bandages, and had a good look at what I'd done. It was shocking. From the elbow down my right arm was a jigsaw puzzle of stitches holding together a useless mass of meat and bone. I stared at my fingers and willed them to move, but alas, they just wouldn't respond. *'How am I ever going to trade again if I can't move my fingers?'* I wondered in despair. Later the surgeon stopped by for a chat. *"The surgery appears to have been a success,"* he said confidently.

"Really? Then why can't I move my fingers?"

"Yes, I know. Look you did some serious damage, and you're lucky to be alive. If the weight of the glass had fallen down through the frame it could have cut your arm clean off! You need to be thankful that you got off so lightly. The surgery went well, I know it did, and I'm confident that you'll heal in time."

"Do you mean full movement again?"

"I can't guarantee that, but yes, I think so. Look Damon, it's going to be a long hard road. Understand that nerves only grow at a rate of one millimetre per day. So based on the length of your forearm it'll take around nine months before you can move them again."

I had a horrible time after that. The wounds healed slowly, and the disfigurement served as an ugly reminder of what an idiot I was. Then a lovely lady with the title of *Hand Therapist* came to see me. She spent a long time customising a strange contraption, and when it was finished she fastened it to my forearm and wired me up. It was a bit like an ukulele but with each string attached to a finger at one end, and a base up near my elbow, at the other. That kept my fingers drawn backward in an extended position, so that the severed nerves, tendons and muscles could heal. Alas, I couldn't move anything, and it was a horrible feeling to be so helpless. So it was that I soon fell into a hopeless cycle of insomnia and depression and that's when I lost my circadian rhythm.

Normally a person's sleepiness follows an autonomic rhythm such that in the evening they feel tired and go to sleep, and in the morning, they wake up and feel refreshed. But my body clock turned against me, sold me out, double-crossed me, and worse. It orchestrated an erratic pump and dump of hormones and neurotransmitters at all the wrong times. Each morning when I awoke, I felt sick, depressed, and ashamed, and I struggled to get out of bed. But then, as the day wore on, I became ever more alert and energetic. By the time regular people were heading off to sleep, I'd be wide awake, and by 3 am my brain was akin to a short-circuiting mesh of electric charge with the power source stuck on full throttle. And though I couldn't sleep, I endeavoured to try anyway. Alas, all I really did was berate myself over and over for not doing the right thing and going to sleep, or else obsess about all the stupid mistakes I'd made. And then, my final thoughts as I drifted into a world of tortured dreams, were my plans to jam a knife into my head to fix it, or in the least, to teach it a good lesson in manners. As Eckhart Tolle said, *"Not to be able to stop thinking is a dreadful affliction. The incessant mental noise prevents you from finding the realm of inner stillness."*

Depression, which I considered the flip-side of insomnia, wasn't what I thought it would be. It wasn't feeling bad or sad or down. It was feeling so bad that I wanted to kill myself and was serious about it. I considered many ways to get it done, but I figured my brother's method – heroin overdose – was the pick of the bunch. And why not? I was trapped in a living hell with insomnia and depression feeding upon each other in an endless cycle.

Eventually, though, I concluded that I was nothing but a hostage to an enemy within, and that professional help might be the solution. I wasn't embarrassed to go and see a psychiatrist, but when he suggested that I take a course of antipsychotic drugs, I said no thanks and moved back to Australia.

I rented a flat in Burleigh Heads and spent the summer swimming, reading, and trying to relax. Then, almost nine months later, I had a dream that I could move my fingers again. When I awoke, it was with a feeling that it might not have been just a dream. Was it time? I held my breath and looked down at my limp right hand. Then, with all my might, I focussed on my index finger and willed it to move. Incredibly, it did just that. I was over the moon. I was on my way to recovery. Or so I thought.

With mobility improving every day you'd think I would have snapped out of the funk I was in. But it just didn't happen like that. In colluding with daytime depression, insomnia was an all-powerful foe that couldn't be stopped by the mere wave of a hand. So I went to see another psychiatrist and explained the situation. *"You'll get through this mate,"* he said kindly, and upon seeing the sincerity in his eyes, I entrusted my brain to him.

For the next six months I took a combination of lithium and olanzapine. The odd part was that no one really knew how they worked, which meant they were being peddled as a prescription for a whole range of conditions. Just as stockbrokers knew all about stocks, but not what their prices would do, the pharma industry knew all about these drugs, but not what their chemicals would do. Indeed, the makers of the stuff, Eli Lilly, were later ordered to pay the largest fine in U.S. corporate history on allegations of false marketing.

Taking antipsychotic drugs had an enormous effect on me. First, I lost my creative edge and the ability to think abstractly. Then my reaction time blew out, and I started doing silly things like reversing my car into a pole at the shopping centre. Previously I'd wondered how people could be so stupid. Now I was the one scratching my head over a broken taillight. Finally, and I could only have perceived this in hindsight, the antipsychotics did something really profound when they destroyed a delusion I'd carried with me my whole life.

For as long as I could remember I'd been compelled to count all manner of physical objects around me. They were like hidden codes left for the benefit of those lucky few that could see them. And the numbers always meant something. I'm talking about the number of bricks in a wall, leaves on a branch, or lines in a pattern. And having counted these things with such obsession, without knowing it was an obsession, for such a long time, I wound up getting pretty good at it. When I went to Starbucks I could quickly determine that there were 18 sticks of sugar in the holder. It wasn't magic. I simply counted them as fast as I could, and after years of training I got to be pretty fast. That's not to say I could look at a bowl of sugar and count the grains – that was impossible – but at least I tried whereas other people never did.

Now if I saw two bottles of water in the fridge or eight slats in the Venetian blind, then that meant *No*. But if it was five minutes past the hour or the elevator was on the ninth floor, then that meant *Yes*. Why? Well, in these cases the system was pretty simple – odd meant yes, and even meant no. But upon such foundation I got to developing some highly elaborate systems for extracting answers out of the world around me. And all the while I never stopped to question whether such behaviour was normal and real, or abnormal and unreal, or as I now believe, normal and unreal. Yes, I'm all but certain that most people suffered from delusions even if theirs had nothing to do with numbers.

But then one day, many months into the treatment, I found myself staring at a tree but not counting the leaves. Startled, I turned my attention to the sidewalk, but I saw no patterns in the concrete. Carefully this time, I stared at another tree. But again, all I saw was a tree. It was then, in a flash of insight so profound it shook me to the core, that I realised the delusive numbers had gone. *'Wait a minute,'* I thought. *'There are no answers here because there is no underlying truth. There is no meaning. There is no yes or no. There is no right or wrong. There is no true or untrue. It is just a bunch of stuff that happens, and that is all.'*

For the next few days I lived in a very different world, and it sure was peaceful not having to count, calculate, ruminate or rationalise every little thing that crossed my path. That's when I discovered the infinite serenity of *no mind*, and just like that, the curse of insomnia faded away.

"I think I'm cured," I said to the doctor.

"I'm happy to hear it." He said. *"I told you it would work."*

"So, can I stop the treatment now?"

"Why do you want to stop?"

"Because I'm bored. I don't exactly analyse things in great detail these days."

"And what's wrong with that."

"Nothing I guess. It's just not me."

"You mean the old you."

"Yes, the old me."

"It's a risk. That if you stop now, you could fall back into the cycle."

"I know. But I feel like I need to get on with my purpose."

"And what's that?"

"To trade."

"And why do you think that's your purpose. There's plenty of other things you can do in life."

"I don't think so. I mean ok, there could be, but I think I've figured something out that no one else has."

"What's that?"

"That there's no truth to financial markets. They don't make any sense and they never will."

We wound down the treatment, and eventually I returned to the smarter, faster version that I used to be. But though my inquisitive nature and interest in the abstract were restored, I retained a clear awareness of my former delusion. So though I was free to count again, I simply didn't want to, and with that I became pragmatic and comfortable with reasoning alone.

As for financial markets, I decided that most analysis was really just a senseless concoction of one's own delusions, biases, interpretations, and imaginings about a bunch of stuff they couldn't possibly know about. So I vowed to never again consume macroeconomic reports, corporate earnings, or fundamental analysis. I would need to find another way to beat the market.

13. PERDU CAPITAL PARTNERS

I flew back to London and found a room in a share-house in Bayswater. Then I set up meetings with a bunch of recruitment agents. As expected, they all told the same sad story about how the economy was bad, and there weren't any jobs for traders. In fact, the lack of jobs had nothing to do with a bad economy. It was because algorithms had made execution traders 10 times more productive, or said differently, there were now 10 times too many traders than the city needed. Nevertheless, most of them said I had a good CV and were happy to have me on their list. So every day I harassed them with phone calls, and even though I was in no position to make demands, I said I only wanted to be a buy-side trader.

One Saturday night I was out eating Thai food at the Walmer Castle with my friend Reff. He introduced me to another guy who was a portfolio manager at a hedge fund. The conversation turned to trading, and I explained how I'd blown up my account during 7/7. *"Well, if you're looking for work then we have a job opening at Perdu,"* he said but then added, *"But you wouldn't want to work there mate."*

"Why's that?" I asked.

"Because the guy who runs the trading desk is a total dick. He just fired the third guy in a row who tried to work with him." We had a few more beers and a few more laughs, and by the end of the night the three of us were rolling drunk.

The next day I was intrigued by what I'd heard about Perdu, so I jumped on the Internet to find out more. Alas, nothing came up. So I called a few friends in the industry, but no one had ever heard of them. On Monday, I got on with calling the head-hunters and reminding them that I was still looking for a job as a buy-side trader. Some had stopped taking my calls, but the guy from Hays was always happy to chat. He was young and knew nothing about anything, and I assumed he only talked to me to learn about the industry. And so it was a total surprise when he said, *"I think I might have something for you Damon."*

"Yeah, what's that?" I replied.

"I'm in contact with a New York hedge fund who've recently set up an office in London. They're looking to hire an execution trader and need someone ASAP. It's a big fund, about twenty-one billion AUM, but they're very secretive so you wouldn't have heard of them."

"What's the name of the fund?"

"Perdu Capital Partners."

"I know them," I said. *"Just get me in there for an interview, and I'll get us the job."*

To my surprise he did just that, and by the end of

the week I'd been in for three interviews at the prestigious Mayfair offices of the obscure hedge fund. He wasn't kidding when he said they needed someone ASAP. At last, I spoke to Jack, the global head of trading based out of New York. I explained that the job seemed very similar to what I'd done at Amrobas, and that I was the perfect man for the job. As we spoke via video conference I could hardly believe the connection speed the firm had under its control. I'd honestly never seen anything like it. Then he said, *"Listen Damon, you're in the top ten percent of traders in London. What makes you want to work for Perdu?"*

It was the most bizarre thing to say, and I sat there perplexed for a moment. How did he supposedly know I was in the top 10% of traders? What did that even mean to say top 10%? Perhaps he'd spoken to someone at Amrobas. *'No way,'* I thought. *'Tanner would have destroyed me.'* I figured it was some kind of trick question to analyse my reaction at being referred to as such so staring back at him confidently, I replied, *"I like the idea that you have a large number of portfolio managers working individually and fighting for their own survival. I like how portfolio managers trade stocks and you in turn trade the portfolio managers. I also like the people I've met so far in the interview process."* Unfortunately, Jack's concentration had moved to his Blackberry, and he hardly noticed when I finished speaking. *"Jack,"* I said, and he looked up. *"These people here, these are my kind of people."*

"Ok Damon, but what about handling stressful environments. What about handling these people when they're in a difficult situation."

"Sure, no problem," I said. *"Like water off a duck's*

back." He didn't reply, just stared at me for a long time through the 50-inch screen. On his face was a look somewhere between amusement and reasoning and I imagined him thinking, *'Famous last words kid.'* Then he smiled and relaxed in his chair. "*Ok, good. We'd like you to take the exam now. Good luck.*"

I left the room to find Charlie, the head of the London office, waiting for me in reception. "*How'd you go,*" he asked in a friendly tone.

"*Good, I think. Jack mentioned something about an exam*?"

"*Yes, you can forget all about the interviews now. From this point forward the decision on whom we hire is entirely based on the results of the exam. It was designed by some of the best psychologists in the world for the exact job you'd be doing. You can't cheat it, and you can't game it, so don't bother trying. My only advice is to just be honest.*"

I followed him into a meeting room where a glass of water, a pad of paper, and a pen were waiting. After I'd sat down he handed me a test booklet and explained the rules. "*Ok Damon, this is a psychometric profile examination. It contains several sections. You can take as long as you wish to complete all sections. But once you give it to me that's it.*"

He left the room, and I started working my way through the gruelling exam. Having been given an unlimited timeframe, I was confident that I could solve any problem. Even so, my strategy was to burn through it as fast as possible on the first run, then more slowly on the second run, and then slower again for a third run. Each time I couldn't figure out an answer I just relaxed and thought, *'I can feel the answer. I know I can figure it out. I'll get it next time.'*

There were questions on problem-solving, abstractions, maths, pattern recognition, and code breaking. Oh, and one final section that could only be described as sick and twisted. It took about two hours to get through the first three cycles and then I was left with about 10 problems that I hadn't solved. Only one of them was in the section on number sequences. I'd tried every angle of mathematical reasoning but I just couldn't crack it. Until *Boom!* I saw the solution. It was an alphabetic code hidden within a numeric code. *'How did I miss that three times over?'* I thought. *'Oh well, it doesn't matter because I got it now.'* They were the kind of questions where you knew immediately if you were right or just guessing, and I was happy that I'd gotten them all right. Then I pushed through two more cycles which were really just checking, before facing the remaining unanswerable questions head on. But no matter my repeated what-if iterations I just couldn't figure out what they wanted me to say in response to, *"Which would you prefer – to hurt a small animal or to lie to your boss?"* I recalled the advice I'd been given, but it didn't help since I had no honest opinion either way. *'What was the lesser evil according to them? What was the lesser evil according to me?'* Then I smiled and answered, *"I want to hurt small animals."* I supposed it was just a trick to break my emotional balance and damage my performance in the rest of the exam.

When I finally handed my papers to Charlie, I smiled and said, *"Easy."* He knew I was joking and smiled back. Then he said, *"Damon, it's been great to meet you. Thank you for your time and good luck."*

I went home and set about increasing the

probability of getting the job over some other guy. Having received several business cards, I could see that the firm used firstname.lastname@perducap.com for all their email addresses. So I sat down and wrote out an email to Jack in New York.

Hi Jack,

I want to thank you for the video interview we had today. It was a good chat but no matter how good the technology it just wasn't the same as meeting in person.

Indeed, I don't think I was able to convey my true personality which is profoundly more passionate and motivated than might have come across the screen. I'm known to be energetic with a zeal for openness and sharing with my colleagues. However, above all, I stand for honesty and integrity in what I do.

If given the chance I will work my guts out for you day in and day out with complete dedication.

Damon.

A few days later I was skateboarding through Hyde Park on my way to a touch football game when I got a call from Vito, the head of the London trading desk. He said I'd been chosen for the job and he wanted me to start on Monday. *"Wow, that's fantastic news,"* I said doing my best to hide the elation. *"I'll see you Monday morning 6:30 am sharp. Thank you, sir, you won't be disappointed."* I hung up the phone and put it in my pocket. Then I picked up my skateboard and threw it into a tree.

My first day at Perdu reminded me of putting on

headphones for the first time and hearing what other people couldn't hear. As Charlie walked me around the office I discovered a clean, modern layout with beautiful artwork on every wall and a fully equipped kitchen. Then we retired to a soundproofed meeting room and talked for several hours. *"Perdu is the quintessential hedge fund,"* he said, *"with exposure to every asset class, strategy and style."* Thus far I'd gained little information about the fund, but now he took me through the firm's marketing material. In it, I discovered that the minimum investment was $10m, though Charlie qualified it by explaining that there was a five-year waiting list before you could even be considered as an investor. The performance I saw on the next page completely blew me away: 15 years of track record, average return 17%, Sharpe ratio 3.1. *'What! Is that even possible?'* I thought. *'Yes,'* Charlie nodded having read my mind.

When I'd finished taking in the last of it, he went on, *"Perdu is different to anywhere you've worked before. We have no logo and no HR department, no politics and no middle management. Staff have just one purpose – to do their job perfectly in every second of every day. We maintain a ruthless pursuit of excellence, and if that's not for you, then you'll be shown the door."* I gulped as I recalled that three candidates had tried and failed before me. He went on, *"As you've no doubt seen, there is no mention of Perdu in the press. That's because we pay them not to talk about us. So while other funds are talking it up, or talking their book, we believe that those who say don't know, and those who know don't say. This is a phrase you'll hear often, and it's the mindset we'd like you to adopt."*

We left the meeting room, and I was shown to my desk where Vito was too busy clicking and typing to say hello. I looked around for a moment and then sat down. It wasn't really a trading floor; it was an office. In fact, it was so quiet, it felt more like a library. *'Just beautiful,'* I thought. *'This is nothing like a sell-side trading floor. Now I won't ever have to listen to CNBC again.'* Finally, Vito finished what he was doing and turned to welcome me. And there started the most turbulent relationship of my life.

Soon the IT guys came by to say hello and after a brief chat Harry, the head of hardware, took me for a walk. Along a hallway, we came to a retina scanner on the wall. He stared at it for a moment and then a door clicked open. It was so well concealed that I hadn't even known it was a door. I followed him in and realised it was the cold room where our server blades were housed. Unlike my time on the sell-side, where tower PCs sat burning under our desks, all the hardware at Perdu ran out of a cold room. And damn if it wasn't the coolest room I'd ever seen. He explained all the gear and said we had our own dedicated cable running under the Atlantic to connect us to the head office in New York. As I stood there wide-eyed, I remembered back to the first time I'd ever used a computer. I was five years old, and the machine was a TRS-80. I remembered it taking my brother and I three hours to type out a simple program in BASIC and then almost as long again to record it onto a cassette tape. Alas, it was all for nothing, for those silly tape drives hardly ever worked. "*Those are yours,*" Harry said snapping me out of the moment. He was pointing to three octa-core server blades, two of which ran

Windows and the other Linux. After I'd thanked him, I returned to my desk to find Simon, the head of software, waiting for me. If I'd thought the hardware was complex, I can tell you it wasn't a patch on the software. Indeed, just to install and set everything up took us over four hours.

I spent the rest of the week watching Vito closely and learning to navigate my way around the seven screens that hung in front of me. As I took it all in the desire to master it yearned deep inside. But there sure was a lot to learn for depending on what I traded, and for whom, I had to choose between 19 different trading apps: TSCN, REAL, FIDS, BEMS, GLTR, AUTB, PASS, REDI, LBTT, XTAS, CURX, HOTS, BARX, ABFX, UBFX, BLKS, LNET, SPRD, IPOS. Plus, I went straight onto live systems, where one bad click could mean sending an error report directly to Ezra, the founder and CEO of the firm.

The portfolio managers were divided into two broad groups. The first, which I called the *old-school* portfolio managers, ran low-frequency strategies such as fundamental long/short, event-driven, risk arbitrage, closed-end fund arbitrage, and global macro. Though they sometimes passed us orders over the phone, we generally preferred them to email or Bloomberg them through. That way, we'd have a clear audit trail should anything go wrong.

The second group were what I called *new-school* portfolio managers. They never passed us orders since the automated trading systems they developed used *FIX connectivity* to shoot their orders straight into the market. Some ran statistical arbitrage models (StatArb) that were offshoots of the Fama and French, or Barra factor-driven variety. They were always market neutral and held thousands of positions at any one time. Others were entirely different and might have taken directional exposure or engaged in cross-asset class arbitrage. Collectively, we referred to all the new-school portfolio managers as *quants* and what they developed as *quant models*. It was our job to manage these on a day-to-day basis since the portfolio managers' time was considered better spent developing the strategy. Plus, all the important guys were based out of New York, and therefore sound asleep during the European session. It was an exciting role, and managing them was an epic responsibility. And though I wasn't fully aware of the sea change taking place, the quant models were fast becoming the dominant force in the market. Though eventually, even the quants would have their day of reckoning.

14. NEW YORK

At the end of my first week, Vito turned to me and said, *"Damon, what do you think about taking a trip out to New York?"*

"New York!" I exclaimed. *"That would be amazing."*

"Good, well you need to meet all the important portfolio managers in the firm, and of course, you need to meet Ezra." Then he handed me a wad of papers. *"Here's your itinerary, hotel details, and what not. Your flight leaves tomorrow."*

"Tomorrow?" I replied but then added, *"Sure, ok. Are you coming with me?"*

"Yes, but I'll be taking a different flight. I'll see you at the office on Sunday night, midnight. Don't be late."

"Midnight? I don't understand."

"Yes, we'll need to spend some time with tech support to get our systems are up and running, and then, of course, we'll be trading European hours."

"Oh yeah, of course. Sorry"

"No problem Damon. You did a good job this week." As he turned to leave, I glanced down at the itinerary, but my eyes froze when I got to reading the office address.

"Wait!" I said. *"Is this right? Is this a joke?"*

"Is what a joke?" He replied.

"Look," I said pointing at the paper. *"The office address is 666 Fifth Avenue. That's the devil's number man!"*

"Ha!" He replied and looked quite amused. *"This is a Jewish firm Damon. 666 has no significance in Judaism."*

"Oh, ok. Right. Well, I'll see you in New York then." And with that he left me standing there in disbelief.

It was 11:45 pm on Sunday night when I stood alone in a patch of darkness on the usually bustling Fifth Avenue. I gazed up and down the 41-story tower trying to learn something, but my eyes kept returning to the searing red glow of the rooftop insignia – the ominous and terrifying numbers of 666. *'Just relax,'* I thought. *'The numbers don't mean anything. There is no underlying truth.'*

I crossed the street and entered the sparse lobby where I introduced myself to a security guard hoping he wasn't the gatekeeper to hell. Instead, he was a friendly old chap who seemed happy to have something to do. He took a digital copy of my hand and fingerprints and then did a retina scan. Together they would give me access to those floors and sections I was authorised to enter. It was cool technology, and the fun of it lifted my spirits.

When the elevator opened on the top floor, I stepped out to find Vito waiting for me in a small reception area. *"Good flight?"* he asked. *"How's the hotel?"*

"Great, everything's great," I said. He led me to a large open plan office where two IT guys were piecing together the last of our flatscreen frameworks. They turned and introduced themselves and then asked what side I wanted Windows and Linux, whether I was left or right handed, and if I'd had my biometrics taken. Then they wired it all up and showed me how to use the scanner to get through the lock-screen. We didn't need to install or setup any software since they'd done a remote clone of our hard drives in London. Then we all passed around business cards, and they said to call anytime day or night if there was a problem.

Having an identical setup to that in London I was comfortable trading in and out BUND, BOBL, FTSE, STXE, CAC, and DAX for an hour before the real action started in the stockmarket. We traded through the night and finished up at noon, before heading to a dining area where we enjoyed the banquet lunch that Ezra had delivered to the office each day. Afterwards, Vito had to go somewhere for an hour and said I was free to wander around and get a feel for the place. As I did, I noticed that everywhere my retina scan allowed me to go I saw the same Mezuzah scrolls on the walls, just as we had in the London office.

When Vito returned we headed upstairs, which was a surprise since I'd thought we were already on the top floor. Then he had me wait on a couch while he went ahead. As I sat there looking around the only thing I could see was a glass-walled conference room with a bunch of people standing around inside. I watched them for a while and eventually realised they were running some kind of experiment with lasers, cords and light bulbs. Each time a light bulb turned on or off they clapped and cheered. When Vito returned to fetch me, I followed him down the hallway, and as we passed the commotion in the conference room, he turned to me and said, *"These guys on the right. They run Bluewave. The portfolio manager's name is Nikolai."* I nodded that I understood it was important and we carried on toward the large airy space in front of us. When we arrived, I was amazed to find a giant square room with a single glass office in the centre. We walked toward it, but about halfway there Vito stopped, turned to me, and nodded. He was saying, *'Look around. Enjoy yourself.'* It sure was a lovely environment, calm and quiet, with lots of light coming in from the glass outer shell of the building. It was an entirely different world to what I'd imagined 12 hours earlier gazing up at the menacing 666.

"In front of us is Ezra," Vito said snapping me out of the moment. We made eye contact, and a subtle nod conveyed that it was game time. The door was wide open when we got there, and Vito knocked softly on the inside wall of the glass box. Ezra looked up and as Vito entered it brought out a smile and a handshake. Then I was introduced, but as I reached out to shake his hand, he looked away at the moment of impact. That really rattled me since where I came from you always looked a person in the eye when you shook their hand. I figured it was just a test of some sort, so I shrugged it off and nodded and smiled. When it was my turn to speak, I said, *"Ezra, I want to express my gratitude for the chance to be part of the firm. Thank you."* Then Vito shook hands with him again and took off.

The two of us remained standing there, but it quickly became awkward since Ezra didn't say anything. I tried to take him in, but it was hard to get a handle on the guy. I mean his skin was so translucent that he appeared more of an apparition than a man. Almost like a ghost. Or a vampire. '*Oh my God*,' I thought. '*The vampire ghost of 666!*'

Then, for reasons unknown, I started to wonder about my grandfather, whom I'd never met, and if he might have looked a bit like Ezra since they were both of Polish Jewish descent. I was about to tell him about it but then I realised what an idiotic conversation starter it would have been since I knew virtually nothing more about it. I decided that he wasn't really a vampire – it was just that when you had a net worth of $10bn you could afford the medical technology to keep living as long as you wanted. If I had to guess, and believe me I was guessing, I'd have said he was over 150 years old.

He was staring at me now, staring deep into my soul, but then he started speaking and I relaxed. He told me all about the fund and how it started, and I responded with a smile and a lot of nodding. He told me about the bedrock of integrity, discipline and excellence, that the firm stood for, and I replied that I understood. Then he told me about Isaac, the most important portfolio manager in the firm, and finished with, *"But he can be tough to work with."* Then he went silent on me and just floated there motionless. I didn't worry since I figured it was a test to see if I could hold my cool. Alas, I just couldn't do it. Somehow his vampire powers took control of my voice box and words started coming out that I'd never intended to disclose.

"I had a brother Ezra. He was schizophrenic. I'm an expert at dealing with difficult people."

"Well, it's a tough job Damon, but somebody's gotta do it. I'm happy to have you on board." I smiled and looked around for a bit and noticed a Mezuzah scroll stuck next to the door. I knew nothing about religion, and in my ignorance, I motioned toward it with my right hand. *"Ezra,"* I said. *"What are these things on the walls? I saw them in the London office too."*

He didn't answer my question but instead asked, *"Whaddayuh done to your hand Damon?"*

"Oh that. Well, the good news is that it's fine now. I had an accident a while back, but I was lucky and regained full mobility."

"Shark bite?"

"Yeah right! Actually, a shark bite is what I tell most people. But actually, I smashed it through a glass door in a moment of rage." He looked into my eyes and willed me to proceed. *"Actually Ezra, it's probably the best thing that ever happened to me. It was the moment when I learnt that pushing the boundaries was one thing, but if I pushed too hard, I'd wind up dead. When I look at it now it's a friendly reminder. A reminder of how lucky I was. And how lucky I am."*

He nodded and then motioned toward the scroll. *"Whaddayuh think it is?"*

"Well, I suppose it's religious.. Jewish I mean.. and.. or.. maybe it's the perfect hiding spot. I mean who's gonna steal a religious artefact? No one."

"To hide what exactly?"

"Oh, I don't know, like maybe old bearer bonds like those UK perpetuals from the Napoleonic Wars. Or those Dutch water bonds from the 1600s. From what I

heard they never defaulted and they're still out there paying interest. Someone owns them and why not hide them in plain sight."

"That's an interestin' theory Damon, but in fact, they contain sacred texts whose purpose is to remind us of our Jewish identity and faith."

"I'm sorry. I'm not Jewish."

"No need to be sorry, okay? You can just view the Mezuzah as a reminder to conduct yourself with discipline and integrity."

"I understand. I will."

Without warning he turned, picked something up from the desk, and threw it to me. I didn't take any chances by trying a one-handed catch which was lucky for what he lobbed at me was significantly heavier than I expected. It was a gold bar. *"Wow!"* I said struggling to come to terms with what I was holding. Not because it was gold but because it was so unbelievably heavy. *"Is this what I think it is?"* I asked.

"Whaddayuh think it is?"

"I think it's a good delivery bar from Comex. Like maybe someone screwed up, and you had to take delivery of some gold futures."

"And why do you think that?"

"Because it's heavy and you're rich! No, I mean, Vito told me that a few years back that actually happened with one of the Comex contracts and it caused all kinds of drama. He said if I ever screwed up a futures roll I'd be fired."

"Yes, that did happen once. So how much do you think it's worth?"

"Oh, well gold's trading around four hundred and fifty dollars now so.. well I don't work in ounces I work

in kilos.. but I mean I could figure it out. Well, there's twenty-eight grams in an ounce so one hundred grams would be a bit under four ounces, let's say three point six, so a kilo would be thirty-six ounces. Now to me, this feels like about ten kilos so that would be three hundred and sixty ounces. And at four hundred and fifty dollars per ounce.. well if it was a thousand it would be three hundred and sixty thousand.. so let's halve that and take off ten percent.. so it's gonna be a hundred and sixty-two thousand dollars' worth. Roughly.

"Actually, gold is priced in troy ounces, right?"

"Oh yeah."

"A troy ounce is about ten percent heavier than a regular ounce. But what if I told you it's worth less than five percent of the figure you came to?"

"I don't know."

"Do you think you made an error somewhere in your calculation?"

"Not really. I mean you saw how slowly I reasoned it out."

"It's not a gold bar. It's gold plated tungsten."

"Oh, I'm sorry."

"Don't be sorry, okay? Be smart. Assumption is the mother of all fuckups, so never assume. Even for things you think you know well. Because the truth is that you don't know shit. See that table there, well if that table represented all the knowledge of, say, the automotive industry, right, then even the best analyst on the street only knows this much. He spread his thumb and index finger about an inch apart and placed them on the corner of the table. "Right?"

"I understand."

"I hope so. Every assumption you make is a

mistake waitin' to happen. And every mistake costs money." With that, he took back the bar and placed it on his desk. I knew my time was up, but before I could say goodbye, he switched to vampire mode and floated back to his chair. *"All right Damon,"* he said. *"Leave the door open on your way out."*

"Goodbye Ezra. It was nice to meet you."

Vito met me outside, and once we were out of earshot, he said, *"He tricked you with the tungsten, didn't he."* I replied with a smile, and Vito laughed and patted me on the back. Then we went for a lap of the floor where I was introduced to all the senior staff in the heart of 666. After that we went downstairs to the first of two trading floors where the teams who ran the big three quant models were located. We headed straight for a conference room, and once I was set up with a notepad and a pen, Vito left me and went home for the day.

I spent the next three hours with a procession of quants and programmers. Some were casual and spent the time chatting like regular people. Others were serious and non-personal and had me struggling to understand them. Finally, I met Isaac, whom Ezra had warned me about, and all at once I understood what he'd meant by *a brilliant Aspergian*. Isaac had hardly said hello before he picked up a marker and started drawing tables and diagrams on the whiteboard. Then he stood to one side and said, *"Doo oooo err oo yoo underr st st and stand?"*

"Yes, I do."

"The en the enn then mem or ise it an der an der and err ase erase it before yerrr le eave."

"Yes, sir."

When I finally left 666 I wandered slowly up Fifth Avenue having no idea what I might discover. I was just happy to have gotten through the day without saying anything too stupid. When I came upon the Saks department store I went inside and bought myself a Mark Jacobs red leather jacket just like Tyler Durden's in Fight Club. Then I went and had dinner with my friend Manny at the Hudson Hotel.

We'd gone to college together back in Brisbane, but I hadn't seen him in years. After chatting for a while about the good old days I eventually said, *"So Manny, what are you doing at Bear Stearns?"*

"Oh, I work on the mortgage desk."

"You mean like in the book Liars Poker?"

"Yeah, something like that. I'm in origination. We securitise all sorts of dodgy shit into MBS and CDOs."

"Yeah cool," I said half listening as yet another gorgeous girl walked by our table.

"Anyway, I'm getting out of this racket just as soon as I get my next bonus. It's all just a scam. It's gonna implode for sure."

"What's gonna implode mate?"

"The whole dodgy mortgage thing. Look I can see what they're doing, and it all seems really noble to want every American to own their own home, but maybe they should think about the fact that not every American deserves to own their own home. Because at the end of the day an unemployed bum can't afford it, and won't pay for it, and it's all gonna end in tears. Sure, it's hypocritical for me to complain, I mean we're the most profitable department in Bear Stearns, but I swear it's nothing but a house of cards."

"Yeah man. Cheers to that!" I thought nothing

more about his comments until years later when those very same securities kicked off the worst financial crisis for 70 years.

The next day, at the end of my shift, I had lunch with Bryan who was my equivalent in 666 for the US markets. To my surprise he asked if I wanted to go and see the floor of the New York Stock Exchange. *"You what?"* I replied. *"I thought that after 9/11 the public was no longer allowed to watch the action from the viewing gallery."*

"That's true, but I used to work there as a floor broker. I could ask my old boss to pass you in as a guest."

I asked Vito if I could go and he said yes, and two hours later I found myself being escorted onto the floor of the NYSE. First, I was scanned and searched like a prisoner. Then I went through a tunnel and met John, Bryan's old boss. He was the senior guy with Kabrik Trading and more than happy to show a young bloke around. He led me into the *main room,* and as we proceeded through a slow lap, he recounted many of the historical events that had occurred throughout its 140-year history. I was so overwhelmed that at one point I stopped walking, looked around, and shook my head in disbelief. It really was a dream come true. What stood out was just how old everything felt. But I don't mean like crappy old. I mean carved stone ceilings, oak and mahogany panelling, and all the elegant classiness of antiquity.

When we arrived at their – well I guess you'd call it a bunker – John introduced me to his team. They explained that despite the rise of alternative trading venues the floor still accounted for roughly 40% of total volume. That's because it remained *the place* to do the big business. Soon we were back out in the thick of it, and though it wasn't the financial warfare I was expecting, they were certainly trading, and I tried to understand what was going on. We arrived at one post just in time to hear a broker say, *"Caterpillar something something."* It was unintelligible to me. The specialist replied, *"500 at 90,"* and the man said, *"Done,"* before shuffling away into a sea of blue jackets. We stood there watching the specialist for a while. He had this odd device about the size of half a keyboard, and he kept rocking his hand back and forth on it. He was pressing buttons with his thumb at one end and his little finger at the other. I realised he was filling orders and making the market. *"Is that Caterpillar they traded?"* I asked John.

"Yeah, why?"

"Well, I know a fair bit about Caterpillar. Maybe stuff you guys don't know."

"Ha! Whaddayuh know then?"

Upon hearing it, a few brokers turned toward us, and then a few more followed their lead. All of a sudden, I was standing alone in the middle of a circle with them gawking at me like I was an animal in a zoo. Then someone said, *"Oh an Aussie! Happy to meet you, Aussie guy. Whaddaya doin' in Noo Yorwk?"* They sure were a friendly bunch, or perhaps they were just bored since it was a slow news day.

"I just started trading for Perdu and my buddy Bryan gave me a pass in with this guy," I said pointing to John who they all knew. *"I got a story to tell you about Caterpillar."* I explained that Australia was in the midst of an incredible mining boom, *"and guys who'd*

· *been working at the post office their whole lives are now making two hundred grand a year driving trucks! Everyone's getting rich man. But not for long,"* I said.

"Oh, another bear huh? Heard this one before," they laughed.

"No, you haven't heard this one. You see my Dad's friend happens to be the biggest Caterpillar importer in Australia. And guess what? He can't buy any more trucks. Really! He just can't get them. So there's all these mines, right, but they can't ramp up because they don't have enough trucks for the job. And the reason? Tires. Rubber tires. So all the trucks are just sitting there on the factory floor unfinished. I mean, what good's a truck with no tires?! So now there's all these mines, who've agreed to deliver this many tonnes of coal to China, but they just can't do it. So now the Chinese are pissed off and their only solution is to build their own trucks to compete with Caterpillar. And you know they will. They'll copy the shit out of them and then sell 'em to the Aussies for half price."

"What's the name of the Chinese company?"

"I have no idea. But I do know they're making contact with people and trying to do deals."

The brokers were aghast, and so was the specialist, and all of a sudden there was action on the floor. Brokers started shouting and the specialist started thumbing his device. I assumed thumbing was selling. Then he said, *"Caterpillar, 10 at 20, 500 up."*

'Damn,' I thought. *'He just dropped the market by three percent.'* More brokers arrived from other parts of the floor wanting to know what was going on. The story was retold, again and again, and each time embellished to make it ever more bearish. I just stood there in the

middle of the crowd, shrugging my shoulders and saying, *"Yeah, it's true."* Everyone was having a great time and with the stock down 5% by now a few were making some good money too. Someone started calling me the *Crocodile Hunter* and then someone changed it to the *Caterpillar Hunter*. I laughed and proceeded to bullshit them with a fabulous story about how I'd fought off a great white shark while surfing the Superbank at Snapper Rocks. They didn't believe me so I rolled up my sleeve and showed them the 85-stitch scar on my arm. *"Whoa! Holy shit!"* they roared. *"This guy fought off a great white shark!"* Soon the brokers were in a frenzy with half of them shouting about my shark attack story, and the other half screaming at the specialist who'd by now taken Caterpillar down 6%. Finally, John pulled me away, and we went to find another post.

When we got there, he spent some time staring at the IBM mobile PC that was dangling from around his neck (this was years before iPads and tablet PCs). Then he said, *"Do you want to trade something?"*

"Are you kidding? Of course!"

"Well, you're not supposed to, but I guess it wouldn't hurt. We got an order here to buy 2k Apple. Go ahead and ask this gentleman for an offer," he said pointing to the specialist.

"Hey pal, Apple," I said trying to sound like one of them. *"Where can I buy two thousand shares.'"*

"Fifty-two," he replied but upon realising I had no idea what he meant he corrected himself. *"Sorry pal, 38.52, how's that for ya?"*

"Done," I said.

"Good," said John, *"Now just click here, and then here on the price, and then here to confirm."* He passed me a stylus, and I did as instructed. *"And you're done,"* he said. "*Now you can say you've traded on the floor of the NYSE."*

15. LONDON

The following week I was back in London and battling a learning curve so steep it might have been inverted. Perdu adopted the military method whereby a new recruit was broken down into a worthless pile of shit and then built back up slowly. For the first month, I wasn't allowed to look at the firm's positions or run my own instances of the quant models. Instead, I concentrated on trading for the old-school portfolio managers, many of whom had specific sector expertise. For instance, we had a three-man team of doctors who traded pharma & healthcare, an ex-BMW director who traded autos & parts, and an ex-Rio Tinto exec who traded mining & resources. And though I mostly traded stocks for them I stood ready to trade whatever could best express an idea. If a portfolio manager could name an instrument, I was expected to be able to trade it.

In my fifth week, Simon installed live instances of the big three quant models on screens 1, 2 and 4 so I could watch them. Still, I wasn't allowed to click on anything, so every time my mouse pointer travelled over their parts of the screen I held my breath for fear of accidentally clicking something. A few weeks later I was chomping at the bit to get involved, and finally the day came when I was allowed to make a few small interactions of my own. The most difficult thing was that there were no *Run Books*. By that I mean there were no instruction manuals, explanations, or notes. It all had to be in our heads, and Vito said anyone caught making notes would be fired. Furthermore, the procedures were always changing. For instance, just as I felt comfortable with a model's start-up sequence, the portfolio manager might go and change it. So I found myself in an endless cycle of learning something, unlearning it, learning something else, then unlearning that. It was a real struggle.

There were a lot of parallels to the video games I'd grown up with – warning lights and sounds, loading and reloading, things obliterating things. But not a moment passed when I wasn't acutely aware that with these games mistakes cost real money. To grind that into me Vito was absolutely vicious in his demands for perfection. He saw any interaction with the quant models as a privilege I had to earn by first doing good in the other half of my job – trading for the old-school portfolio managers.

Eventually, he let me take full control of the models for an hour or so during the quiet times. *"Vito is out,"* he'd say and, *"Damon has control,"* I'd respond. Then he'd sit back in his chair and stare at every mouse click and every key that I pressed. If I did one little thing wrong he'd scream, *"Stop! Do not hit enter! Kill that xterm. Damon is out. Vito has control. You're banned for the rest of the week."*

And just like that he'd take the game away from me. Often, he wouldn't even explain what I'd done wrong. He'd just say, *"Damn it, Damon. Think about what you were just about to do!"* and I'd say, *"But you made me kill the xterm. How am I supposed to figure it out now?"* Then I'd spend hours trying to recall what I'd done and how it was wrong. *'I got the ETB file. I FTP'd it to the server. I waited for the heartbeat. I ran the locates script. No, I didn't. Vito stopped me before I ran the script. Why did he stop me there? What did I do wrong? Damn it.'* I can admit though, that as infuriating as it was, it was a highly effective way to learn, for when I finally figured it out it, it burned itself into my memory forever.

Nothing about running the models was easy, and in large part it was because they'd been developed over a 10 or 15-year period using old languages and methods that were clunky and esoteric. And it was upon those foundations that they'd forged ahead in developing their strategy without ever finding time to step back and make them easier for us to interact with. As such, there were all kinds of bugs that we had to watch out for, and Vito had to catch me by screaming things like, *"Don't click that! If you click that you'll crash the whole system!"*

"But I'm just resizing the window."

"Exactly! Don't ever resize that window. If you pull on the edge, it'll crash the system!"

Sometimes I couldn't tell if he was exaggerating or straight out lying. After all, he was just about the most neurotic person I'd ever met. And why would a sophisticated quant model crash just because I pulled on the edge of a window? Whatever the case, you can be damn sure I didn't try it. Furthermore, I eventually discovered that no matter how good a programmer was, things would always go wrong in the blossoming world of automated trading. There were so many exogenous links between the models, the in-house systems, the FIX brokers, and the market, that not a day went by when one of those links wouldn't cause an issue. As such, most of the models were still a long way from being fully automated. They needed constant attention, decision making, and human intervention, and if I couldn't figure something out, I had to call the portfolio manager directly. As Ezra had warned, *"Assumption is the mother of all fuckups,"* so I took no chances.

An example of the Pareto Principle is that societies tend to evolve such that 20% of the people control 80% of the wealth. Well, it was the same at Perdu where despite having over 100 different portfolio manager groups, the majority of the firm's capital was managed by just three quant models. First, there was Interweave that ran a StatArb strategy with around $3½bn. Avi, the portfolio manager, was one of the nicest guys I ever met. He was genuinely happy that I was there to spend my days fretting over his model. And I certainly didn't mind since Interweave was highly interactive and gave me an excellent education in StatArb.

Then there was Isaac's model, Phoenix, that ran a $5bn Managed Futures strategy. It traded all the major contracts around the world – energy, agriculture, FX, government bonds and stock indexes – but it couldn't be categorised as trend-following, mean-reversion, or any other common strategy you might have heard of. Instead, it leveraged off Isaac's 20+ years at the vanguard of applied mathematics. He'd explored everything from the nonparametric estimation of probability density functions, to the shape of plasma, and the orbits of comets. But though he was considered the alchemist of code, he could be an utter nightmare to work with. Waking him up at 3 am with a system problem could elicit an earful of Aspergian abuse no matter who was to blame.

Finally, there was Nikolai's model, Bluewave, that managed around $8bn. It too was a StatArb model, but it ran at the cutting edge of high-frequency trading (HFT). It was about as close to being a fully automated black box as any model at the time. Indeed, I couldn't even see its trades because they were too fast and too many for a blotter to display in real-time. So when there was a problem, which there always was, we'd receive a bunch of arcane messages and do the best we could to find a solution. Alas, more often than not, we had to wake up various people in New York who had access to those parts of the model we weren't allowed to see.

16. VITO

It wasn't unusual for Simon to come over to the trading desk 20 times in a day, such was the complexity of our systems translating into so many problems. But he was brilliant in his ability to figure it all out, and the running joke was that he'd say it was user error, i.e., my fault, and I'd say it was an app error, i.e., his fault. But he was a wealth of knowledge and didn't mind me bugging him with a thousand questions about every little thing. Vito, on the other hand, never dared discuss the innermost secrets of the firm. Indeed, I suspected he hid a lot of information from me that was pertinent to my job.

Eventually I set up a meeting with Charlie to complain that Vito was being a dick and treating me like a temp worker. I wasn't exactly sure what I was hoping to achieve. I suppose I just needed to have a good rant. Though he was the most senior person on our side of the Atlantic, Charlie had no involvement in the trading aspects of the firm. Instead, his role was to present and promote an ultra-calm presence to stabilise what might otherwise spiral out of control. So it was that Charlie spent his days in a zen-like state of calm while Vito and I screamed into our phones and clicked for our lives just a few meters away.

I met Charlie in the last meeting room at the far end of the office. I didn't want Vito to know we were having a meeting. After we'd sat down, he said simply, *"It's ok if you want to quit. I understand. This job isn't for everyone."*

"I don't want to quit," I replied. *"It's just that, well, I was warned that Isaac was hard to get along with, but no one said anything about Vito being even worse."*

"Yes, I'm sorry that you weren't forewarned. I considered mentioning it during the interview process but felt it was better left unsaid. But look, what's done is done, and you have to accept that he's not going anywhere. And that means that if you want to stay you'll have to find a purpose in your suffering."

"Ok," I mumbled.

"The truth is that not everything is Vito's fault. A lot of it is your own stress at being unable to do the job. But that is to be expected during the first few months, and no one is criticising you for it. I'm sure that if you can just hang in there the learning curve will start to flatten out."

"Yeah ok, but a lot of it is Vito too. He's always looking to start shit," I countered.

"Be that as it may, your job is to tolerate him and his shortfalls. Has anyone told you what happened with the last guy?"

"No, what happened?"

"Well, basically the guy just snapped. They were having some kind of argument about futures, and then all of a sudden, he just picks Vito up out of his chair and slams him against the wall. I was sure he was going to punch his lights out, but thankfully, he just shook his head and walked out the door. We never heard from him again."

I couldn't help but laugh out loud, and all at once I felt a lot better. I never felt rushed in Charlie's presence, and for a while, we sat in silent contemplation. I got to thinking about what I'd said to Ezra, *'I know how to deal with difficult people,'* and gradually I became aware of why Vito was getting under my skin. It was because I'd been through it all before, yet hadn't quite accepted, that it was time to go through it all over again.

When I was growing up, my brother had been a paranoid schizophrenic heroin addict – and a violent one at that. And being seven years younger than him, there wasn't much I could do about it. In our house, everything was temporary – windows, TVs, front doors – all just waiting to be smashed in a rage, or stolen to pay for his addiction. He also bred these nasty pit-bull fighting dogs that scared the hell out of me.

Well, one day he came around and I knew he was in a bad way. Some friends of mine happened to be there, and in an instant I decided to hide everyone behind the kitchen bench and pretend no one was home. But he knew we were there and started screaming bloody murder and demanding that we open the door. When we didn't he started smashing in the windows with a block of wood. I remember whispering to my friends, *"Stay down. Be quiet,"* as the glass rained down. If it weren't for the security screens he'd have jumped right through, or else sent one of the dogs in for him. By the time he screeched off in his V8 Monaro one of my friends was pretty shaken up and turned to me and said, *"Your brother's a dick man!"* to which I replied, *"Yeah, I know. Just be glad you get to go home after this."*

Now, 10 years later, I realised that I was once again in the company of a clear-cut nutcase. But no matter Vito's OCD, bipolar, and near constant state of abuse, he wasn't a patch on my pit-pull wielding maniac brother. So I vowed to Charlie right then and there that I understood what needed to be done and that I might just be the only one in the world who could do it.

A few weeks later Vito arrived late wearing his sunglasses. I'd seen that a few times already and figured he'd been up all weekend on a coke binge. For the next few hours he had me do all the work on the desk, while he sat by my side criticising me and explaining how I should have done it better. He looked angry, he talked angry, he was just so unhappy. Then he received a call from the Porsche dealership and got really agitated about the new 911 he'd ordered. *"No! No! I told you I wanted red leather on the dash. Bordeaux Red!"* He screamed as though he were talking to Hitler.

I went outside to get some lunch. Vito never ate, just drank coffee all day, so I brought a Snickers bar back with me. *"Here, I got you something,"* I said and held it out for him. He responded by glaring at me as though I was now Hitler. Finally, he took it and placed it on the desk under his second screen, drawing careful angles in his mind and calculating the least number of linear perspective breakages. Then in a sheepish tone, he muttered, *"Yeah ok. Thanks. I'll just leave it there for later."* Then he made one last change to the chocolate bar's position. *'Guess he doesn't like Snickers,'* I thought and went on with my work.

Later I was chatting to Simon, and I told him about my latest nutcase Vito story since it was something we both had to endure. *"Actually, I think I know what that's about,"* he said. *"Right before the last guy left he gave Vito a Snickers, and now he thinks those are related events. Remember this is a guy who can't go through a door without twisting the knob back and forth five times."*

Well, the next day all hell broke loose. I was at work at 6:15 am when I received a call from Simon. *"Hey Damon, there's something you need to know."*

"Yeah, what's that?"

"Vito's dog died last night. Yeah, it's really bad mate. That dog was his best friend in the world, through the divorce and everything, so just go easy on him today ok."

"Yeah, of course. No worries, I totally understand."

Vito arrived just as the stockmarket was opening and I was too busy to turn around. I confirmed on screen 1 that Bluewave was balanced and trading. I sold futures on screen 6 for Phoenix, and I jumped in and out of screen 4 to get Interweave up and running. With the big three out of the way I worked my way through the orders from the rest of the portfolio managers, and about 10 minutes later I was all done. I turned to Vito and said, *"Hey mate, I'm sorry about Buster,"* but he responded with silence and evil in his eyes. Then he leaned forward and picked up the

Snickers before angrily and dramatically slamming it into the bin. Then he turned to me and said. *"I knew it was bad luck. You killed Buster!"*

If there were any chance of it being a joke, I might have laughed. But it surely wasn't so I kept my mouth shut. For the rest of the day, he made me do 95% of the workload of European trading, and there began a great battle of wills between us – him trying to break me and me just trying to survive. For weeks I endured his abuse, torment, and threats until the day I almost quit. I'd just finished trading futures for Phoenix when he ripped into me saying, *"Why did you trade that at Barclays? You know Lehman is first prime for futures!"*

"Because," I responded defiantly, *"we're short at Barx, and I'm buying. I'm working to flatten the position."*

"Never you mind about that! We're still a week from expiry, and the model knows to flatten by broker when we turn Auto back on."

"Well, how was I supposed to know that? I didn't write the damn code, did I? Just tell me this – why won't you help me? Huh? Why won't you help me!!" Then I stormed over to the closet, took my coat from the rack, and started swinging it around in the air like a madman. Alas, from the coat pockets, loose change started spraying out all over the place, smashing into walls and windows, and making a hell of a racket. Then I stomped my way out of the office with no intention of ever returning.

I sat alone in Green Park wondering how it had all gone so wrong. But then I thought about the quant models, and how much I'd miss them, so half an hour later I was back in the elevator heading up to apologise. As I exited on our floor I found Charlie waiting for me in reception. He led me into a meeting room, and after we'd sat down, he said, "*Look Damon. You have to make up your mind. This is going to be your last chance. I hope you decide to stay because we're all happy to have you here.*"

"*Yeah but Charlie, he's a complete nutter.*"

"*I know he is.*"

"*He thinks I killed his dog!*"

"*He whaaaat?*" A great big smile took over his face, and after I'd explained the story we both laughed our heads off. Then I went back to the desk and apologised to Vito. I admitted that I couldn't handle the business by myself but promised that I'd keep trying to get it. He accepted the apology but, alas, things only got worse from there. Each day the war between us started afresh, and I was reborn to suffer and die, time and again. But then a curious thing happened. I became glad for having to do all the work because I didn't want anyone else screwing around with the quant models – my quant models – for only I could run them the way they deserved to be run.

When I reached the end of my six-month probationary period, I was pretty nervous. Vito took me into a meeting room where a stack of papers lay on the desk. Then he reprimanded me for every single error I had ever made. It was an exhaustive list and a brutal assessment, and I was ashamed of my performance. Then he told me to go home and think about it and email him an explanation for why I had underperformed as a trader.

Later, sitting alone at my kitchen table, I struggled to come up with a reasonable excuse. I mean what could I say? That I was having trouble sleeping at night? That I was a former insomniac who was terrified of the disease returning? That I didn't like Vito? That I just wasn't good enough? In a lot of cases, I hadn't even known I'd made an error because he never told me. Plus, there were many cases where the alleged error was just a reflection of his own neurotic nonsense, and which never harmed or risked the firm at all. But I couldn't say that. I had to toe the line to keep my job. And so I responded as delicately as possible.

The next day as I approached the desk Vito told me to stop. *"Don't sit down Damon. Today you will not be trading. Go and see Charlie in the conference room."* I found him there with another guy whom I didn't know and to my astonishment, Ezra himself. *'I'll be damned,'* I thought. *'Ezra has left the perimeter of 666.'* We all said hello and shook hands and Charlie introduced the third guy from Caliper Corp – the same firm that had written the psychometric exam I'd done before joining the firm. The Caliper man was friendly enough, but he wasted no time in putting me through a series of multitasking tests. The first consisted of picking up and putting down a pen, a pencil, and a coffee mug in various sequences. Simple as it sounds, the manner of instruction rendered it very difficult. Then he put me on a laptop where I did a bunch of clicking and typing exercises. Again, it was very difficult. Upon finishing, there was no need to wait for the results, since it was obvious that I couldn't do most of what was asked of me.

Then the Caliper man said, *"Your level of performance over the last few months coupled with the cognitive and multitasking abilities shown here today are well below the requirements of a Perdu trader. You are suffering from numerous errors of perception, and though you've not made a serious trading error so far, the probability of it happening is too high for the firm to accept."*

Ezra didn't say anything. Just sat there staring into my soul. The Caliper man went on. *"Your brain, your thoughts, everything that you feel, they all boil down to a series of chemicals, reactions, and electrical impulses. There are times when your brain tricks you, lies to you, or in the least, misrepresents and distorts the facts. You need to learn to get a handle on that."*

'And just who the fuck are you anyway pal!' I felt like saying. *'You have no idea what I've been through!'* But I kept quiet and just stared back at him. Then Charlie spoke, calm as always. *"Damon, the job is bombarding you with an overwhelming amount of information, and you're not able to take it all in. You focus on one thing that is happening, the most important thing to be sure, but you miss many others. It is a common delusion that most people think they are good at multitasking. In fact, they are shifting attention between tasks sequentially, and they cannot multitask at all."*

I responded, *"Well it's true what you say. I'm working with seven screens, and I feel like it's impossible to focus on all that is happening. Things are beeping and flashing all over the place, and all of them are the equivalent of urgent."*

Then Ezra spoke. *"Damon, don't worry about the test. Everyone fails. We're all born neurologically defective to some extent, right. The point is to find your deficiencies and fix them."*

"Fix them?" I asked.

"Look I'd prefer to have no human traders at all but we're not there yet. We need you for all those things that computers can't do, like screamin' at brokers, which I hear you're pretty good at." Everyone laughed, and the jab changed the atmosphere in the room. He went on, *"Your brain can not pay attention to everythin' that is goin' on so you're prioritising what you consider most important. Your job is to go further and master your visual environment so you can pay attention to everythin' that is happenin', right. First, we'll have Simon remove three of your screens so everythin's in your field of vision. Then we'll fix your eyes."*

"Huh?"

"We've long been investin' in the cuttin' edge of technology to improve our vision. Because when your vision is improved it opens up a whole range of cognitive benefits. All of us here have had the operation performed, okay. Whaddaya think? Will you consider it?"

"Operation? What do you mean?"

"Well, the gentleman here can fill you in on the details in a minute because I have to go. But let me just say this, right. It's ok if you say no. We understand it's not for everyone. But if you don't proceed you won't be able to handle the requirements of the job." With that he stood and made ready to leave but as quick as a flash I followed his lead and stood with him. *"Ok Ezra,"* I said. *"I'll do it,"* and held out my hand. He nodded, looked me in the eyes, and we shook hands.

17. WINDOWS TO THE SOUL

I was told to go home and rest. No TV, no reading, just drink a lot of water and keep my eyes closed as much as possible. The next morning, I caught a cab to Harley Street where I found the nondescript building I was looking for. I went in, sat down and waited, and finally my name was called. What happened next was the most terrifying experience of my life.

The first machine's purpose was to emit an arc of electricity through my eyes and into my brain. The idea was that a normal brain running at 20 watts was underpowered and the principle cause of taking cognitive shortcuts. Zapping me in just the right way would permanently increase the brain's baseline energy consumption. Unfortunately, the procedure was the practical equivalent of a controlled and prolonged epileptic fit.

The doctor didn't say much. In fact, beyond "Hello" and "Sit" I wondered if he could even speak English.

The first thing he did was fit me with an EEG-type headpiece. But from the sheer weight of the electrodes protruding from it, and the heavy duty wiring they connected to, I suspected it had little to do with measuring electrical activity. Rather, I was to learn that the entire hat was a special kind of distributed cathode, and what I was about to receive was an advanced form of electroshock therapy.

A moment later I found myself being strapped to a table. Then the doctor rolled out a thing that looked more like military hardware than medical equipment. I started to wonder if he was even a doctor, or just a mad scientist with a rich client base. The machine, whatever it was, culminated in a binocular headpiece, which he duly fastened to my head with tight Velcro straps. Then he went about adjusting the fit of each nozzle, and when he was done I found that no matter how hard I tried to look away, each lens tracked perfectly to the motion of my pupils.

It all happened so fast. There wasn't a lot of hand-holding or reassurances. It was just suddenly alive and crackling like an arc welder or a downed power line in a storm. Then he cranked up the voltage and blasted me to pieces. There was no physical pain since he'd given me anaesthetics, but psychologically it was terrifying because no matter how hard I tried to look away the arc came straight at me in the middle of my vision. At first, I saw strange shapes and colours, but then the arc turned nasty and transformed into the visual equivalent of a dentist's drill. Then I lost control and fell into a raging fit.

Eventually, I relaxed, and then you wouldn't believe it, but I actually started to smile. Then I almost burst out laughing. However, a few moments later I was back to fighting it again. I swung several times between despair and elation, and it seemed to go on for an awfully long time. Then, I started to really freak out and tried to physically rip the thing off my head. Alas, my arms were strapped to the table, and there was no escape. Finally, the doctor flipped a switch, unstrapped the binocular headpiece, and withdrew the monster.

I lay there wide-eyed and terrified as I stared at the blurry confusion that was now my entire perceptive reality. I wanted desperately to close my eyes but I couldn't because they were taped wide open. Soon he was back and with careful hands he removed the electrode hat from my head and set it down on a nearby table. The next thing I knew he was wheeling along the business end of a Lasik machine and after he'd parked it next to me he covered one of my eyes with an eye patch and then positioned the single nozzle of the machine over the other. Again, he strapped me to it so I couldn't escape. And then he flipped a switch and the awful thing crackled to life.

A faint red light appeared and started to grow, and as the one-eyed monster peered deep into my soul, I thought of Ezra. Then it changed form, and suddenly I was standing in a dark tunnel in the path of an oncoming train. Alas, I was trapped and couldn't get out of the way. Then he cranked up the power, and suddenly there were screaming trains coming at me from all directions. Then I saw shapes and rainbows and colours, the likes of which I'd never seen before. Then they gave way to a burst of intense red light so powerful I feared it might burn a hole right through my head. I decided I couldn't take it any longer. I wanted it to stop. I needed it to stop. But then the unthinkable happened when I smelt the stench of burning flesh. My flesh. My eye was on fire.

Finally, he turned off the power, unstrapped me, and pulled the machine away. Then he retrieved a thick bristled toothbrush from the table and came in close. The next thing I knew he was scrubbing my eye out as though he were cleaning the windscreen of a car with a wet broom. I could do nothing but give myself up to the sick torture of a madman. When he was done he covered the eye with a second patch, but it made no difference, for the eye had already given up on seeing. Then he removed the first eye patch and positioned the nozzle of the terrible machine over it. When he was satisfied with the fit, he secured the straps and once again jacked up the power. Same cracking sounds like an arc welder. Same shapes and colours. Same feelings of terror and that same awful smell of burning flesh. Then the lightning storms faded, and the colours faded, and darkness crept in from the edges. *'Please no!'* I begged, but I couldn't stop the fade to black. *'Forever,'* I thought. *'I will be blind forever.'*

He unstrapped me again, but as he pulled the machine away, I saw no light. I wanted to tell him, *'Something's wrong! I'm blind you nutcase! I'm blind!'* But I just sat there frozen in a state of semi-consciousness as he attacked me with the toothbrush for the second time. Then I remember him peeling off the tape and saying, *"Quickly, close eyes now. Do not open again!"* Then he walked away, turned off the lights, and closed the door.

Five minutes later he was back and standing over me. *"Ok friend, now we go,"* he said. *"Keep eyes close."*

We walked together bumping into things and finding doorways in the darkness until eventually I was seated on a couch and told to relax. Ten minutes later I found myself wondering, *'Did he say I can open my eyes now?'* Over and over I asked myself until finally, I summoned up the courage and just went for it.

In an instant, I knew I wasn't blind, and the relief was enormous. I looked around the dark room, and though my vision was blurry, I made out the shape of a man sitting nearby. It was a huge surprise since I'd thought I was alone in the room.

"How do you feel Damon?" Charlie asked.

"Charlie! What are you doing here?"

"It's my job to be here. So how do you feel?"

"Scared. Relieved. Scared. I'm glad you're here."

"Well, you needn't be scared. Your vision will recover quickly. In fact, by tomorrow you'll be better than new."

"I hope so."

"I wondered if we might have a chat. Some of the concepts might be quite deep so just take your time."

"You.. you.. want to do this now?" I stammered.

"Yes, if you don't mind. Perhaps I should explain. I'm a neuropsychologist by training."

"So you're here to brainwash me?"

"Ha!" he laughed. *"Well, it's true that your mind is very absorbent right now, and there's a lot of things we want you to think about, but I promise it's all for a good cause. Now close your eyes and relax."*

I swung my feet up onto the couch and pulled some cushions under my head. *"Right,"* he said. *"Let's get started. What do you think about delusion?"*

I felt blank. *"Take your time,"* he said. *"Just relax*

and be honest and let it flow."

"I think most people are delusional to some extent, but they're too dishonest to admit it."

"Go on," he said.

"I was delusional. Then I took lithium and olanzapine and now I'm cured."

"Why do you think you're cured?"

"Ok, well not completely cured. But I'm way ahead of most people."

"But you still have much to learn and overcome."

"Like what?"

"Like how to recognise and overcome your emotional responses. You're prone to acting first and thinking second, and almost always too aggressive when buying a stock."

"How do you know that?"

"We've analysed your trading record since you joined the firm, and you cross the spread too often. In fact, you only do it when you're buying but not when you're selling."

"Oh, ok sorry."

"No need to apologise. All people suffer from biases, and you're no different. I'm referring to errors in judgement that reoccur time and again in similar situations. As a trader, every bias you have is really just a loss waiting to happen. When you're impatient, the market will make you pay for your impatience. When you're over-confident of a trend, the market will revert. As dynamic self-organising systems, financial markets will always move in the direction and the manner to take the most money from the most people. And it does so by targeting first the aggregate biases of the trader population, and once they're wiped out,

targeting the individual biases in whoever remains. At the end of the day, the abstractions of fear, greed, hubris and impatience are transformed into real losses for the firm."

"That sounds like the market I know."

"So how do you think physiology affects your trading?"

"A lot, which is why I've always eaten well. And I also drink a lot of water through the day."

"Are you drinking coffee and eating sugary foods?"

"Yes."

"I'm going to ask you to stop that. It's just not worth it. And you'll see for yourself the benefits that will arise. As for the rest of your diet, I'm happy to hear that you take it seriously. Your gut is a major source of serotonin which is one of the key neurotransmitters associated with happiness. If you eat poorly, your gut will be unhealthy, and your serotonin production will be too low."

He stopped talking for a while, and I wasn't sure why since my eyes were closed. Then he apologised and explained that he was taking notes. Finally, he continued, *"Ok, let's move on. Some people describe the mind as a transcendent and perhaps magical concept where the processes of reason and understanding take place. We don't share that view. We consider the mind and the brain as one and the same. The concepts of consciousness, thought, and reason, are just the outputs of a physical organ, of neurons and neurotransmitters, and other biological phenomena. That said, the complexity is far from being understood by either science or individuals. So if you think you understand your mind, you're wrong. Dead wrong. Your understanding is a poor joke at best."*

"Wow, that's a bit harsh."

"Think of something you want or don't want, or believe or don't believe. One could easily change your mind with an injection of the right neurotransmitter in the right place."

"Seriously?"

"Theoretically yes. But as of now, it's not really practical. For example, we don't have a syringe small enough and probably couldn't pinpoint the exact right synapse at the exact right nanosecond."

"So in lieu of that, I'm still my own person?"

"Not really. Despite your assertion to owning your own mind, to forming your own judgements, to having free will, you are in fact highly suggestible and more often than not the victim of manipulation."

"By who?"

"Who do you think?"

"The media."

"Yes, the media but also everyone else. Every parent, every teacher, every politician, every friend. What you believe are just those illusions and delusions that you find most palatable at the present moment. And palatable is where the real source of manipulation takes place."

"How so?"

"Palatable means two things: first it means those neural pathways that are most conductive to electricity; and second it means those pathways that lead to the release of happy neurotransmitters such as dopamine, endorphin, oxytocin and serotonin."

"Are there any unhappy chemicals?"

"Yes, and the main one is called cortisol. It is your

job to understand these chemicals. You need to recognise when they're released, why it happened, and the effect they have on you. Dopamine might be one of the most important. It provides the motivation to keep going through tough times so you can reach your goals, or more accurately, your rewards. But you need to find a stable source of motivation to trigger it."

"You once told me to find purpose in my suffering."

"Exactly, and it can be anything at all. For example, just getting to the end of the day can be the reward that produces the dopamine to motivate you to get there."

"I think just being part of the firm is a huge motivator for me. I have so much respect for the people and the standards that I feel immense pride in being part of it."

"Ok that's good but what you're describing is more likely oxytocin or serotonin. And I'm certainly happy to hear it because most people struggle to find that at Perdu. It is, as you know, mostly a place of solitude and individualism. But if you can feel a kind of loving and loyalty to the high standards of our people then that's great because you've found your source of oxytocin. And if you can identify with those high standards and seek praise for your work then that's great because you've found your source of serotonin."

"Yeah, I have, and I do. Obviously not from Vito, but from others in the firm."

"Fantastic. Now the flip side of the coin is cortisol, and for you, it's going to be the more important thing to think about on a daily basis. You can recognise its release when you feel bad or become aggressive. Feeling bad might mean fear, anxiety, emotional pain,

or stress. But here's the thing – because it doesn't come from the verbal logic of the cortex it won't make any sense to you. You just feel bad, and you don't know why. But I'm here to tell you that you can overcome it. It's very difficult, and it will take a lot of training, but you can overcome it."

"How?"

"By reframing your mind and your perspective to a state that either reduces cortisol production or increases dopamine to mask it. What I propose is a three-step plan, but it's up to you to implement it in whatever way works. Ok here goes. Say you're halfway through the day, and suddenly you feel bad. It could be something that you did wrong or something that someone else did wrong or something that you can't even link to feeling bad. The first step is to accept that cortisol production is a normal biological function that happens in everyone. The second is to recognise that you don't need cortisol in that moment. The third is to take action to overcome it."

"What action?"

"In the beginning, it's helpful to make a physical change to your circumstances of sitting in your chair and staring at your screens. For example, sit back and practice deep breathing, or get up and stretch, or go for a walk to the kitchen. Once you get there, make yourself a cup of tea. And once you've finished it chew some gum. All of these things can work to either reduce cortisol or increase happy chemicals to mask it. Eventually, however, and as I said this can take a very long time to master, you'll discover that it's possible to reframe your mind just by thinking calmly."

"Ok, I'll try."

"Now it helps to understand that it's the amygdala and the hypothalamus that are responsible for your emotions, and they are far more powerful than the prefrontal cortex, which is responsible for what you might call intelligence. That's why people often override rational decisions with emotional ones. But you're not a slave to them. You can learn how to remain present in the now, and that will save you."

"By thinking about a happy place?"

"Not really. Remember the three-step plan. First, you accept that a cortisol release isn't bad or wrong. It's just a warning system, and it's doing its job so you can thank it for highlighting a potential threat. Then, having assessed the situation, you recognise that the threat was exaggerated and has made you unhappy and aggressive. Then you can get your mind into a calm state and deal with the situation from that calm state."

"Sounds like meditation."

"Sure, you could call it that. Only meditation is practised over many hours whereas what I'm proposing can be done in ten seconds."

"Really? Ten seconds!"

"Eventually, yes. But this is a skill, and it's gonna take a lot of hard work to master it. But once you do you'll be able to turn the unhappiness of a cortisol release into the happiness of another neurotransmitter release. For example, say you're checking one of the StartArb models, and you see a problem. Maybe it tried to hedge but it didn't get filled, and now it's short beta and the market's moving higher. Well, you're going to get a surge of cortisol and think, 'Oh no, what the hell is wrong with this model. It's been losing money for the last half hour and it's all my fault for not paying attention to it.' But that situation can be turned around quite quickly by the release of dopamine that would accompany the search for and discovery of the error that caused the problem. And once you've fixed the problem you'd likely produce a surge of serotonin that would leave you feeling proud of the actions you took and how everyone will be glad you saved it from losing any more money."

"What about adrenaline? I asked.

"Adrenaline is similar to cortisol in some ways. But whereas cortisol is the feeling of fear and unhappiness, adrenaline is an immediate burst of raw energy. Of course, you don't want that screaming at you for quick action when it would be better to proceed with cautious optimism."

"So avoid adrenaline?"

"Avoid is the wrong word. Neurotransmitters are released as an autonomic response and therefore out of your control. Instead, you should concentrate on recognising why and when they are released and trying to turn that to your advantage."

"You describe the mind as a bunch of wires and chemicals but what about the concept of reality?"

"I'd say you should forget about reality. Whether reality exists or not is one of the big philosophical debates of our time."

"Is that what we're discussing, philosophy?"

"We are. But you have to understand that most knowledge starts out as philosophy. The science of biology started out as philosophy. So too did astrophysics. In fact, most pre nineteenth-century science was initially classed as philosophy. The functioning of your brain, the nature of your thoughts *and memory, your perception of reality – these are areas of enquiry that are undergoing a radical shift from speculative philosophy to hard science."*

"And I guess the conclusions are going to upset a lot of people?"

"Indeed, but that is still some way off in the future. For now, such knowledge remains privately held by those financing the research."

"Like Perdu?"

"Yes, we spend about twenty million dollars a year on neuroscience research. And we're certainly not going to release that into the public domain. The point is, don't get too attached to yourself. Don't be too quick to ascribe much meaning to anything. You're largely a product of what the agenda wants you to be."

"Wait, are you talking about me specifically or everyone in society?"

"Both. You are targeted specifically, and all of society is targeted generally."

"Ok, so who.."

"Let's move on. You've probably seen or heard about a portfolio manager who blew up and lost everything in a single moment of madness."

"Yeah, it happened to me."

"Oh, well I'm sorry to hear that Damon. So what did you learn from the experience?"

"That it wasn't the result of bad luck. I simply couldn't control the storm of bad decisions and indignant actions that arose within me."

"Ok and what do you think caused that?"

"Bad mood?"

"Exactly, but what is mood?"

"Brain chemicals."

"Correct. Hormones and neurotransmitters. Any mood but a flat one is the wrong mood for trading. So when you feel any deviation from the centreline you must reset and overcome the moment before taking any further action. The fact is that the stress of trading is almost unparalleled in its potential to release exactly the wrong neurochemicals at the wrong time. Unchecked they can destroy your judgment and your memory and lead to disaster. Your job is to be able to objectively diagnose yourself and recognise the tell-tale signs of neurochemical release."

"Ok but assuming I can do that how do I take the next step. How do I reframe my mind?"

"Since all of your reality is fabricated it is within your power to fabricate whatever reality you wish. Just think about people who see Jesus in a grilled cheese sandwich."

"Ha! Or the man in the moon."

"Yes, there are all kinds of pareidolia out there where people see whatever they want to see. But you also have a prefrontal cortex, and that means you can overcome your autonomic neurochemical brain if you try hard enough. Notice I said overcome, not override. You cannot override it. But you can deal with the immediate aftermath and move around the problem. How would you react if I gave you an order to sell thirty million shares of BHP?"

"That's a huge order. I'd probably receive a burst of adrenaline."

"I'm sure you would. And it wouldn't matter how long you'd been trading for. A size order always prompts a neurochemical response."

"Yes, I probably get them five times a day!"

"Well, that's just plain dangerous. Trading, or more accurately, decision making, is not helped by the fight or flight response of adrenaline. In fact, it is severely impaired by it."

"I agree, and I wish I could turn it off."

"As I said, the best you can do is manage the immediate aftermath by reframing your mind. It is within your ability to push your subsequent thoughts down alternative neural pathways to those they naturally want to go down."

"If you say it's possible then I believe you."

"Let's talk about assumption and confidence."

"Assumption is the mother of all fuckups," I said doing my best impression of Ezra.

"Mmm, yes, and here's another one – 'Most people are more sure of everything than I am of anything.'"

"Yeah, I like that."

"You see when something is small and meaningless most people have no problem admitting that they don't know much about it. They might even combine it with a statement like 'who cares.' But when dealing with big topics, like which politician to vote for, or what investment to fund, the ego cannot accept that they don't know what they're talking about. So they take whatever tiny snippets of information they can acquire and they satisfy themselves that they're now informed. Worse, they believe that any increase in information is the same as an increase in knowledge. Alas, it's likely to be just the opposite since most public information is either taken out of context or biased to one side of the truth. And snippets are all that most people can be bothered acquiring."

"So how does that apply to markets?"

"Financial markets embody the epicentre of misinformation and subjectivity disguised as objectivity. Take corporate results. Let's say Vodafone announces a good profit for the quarter. Well, the truth is that you can never know if they actually made a profit or not. First, accounting laws are so complicated and have so much leeway inherent to their application, that no matter how smart an analyst is, a company can always mislead them. Second, it's human nature to cheat to get an advantage. So time and again we see companies go bankrupt out of the blue, yet still people cling to the belief that corporate results are a good guide to the underlying truth. Why? Because their egos can't accept that what they're being fed is just a manipulated version of what's really happening with the company. Government data is even worse. The wiggle room for calculating inflation is mind boggling. And yet people latch onto the announcement of CPI as though it is truthful and useful. It's probably more useful to count the number of ducks on a lake in Uzbekistan than to believe the government's CPI figure. Same goes for GDP and unemployment."

"Are you saying they're all fabricated?"

"Sometimes they are, and sometimes they're not. But it doesn't even matter because such knowledge can never be objectively and accurately obtained. Take GDP. First, no one can agree on how to measure it. Second, no one can get accurate enough data for it to be worth calculating anyway. Did you know that up to a third of all economic activity occurs on the black market? And that in most models none of it is included in the analysis? So the idea that GDP increased by two percent this year, when thirty percent of the data was

missing, is utterly ridiculous. The point is that no one knows what GDP is, was, or will be. So when someone claims it 'went up' it does nothing to increase your knowledge about it."

"You know, I happen to agree with everything you're saying. Yet, I still find it hard to reject in its entirety."

"Well you must if you ever want to be free of manipulation and make your own decisions. My advice is to do everything you can to prevent such things from entering your mind. They exist only to misinform you. Now look, I don't want you to think we're being overly critical of you. We're quite satisfied with your performance in a number of areas."

"Like what?"

"Like your absence of group bias and herd behaviour."

"Yeah, I really don't give a shit what other people think about the markets. My assumption is that no one knows anything."

"Those who say don't know, and those who know don't say."

"Truest thing I ever heard."

"Ok let's talk about Vito. How would you describe him?"

"Irritable. Unhappy."

"Yes, but he wasn't always like that. It was the job that changed him, and if you don't want to go down the same path, you'll need to take preventative action now. We all have the ability to make the effort to overcome our biological responses to stress. Vito is a stubborn person, and thus far has not been able to adequately address them. But we've not given up on him, and we

don't intend to. The same goes for you. It is in the best interests of the firm that our traders be adept at mind-switching because when the shit hits the fan, and it always does, it can be the difference making or losing millions of dollars. In this regard, you can help."

"How?"

"By not making it any harder for him than it is. By being respectful."

"And subservient?"

"Yes, for now."

"Ok, I will."

It was around 3 pm when Charlie helped me into a taxi and I headed home. When I got there, I had a quick bite to eat, donned my swimming goggles (to stop me scratching at my eyes) and climbed into bed. I slept fitfully, in tortured dreams from which I couldn't escape, until finally, I found myself sitting bolt upright and wondering what the hell had just happened. Eventually I got out of bed, walked over to the window, and drew the curtains. A moment later I was shaking my head in disbelief. Lights were like fireworks with each one tearing a shining beam into my mind. Everywhere I looked was like New Year's Eve.

I figured I'd never get back to sleep, so I had a shower, got dressed, and went for a walk. When I got to Marble Arch, I kept right on going instead of turning down Park Lane. It was too early to go to work, and besides, there was just so much to see. I continued up to Oxford Circus, took a right down Regents Street and wound up at to Piccadilly Circus. And there I sat, with a couple of drunken tourists, smiling at the world and feeling fantastic. Encircling every source of light were concentric rings of halo rainbows, and everywhere that light reflected left millions of tiny sparkles in their wake. It was as though I was living in a superior state of existence, and I was reminded of how old paintings showed halos around the heads of divine figures.

In the months that followed my performance at work skyrocketed, and I became the trader the firm had always expected of me. I learnt to react and adapt but with ample time to pause and consider before leaping into action. And nothing, not absolutely anything, that flashed across my screens could escape my eagle-eyes. It was then that Vito's appraisal of me changed, and he stopped treating me like a child, a Nazi war criminal, or a useless pile of shit. Indeed, we started going out with the sell-side where he'd speak of my work with a kind of respect I'd never thought possible.

18. THINK LIKE A QUANT

Two years went by, and the firm continued its impressive string of returns, adding 11% in 2005 and 17% in 2006. Meanwhile, our AUM rose to $27bn, Ezra's pay doubled to $1.3bn, and just to be fair, he doubled mine to $300k. Of course, I wasn't there for the money. I would have worked at Perdu for free.

But though I was at the top of my game the work remained a challenge. There was always some kind of crisis unfolding – either in the world or in the firm – and I felt like a competitor in an endless series of Olympic finals. I was so drained by the end of the week that a typical Friday night consisted of meeting friends at a bar, and then falling asleep on the bar three hours later. As for having a girlfriend – well that was close to impossible since no one wanted to date a guy who could barely keep his eyes open outside of working hours. Indeed, I could understand the appeal and widespread use of cocaine throughout the industry, and

I suppose the few times I ever did pick up a girl was when someone twisted my arm and said, *"Come on man, she likes you. Just have a few lines and stay out tonight."* But those nights were rare for I was terrified that screwing around with my neurochemistry could propel me back into the days of insomnia.

Lehman was our main prime broker (PB) and held almost all of our cash and positions. They were also our main executing broker for most asset classes. As an example of how close we were and the lengths they went to keep us happy, Matt, our relationship manager, once flew Vito and I up to Scotland to play golf on the Old Course at St. Andrews. In fact, the whole street was willing to do just about anything to impress us, and had we wanted, we could have gone out every night of the week to the best restaurants in London. But work was so draining that we just couldn't do it.

Vito was a huge foodie and always chose the restaurant from the latest edition of the *Hardens Restaurant Guide*. It was nice to finally be the client and not the broker, and I came up with several new versions of the KBC special. One night a sales-trader from a second-tier broker met us at Umu, that posh Japanese restaurant just around the corner from Berkeley Square. But as we neared the end of our dinner, Vito and I were so bored that we decided to cancel desert and leave as soon as he got back from the bathroom. Then Vito said, *"Yeah and this douchebag is wearing a Tag Heuer, right?"*

"What do you mean?" I asked.

"His watch. He's wearing a Tag Heuer."

"What's wrong with that? I used to have a Tag."

"Used to have a Tag, exactly. And when was that?"

"My parents bought me one for my eighteenth birthday."

"Yeah well, no offence Damon, but a Tag is a poor man's Rolex. And we can't come to a place like this with people like that." It was a typical Vito comment and not surprising since his father was a billionaire. But actually, he was right in one way – the place was incredible. It might have been the best food I ever had.

"Yeah, you're right," I said. *"This guy's pretty annoying. Let's just use him for toxic flow."*

"Let's 'tag' him then," Vito said with a smile. And just like that *tag* became the term for a sales-trader we didn't like but kept up a relationship with anyway. It always paid to keep a patsy on standby, ready to take the other side of our deadliest trades. And of course, to take us out to the best restaurants in London.

By now Bluewave was executing about a million trades per day and sending 10 times as many FIX messages. Lehman was exceptional in handling the flow, and I'd say they were the best high-frequency PB in the world. We traded our stock orders as CFDs in the UK or equity swaps in most other countries. That meant the stock technically belonged to Lehman, but we received all the economic benefit of ownership. In the UK, CFDs were used to avoid paying stamp tax, and if that sounds like a tax scam, that's because it was. But there were good reasons why every hedge fund did it, and no one ever got in trouble. You see the UK was the only major country in the EU that charged stamp tax on trading. So one year the investment management industry lobbied the government to eliminate it and produce a level playing field with the rest of Europe. They agreed and promised to get rid of it should they win the next election. But no sooner had they won, they reneged on their promise and kept the tax in place. In response, the industry simply asked their brokers to offer side bets, called CFDs, so they wouldn't have to trade in real shares. This allowed the same economic benefit of ownership, except that as a bet, it came under gambling law and wasn't liable for stamp tax. And even when the broker hedged in the underlying market they didn't have to pay because of a long-standing rule that exempted brokers when trading for their own account. Seeing that they'd been outsmarted, the government quietly agreed not to prosecute anyone, and so the system lived on.

Outside of the quant models I traded all strategies and asset classes. I learnt about money flow and contagion. I had access to an astonishing amount of information and watched everything from the Baltic Dry Index to the carry trade. I saw correlations last for months and then totally break down for no apparent reason. But it was the little things, such as Vito's repeated assertion not to be, *"Penny wise, pound foolish!"* or *"If the model wants to sell then bloody sell!"* that advanced my understanding of risk/reward in a way I could never have leant on the sell-side.

The majority of portfolio managers came and went like a revolving door. Hardly a week went by when we wouldn't receive an email from Ezra that so-and-so had been fired and we were to liquidate their book. But just as often we'd get the opposite kind of email welcoming a newcomer and authorising us to begin trading for them. With the smallest portfolio being $50m and the average almost triple that, you might have thought the transaction costs of so much turnover would be excessive. Not so. It was well worth it to weed out the bad apples. The problem was that even with extreme vetting there were very few people in the world who could actually beat the market.

One day after the close I got chatting to Bryan in 666. We spoke frankly about what we thought of the portfolio managers we traded for and agreed that most would be fired within a year of joining. But we saw a common trait in those who lost – a belief in the fundamentals and a claim that they *knew* the market or *knew* the industry. But it didn't matter what they knew, how smart they were, or how well respected in their previous positions as global head of this or that. People might have said, *"No one in Europe knows more about semiconductors than Justin."* And yet it was precisely those guys who lost the most. I asked Bryan why we bothered to hire them at all, and he replied without skipping a beat. *"They're just here as a smokescreen to hide what the firm is primarily engaged in – quant model trading."*

"So why are the quants so much more successful than the fundamental guys?" I asked.

"Because they never listen to the media. They don't care what the Fed said, who got bombed in the Middle East, or whether GM might go bankrupt. In essence, they have no interest in anything other than the factual prices at which stocks have traded."

"Because the media is all fake news?"

"It's somewhere between fake and meaningless. Wait, let me clarify. Ninety percent of it is fake and meaningless, and the remaining ten percent is almost impossible to identify as being true or important in advance. Take economists for example. These are

people who consume endless amounts of news and economic data. And yet they are almost always wrong. But they can always count on the fact that people are impatient and forgetful. So by the time a few years have passed, and it's time to judge their accuracy, no one can even remember what they'd said. Of course, by then, they'll have either reworked the old theory or replaced it with something even more compelling. This forms the basis of the perpetual cycle in which economists are never assessed on their actual utility. Their focus is first, last and always, to sound really smart and be really persuasive. And as you know, the best ones are damn good at it. Now I've no doubt that they're bright, hardworking people, but to make it to the title of Chief Economist they need to be able to sell ice to an Eskimo. And it gets worse because for every economist there's an equal and opposite economist. So if you go talk to UBS you might go away thinking interest rates are heading higher. But if you go talk to Deutsche you'd go away thinking interest rates are heading lower. So you have a choice. You can pick the assertions of the guy you liked the best, or you can believe both of them at the same time. This is cognitive dissonance and exactly where most people who consume it unknowingly reside."

"Wow, you really hate economists," I said.

"Yes, but no more than any other salesmen."

"So what did you study at university?"

"I studied economics at Wharton."

"Cool."

"You think so?"

"Well, I studied economics at UQ, which at the time was the best university in Australia. But I can tell you it was all bullshit."

"*Same here bud. Wharton had one of the highest-ranked economics departments in the country. But it was all rubbish. Probably the same rubbish they taught you.*"

"*Efficient markets theory?*"

"*Ah yes, let me try to remember. 'A stock moves only in response to new exogenous information.'*"

"*Yeah, that's the one. But don't you think that for anyone who's not a trader they wouldn't ever see how utterly incorrect it is.*"

"*What do you mean?*"

"*I mean the only reason a stock moves is because traders move them – because our orders hit the market and obliterate bids and offers. There's no invisible hand guiding anything to some fairy tale level of equilibrium. There is no equilibrium. Never has been. Never will be.*"

"*Exactly,* he said. "*And the kicker is that the vast majority of orders don't come from fundamental portfolio managers. They come from model-driven trading and risk management.*"

"*Which is to say they have nothing to do with the company whose name is on the stock.*"

"*That's right, and it's not just the case in the hedge fund world. It's the case in the vast majority of all trading activity. Honestly, I feel like calling Wharton and asking for my money back.*"

"*You could start a class-action lawsuit. Isn't that what you Americans do?*"

"*Ha! That's a good idea.*"

"*Ok Bryan, I gotta go.*"

"*All right. I'll talk at ya.*"

I sat around for a long time thinking about financial

market speculation. You see it wasn't my job to speculate for any longer than a few hours at most. Indeed, most of the orders I received were market orders, and that meant I got them filled as fast as possible. But every trader dreamt of being a portfolio manager one day, and that meant a full cycle of initiating and liquidating for a profit. The problem was that after six years in the market I found that the more I learnt, the worse my predictions became.

I suspected it wasn't a problem of information overload but of the manipulation of information, for the fact was that even the best analyst, who knew everything about a company, and its place in the industry, and its industry's place in the economy, still had close to zero ability to predict its stock price. I wondered how that could be and the answer I came up with was that stock prices were highly sensitive to their initial conditions, which in the case of fundamental analysis, were the valuation inputs. So if one little thing changed, and it always did, the entire forecast would be invalidated.

Now outsiders might have thought that things like IB Chat (Bloomberg's chat room application) were the equivalent of a secret old boys' club where you could get the *good word* on what the *smart money* was doing. But that was all crap. None of us on the buy-side knew anything that was golden, and you can be damn sure the sell-side didn't know anything either. And so it was that I finally drew a line in the sand and concluded that qualitative information about the real world was essentially useless in the business of predicting stock prices. In essence, I started to think like a quant.

19. THE TREACHERY OF FAKE NEWS

One day the market was very volatile and closed down almost 3%. That left it -6.5% for the week, yet the media didn't say a thing. A drop of half that size normally had them screaming, *"OMG! You're all gonna die!"* It infuriated me that sometimes they'd see a sun-shower and declare it was a hurricane, only to later see a hurricane and declare it was a sun-shower. The only conclusion I could draw was that the media were totally dishonest and being paid to say whatever the promoters wanted them to say.

To keep it all going they went to considerable effort to create a false dichotomy between reporting and advertising. But there was no dichotomy. It was all paid-for manipulation. Every story on every news channel. Every article in every paper. Paid-for lies. A constant barrage of lies! And more often than not it was designed to make people anxious, desiring, or scared. It was as if they sought to induce a measure of cortisol into the bloodstream of anyone who consumed it. To me that was just plain evil, yet apparently, no one else seemed to care. For when pressed they defended the media or claimed it was harmless and inconsequential.

It was late one Friday afternoon when I got a call from the back office. *"Hey Damon,"* said Vic who was the head of operations.

"Hey Vic, it's five to the close. What's up?"

"Ah, we might have a problem here. Did you short a million Mitchells & Butlers last week with Merrills?"

"I don't know. I trade hundreds of orders per day. I don't remember what happened last week."

"Ok, well it looks like you might have forgotten to enter it into the system."

"Mate, are you telling me or asking me? Figure it out and let me know as soon as possible."

"Yeah, we're trying to. We only just got the call from Lehman about it."

"But you said it was last week. How can a trade break go on this long?"

"Look I don't know. Let me come back to you."

A typical trade cycle went like this: Either a portfolio manager or his model would tell me to buy or sell something. I could either trade electronically (on a stock exchange) or over the phone (against a sales-trader). The decision would be based on the size of the order, the liquidity of the stock, and the urgency with which it needed to be filled. A week earlier I'd received a call from José, an event-driven portfolio manager, who'd asked me to short 1m shares of MAB LN (Mitchells & Butlers). I checked the stockmarket, in this case the London Stock Exchange, but there were only 80k shares on the bid which meant my order to sell 1m shares would have taken forever. However, I knew a sales-trader at Merrill Lynch who had a lot of flow in the stock, so I called him up and he agreed to buy the full size on the touch. Great. So I sent José his fill, timestamped a physical ticket, and got on with my other work. But whenever I traded over the phone I had to enter it into the firm's system. Otherwise, the firm's position would be wrong, and no one would know about it. I usually entered them in immediately, but on this occasion, something urgent had intervened, and I'd forgotten to come back to it. It was my error, plain and simple. That said, José should have seen that the position never showed up on his book – after all, he's the one who gave me the order, and I did send him a fill, but somehow, he forgot about it too. That meant the missing position was now my error position.

Vic didn't call me back for another 15 minutes, at which time he confirmed the position was real and that I'd failed to enter it into the system. By then I'd also found the physical order ticket on which I'd written *filled-ML*. I confirmed it with Vic and said I'd try to reverse out of it immediately. We'd recently hired a new trader, Archie, to sit between Vito and I, and we got along great. But no sooner had Vito said, *"Sort it out Damon!"* and gone home, Archie grabbed me by the arm and ushered me into the nearest meeting room. *"You need to get out of that position right now,"* he said.

"Yeah well, what do you want me to do? The market's closed, and the back office couldn't give me a definitive answer until it was too late. There's nothing I can do. We'll just have to run the risk over the weekend."

He came in close and dropped his voice to a whisper despite the soundproofed room. *"No, we are not running that risk over the weekend. You need to get out of that position right now!"* It was unusual for Archie to talk like that. We were very respectful of each other, and I never treated him as Vito did. But on this occasion he was assertive almost to the point of being rude. I looked at him in bewilderment and searched my mind for an explanation. Then I looked him deep in the eyes and said, *"Archie, what's up mate? Do you know something?"*

His pupils had been dilated since entering the room, but now they returned to their normal size. That meant he'd given up fighting the stress of the moment and was about to spill the beans. *"I heard from a friend,"* he said in hushed tones, *"that Mitchells & Butlers are getting taken over by Punch Taverns."*

"What? I never heard that. How do you know that?"

"Look mate, it's all been fixed up. The Sunday paper is going to print a big story about a takeover at a twenty percent premium."

I was dumbfounded, and I just stood there in silence for a moment. Then I said, *"I'll tell you what Archie. Don't you worry about it. I'm going to get out of this right now. And thank you for telling me. I'm glad you're with the firm, and I appreciate that you've shared this with me."*

We returned to the desk and I started calling sales-traders to ask for a favour. Normally they were happy to oblige, that is, to make a deposit into my *favour bank*, but no one was interested in making a deposit that day. *"Sorry pal,"* they said. *"The trader says he doesn't want any more risk over the weekend,"* or, *"Sorry, you've just missed him. The trader's gone home already."*

"Gone home already? The market has only just shut!" Call after call confirmed that Archie wasn't the only one privy to what the Sunday paper was going to print. The whole damn street was in on the scam. Finally, as he made ready to leave, Archie patted me on the shoulder and said, *"Good luck mate."* We both knew that a 20% rally in the stock would cost the firm £1m and me my job.

That night I met my friends at *All Bar One* which was one of Mitchells & Butlers' flagship brands. I told them about the million-quid loss I was facing, and they shook their heads in disgust at the corrupt dealings of the media. Then I explained that we had one chance to make it right. *"Just tell us what to do,"* they said.

I'd come to know the company pretty well over the years. I knew which pubs in London they owned and which were the most important. My plan was to carry out a pub crawl of sorts, and in each location, we'd tell the same outlandish story to the staff, in the hope that someone would pass it on to the Investor Relations department (IR). It was IR's job to comment on such matters, and I needed their official response before 8 am Monday morning. So off we went from pub to pub, ordering shots and causing a ruckus.

"Hey! Another round of shots!" I called to the barmaid.

"Blimey. Wats dis den. A celebrashun or sumfink?" she replied.

"It sure is! We just made a killing in the stock market. Well, not yet, but we're about to. A friend of

ours got some inside information that Mitchells & Butlers is getting taken over by Punch Taverns."

"Gawdon Bennet! We werk fer Mitchells & Butlers. This is a Mitchells & Butlers pub innit!"

"Oh really? This pub? You know, you could be out of a job soon. That's what normally happens in mergers."

"'Oo told ya dat den?"

"Sorry, that's inside information. But you'll read all about it in the Sunday paper."

With that, she turned and passed it on to her boss who upon hearing it looked just as bemused as she did. We ran that story over and over in at least 15 bars that night, and they all thought it was simply outrageous that I claimed to know what the Sunday paper was going to print two days in advance. On Saturday, we kept up the charade, but this time we hit the west-end pubs with our whopper lie about making a killing in the stock market because their company was about to be taken over. In the end, I was satisfied that half of London knew about it, and more than one panicky phone call had been made to the higher ups in the company.

I awoke Sunday morning with a shocking hangover and wandered down the street to buy the paper. I turned to the business section and right there, in giant font taking up half the page, were the headlines I'd been dreading:

PUNCH TAVERNS TO BUY MITCHELLS & BUTLERS
Deal to create UK's largest pub chain

It was a huge article and quoted all kinds of experts explaining how the merger *made sense* and would be a *fantastic deal*. I must admit that seeing it in print filled me with dread, for it was entirely possible that they really were merging, and it was just a simple case of mass trading on inside information.

On Monday, I got to work early, and after setting up the quant models, I called the sales-traders to see where they'd trade MAB LN in the pre-market. As expected they quoted the stock up 20% from the previous close of 620p and my dreaded £1m loss looked like it was going to become a reality. At 10 minutes before the open, I had Bear Stearns on the phone. *"MAB LN in five hundred k,"* I said.

"740 at 750," he replied.

"No mate. That's bullshit. Nothing done." I said and hung up.

Since the stockmarket opened at 8 am in the UK, most front office staff were at their desk around 6:30 each morning. Meanwhile, the rest of the city turned up somewhere between 8 am and 9 am. That was a key point in understanding why media manipulation of the stockmarket was so widespread. You see if a Sunday paper printed a story about a company then the stock would trade on that information until the IR department issued a formal statement. But there was always a delay because they had to get to work, discuss the matter, and then prepare the statement. The crux of my plan was that the IR department of Mitchells & Butlers would hear the rumours, see the confirmation in the Sunday paper, and then make a special effort to do something about it before the market opened on Monday morning. Alas, to my disappointment, they hadn't done anything at all.

I sat on the edge of my seat counting down the last few minutes and watching the exchange's order book build with bids and offers. The stock was indicated to open at 730p, and I was two minutes away from disaster. I leaned back in my chair and for no particular reason I looked around and I saw the Mezuzah scroll on the wall behind me. Then I shook my head and thought, 'God help me,' and turned back to my screens. It was then that my news panel lit up with fresh headlines:

07:58 MAB LN: "KNOWS NOTHING ABOUT ALLEGED MERGER"
07:58 MAB LN: "HAS HAD NO CONTACT FROM PUNCH TAVERNS"

"Holy shit!" I said. *"There's no merger. Mitchells & Butlers says no merger with Punch Taverns!"* I wasn't so much relaying the news to the other guys as I was confirming it to myself – that the marvellous IR team had done their job and set the record straight. And only just in the nick of time. Suddenly my IB chat pinged like mad as sales-traders all over the street pulled their quotes. *"Off that. Pull that. Cancel that,"* they said. It must have been a terrifying moment for the bullish manipulators who'd gone from an easy win to being utterly wrong. And all just two minutes before the market was set to open.

"Where are you now?" I pinged back on IB chat, but no one answered. I watched the liquidity in MAB LN disappear from the exchange, though it still indicated to open way up at 680p – a full 10% higher than Friday's close. Without barely thinking I jammed in an order to sell 300k shares at market and when it hit the order book it crushed the indicated price down to 595p, which was -4% on the day.

"What the hell are you doing Damon!" yelled Vito. *"Pull that order. You're supposed to be buying, not selling."*

"I know Vito. I will. Just give me a second here. I know what I'm doing."

I pulled on my headset and hit the speed-dial for Bear Stearns again. *"It's Damon. Where are you now? No. No. I wanna market in five hundred k. What? What! Then you're off my list!"* I hung up and hit the speed-dial for Deutsche Bank. It was 30 seconds till the open. *"Hey mate, MAB LN, where can I buy five hundred k?"*

"Well did you see the news that.."

"I didn't call for a news update mate. I want an offer in five hundred k!"

"Ok then, 630p."

"WTF! You got delayed quotes or something? Can't you see it's 595 on the screen! Nothing done!" I screamed and hung up. With 15 seconds remaining I hit the speed-dial for UBS. *"MAB LN. Where can I buy five hundred k?"*

"597."

"Done!" I said.

"Any more behind?"

"Yes, another five hundred k."

"Same level."

"Done."

"Ok, total you bought one million MAB LN at 597."

"Agreed, thanks."

With five seconds to go I pulled my sell order from the exchange and watched as the stock opened at 602p. But I didn't care where it opened for I was out of my error and I'd survived my brush with death. *"My man!"* said Archie as I turned to give him a high five. Vito shook his head in mock condemnation but he couldn't suppress the smile that broke across his face.

"Good job Damon. Now promise me you'll never do

that again!"

An hour later I wrote out my error report to Ezra. It didn't matter what I'd done to resolve the situation or that my error had actually made a profit (which wound up on José's book). What mattered was that I'd caused the error in the first place and Ezra would be pissed about it. As to whether José had actually failed to note the missing position, or whether he'd actively taken an option on me, well that's something I'd never know.

20. TRADING ON PSYCHOLOGY

As an event-driven portfolio manager, José had a few neat tricks up his sleeve. One day he explained how he combined the psychology of priming with a targeted use of firepower. What he'd do was wait for the release of a major economic figure, say NFPR, that everyone on the street would be watching. Now let's say the figure was 120k new jobs created and that was a good number because the street was expecting 85k. Well that number, 120, would be imprinted in the mind of every trader as a good number. José would say that everyone was primed to 120. So he'd go through every stock in Europe and find the ones that were trading just under €120.00 or €12.00 or €1.20. Then he'd pick two or three stocks and have me buy them aggressively. He said it was important to push them through the level from below, and once they crossed, to just keep on buying.

More often than not a wave of buying interest

would develop and when it did he'd suddenly call and say, *"Ok Damon, stop buying. Now sell everything you bought working twenty percent of volume."* The theory was that other traders watching those stocks would see they were on the move and get the overwhelming urge to join in the buying. They most likely had no idea why they wanted to buy it rather than fade it (sell it). Of course, it was because they were primed to see 120 as a *good* figure and in that moment, they only knew that they felt good about it.

Until José joined the firm it had always been my experience that being aggressive about buying a stock was a bad idea, for just as soon as you stopped buying, the thing would fall straight back down again. But with José using his priming technique, I almost always saw clear follow-on buying. Alas, the opportunities were few and far between, and as a purely short-term day trade, the profits were small too.

The firm was always on the lookout for portfolio managers who strayed from the strategy they were employed to execute. That usually happened when they lost their edge, but couldn't admit it, and so kept on trading with more hope than confidence. Unfortunately, José was one of those guys.

The stock was Rentokil (RTO LN) which was trading around 150p and printing about 10m shares per day. Well, José was managing a $200m book so when he told me to buy $10m worth of RTO LN, I thought nothing of it. It was, after all, perfectly reasonable to have 5% of his book in one stock. I explained that the street had no flow and that it could take a few days to work it on the market. *"No,"* he said. *"I want to buy it all today."*

"José, it's like a third of the ADV."

"Yes, I know. Just get it done."

ADV stood for *average daily volume,* and a rough guide was that if you traded more than 25% of ADV, you'd push the price. I figured he was expecting some imminent news so I got on the job and bought all the stock I could. By the time the closing auction came around, I still had $1m worth to buy. *"Hey José,"* I said. *"You bought nine million dollars' worth so far. Stock's up six percent. Do you really need another million bucks' worth today?"*

"Yes, I need it today."

"Ok but if I do this, it's probably gonna close up eight percent. I suggest we step back and finish it tomorrow."

"No, just get it done," he said.

That night his book showed a nice profit since his average price was well below the closing price. But the next morning there was no news out, and by lunchtime, it was trading back down near his average from the previous day. That afternoon he called up and asked me to work another buy order all the way into the close. Again, the size was more than the market could handle, and so again it put on a decent rally that left his book showing a decent profit. For the next week we kept doing the same thing but only if the stock was weak. When it was strong, we left it alone. Eventually, however, I started to wonder exactly what event José was waiting for. So I went over to his desk and asked him straight up. *"It's a takeover play,"* he said.

"Ok, well you got some decent size on now. Do you want me to tell the street?" I asked.

"No, just keep it quiet."

Soon he was long $20m worth of RTO LN, and I started to get nervous. Then some sellers appeared, cautious at first, but they grew stronger as the days went on. José had me buy more stock to defend it, but it didn't work, and he was soon under water and holding $40m of stock.

That's when I started making some calls and learnt that absolutely no one thought RTO LN was a takeover play. Was it possible that José had nothing up his sleeve and he was just trying to bully the stock? After the close, I had a chat to Vito about it. He agreed that it was suspicious and told me to give Ezra a call.

I picked up the phone and dialled 666 and Ezra answered on the first ring. *"Yes,"* he said.

"Hi Ezra, it's Damon." Of course, he knew it was me and didn't bother replying. *"Ah, well, I just wanted to highlight something that looks a bit suspect."*

"Ok."

"It's José. He has twenty percent of his book in one stock."

"I know."

"Ok, well, I just thought it was a lot to be betting on a takeover play that no one else has heard of."

"Says who?"

"I had a quiet word with a few people."

"And whadda they sayin'?"

"Nothing much. Just that they don't understand the surge in volume since nothing's going on that they'd heard about."

"Okay, go ahead and liquidate the position."

"How so?"

"Work to sell it at twenty percent of volume and use the house account. And don't tell José that you're

tradin' against him."

"Ok, and what if he gives me more orders to buy?"

"He won't."

"Ok then. I'll keep you posted."

Silence.

"Well then, thanks, bye."

Click.

Poor old José had no idea that I was quietly selling every day for the next two weeks until the house account was exactly short the amount he was long. Unfortunately, the stock drifted lower, and there was nothing he could do but take the losses.

We enacted that kind of risk management every now and then. The reason we traded in secret against them was to avoid the upset to their emotional balance that can accompany being forced out of a position. It was better to let someone operate in peace if you wanted to get the best out of them. Plus, they were each entitled to a cut (somewhere between 12% and 20%) of the profits they made on their trading book. Anyway, it wasn't long before I received the email I'd been expecting: *"José no longer works here. Please liquidate his book."*

21. THE SICK SALMON

Most portfolio managers were quiet introverts, but Ed was different. He was brash and loud, and we spent many nights drinking beers at Nobu across the street. He was what the old timers would have called a *plunger* which meant he wasn't afraid to go big when the odds were good. Well, one day I stumbled across an article that I thought he'd find interesting since his expertise was in food & beverages. *"Hey Ed,"* I said as he picked up the phone. *"You know anything about Salmon?"*

"Yeah, it's a crime to cook it."

"I'd normally agree, but what if there's an outbreak of fish disease."

"What? Where?"

"Norway."

"I'll be there in two minutes."

He came over with an excited look in his eyes. *"Damon, where did you hear that?"*

"Here look, it's on this website."

He had a quick read, asked me to send it to him, and then hurried back to his desk. Half an hour later he called. *"This is big bro. Nice work. I want you to short five million dollars' worth of Marine Harvest."*

"What's the stock?"

"Marine Harvest."

"I never heard of it."

"The ticker is MHG NO. Can you trade Norway?"

"Yeah, we got DMA in Norway."

"Ok good. I doubt you'll find any flow in it, but you may as well have a look anyway. Just go through your messages and IOIs but, please, don't reach out to anyone. It'd raise too much suspicion if you go asking around all over the place about a stock hardly anyone ever trades."

"Ok, I understand. If I can't find any flow how do you want me to sell it on the market? Aggressive?"

"Yes, be aggressive."

"You want to give me a low?"

"You can take it down five percent. Work to sell it over half an hour."

I'd traded thousands of European stocks in my time, but I'd never heard of the company before. I typed in MHG NO Equity DES <GO> and to my surprise it happened to be the largest farmed salmon producer in the world. I hit BBO <GO> and saw that liquidity wasn't great. I mean it wasn't that bad but to sell $5m worth was going to be tough. As he suspected no one had any flow and the IOIA <GO> screen was blank.

I started small and sold about $500k worth, and it fell a few ticks. Then I waited for about 20 seconds but, alas, no buyers showed their hand. So I kept at it until it was down 3% before sitting back and taking another break. This time I left it alone for several minutes, the idea being that anyone watching would conclude I'd finished selling. Unfortunately, no fresh bids emerged, and the market just sat there in eerie quietude. *'Ominous,'* I thought. I could've waited longer to confirm that they weren't just gaming me, but Ed had said to be aggressive. Also, I figured that since I appeared to be the only seller, the locals mustn't have yet heard the story. But soon enough they would, and then they'd freak out and start selling too. Suddenly my IB chat pinged.

> ED: Update
> ME: Sold about $2m worth
> ED: Order now $20m. Get on with it

'Twenty million!' I thought. *'What a nutter!'* At that point I was in complete control of the market since it was just me against a bunch of resting limit orders. So I got busy and sold another $1m worth. Then another $2m worth. *'Damn that hurt it!'* I thought as my order obliterated six levels in one mouse click. Not only were no new bids coming in, but existing bids started getting pulled. Upon seeing the action on his screen, Ed came running over to watch it first-hand. He stood behind me pointing and laughing at the GIP chart as I smashed the stock into oblivion. When it was down 15% I said simply, *"Down fifteen Ed, I'm gonna stop here for a minute."*

He came in close and squinted at screen 2 where I traded stocks, but before he could see anything I hit ⊞M to minimise it. He wasn't allowed to see what the rest of the firm was doing. *"Ok,"* he said. *"What have you done so far?"*

"Sold two point three million shares at 25.06.

About ten million dollars' worth of stock."

"Ten bucks? Come on matey. Get a gait on."

"Ha! You're kidding right. I couldn't possibly sell it any faster. Hang on, look! There's a buyer." Just then a decent bid emerged on the order book and then someone started lifting offers – my offers – since I was virtually the entire market.

"Ed let's just chill for a moment and see how high they can take it."

"Ok," he said and we both relaxed.

"So what's the story?" I asked.

"Well, in the past these farms used to use a shitload of antibiotics, but you know the danger was that the bacteria could develop immunity, and then they'd wind up in all sorts of trouble. So these days they've really cut down on that. But what it means is that when you do have an outbreak, it can wipe out a significant portion of the population. Now after the merger last year my bet is that they're using the same techniques across all the farms. So even if they keep them gated, that is, physically disconnected from one another, it's still possible that multiple pools can be contaminated. Imagine for example if the source of the outbreak was the fish food. Anyway, at this point I can't say how serious it is but then neither can anyone else. It's all about uncertainty, and there's no reason the stock shouldn't close down twenty percent today."

"But how do you know the fish are even sick?" asked Archie. *"It could be fake news planted by a competitor."*

"True," replied Ed. *"But this isn't some dodgy website. It's the leading publication for the food sciences industry in Europe. Plus, what do you think*

I've been doing for the last half hour? I've been on the phone with the company's IR department and the journalist who wrote the story."

"*Yeah Archie,*" I said. "*It's not the bloody Sunday paper, is it?*" We all laughed, though Ed didn't quite get the inside joke.

At that moment Vito finished up what he was doing and turned to us and said, "*Well if you wanna sell then quit stalling and get on with it."*

I raised an eyebrow to Ed, but he nodded. "*Vito's right. Let's get on with it."*

The rally had petered out by now leaving the stock down 12%. Click.. Click.. Click.. I walloped it with multiple market orders, and it fell to its lows of the day, down 15%. I paused hoping the buyer might re-emerge to defend his level, but nothing happened. So I hit what scrappy bids remained and kept going. "*Looks like this might take some time. Give me a call when you're done on the full twenty bucks,"* said Ed before heading back to his desk.

Half an hour later I called with his fill. "*Ok Ed, you're done. Sold 4.6 million shares of Marine Harvest at NOK 24.62. Stock's down twenty percent and.. still falling actually.. more sellers coming in.. getting some Bloombergs now.. people starting to talk."*

"*Good job. Hey, what are they saying?"*

"*Nothing really. Just dumb shit like, 'Have you seen MHO NO today? WTF?'"*

"*Ok then get on the blower and tell everyone you've hearing about a possible outbreak of Infectious Salmon Anaemia Virus (ISAv). Tell them it's like Ebola for fish, but worse since they show no signs of being sick until they all suddenly drop dead."*

"Really? Is that true?"

"Could be. Certainly sounds like ISAv."

I did as instructed, and 10 minutes later I was pretty sure no one in the financial world would be ordering salmon for dinner. Then I thought about the millions of fish whose deaths we were going to profit from. *'Oh well,"* I thought. *"I guess they were gonna die anyway.'*

It was about half an hour before the close when Vic came running around the corner. *"Hey! Tell me it's not true. Did you guys just short a shitload of Marine Harvest in Norway?"*

"Yeessss," I said slowly. *"Why?"*

"Where did you get the borrow?" He demanded.

"No, we didn't get any borrow. Why.. is.. that.. a problem?"

"Fuck! Lehman's on the phone flipping out. It's not an ETB stock!"

"Damn it," Vito said. *"Ok Vic, just do what you can and keep us updated. In the meantime, we'll work to cover."*

You see it was perfectly legal, reasonable, and commonplace to sell a stock that you didn't own (known as *short selling*). But you could only do that if you first borrowed it from someone else. Of course, they were paid a fee to make it worth their while. Now in a highly developed marketplace like Europe, virtually every major stock was what we called *easy to borrow* (ETB). That meant there was heaps of it available to anyone who wanted to short it. So much, in fact, that we never even bothered to check. Now in those rare and special cases, where a stock was tightly held and unable to be borrowed, then it was up to the portfolio manager to know about it, and he had to warn us before telling us to short it. I suppose that being new to the firm, or perhaps in his haste to get the position on, Ed had failed to do so. Or maybe he just assumed as I did, that Norway was a big enough market that all the major stocks were ETB.

The phone rang. It was Vic. *"I found a million shares,"* he said.

"That's it? You can't borrow any more?"

"Very little chance but I'll keep looking."

"Ok thanks."

Vic might have been the best operations manager in Europe. He knew absolutely everyone in the stock lending world, and if there was borrow to be had he would have found it. But just a million shares? Well, that was bad because it meant we had to buy back 3.6 million shares by the end of the day. And if we couldn't we'd wind up being *naked short* which was both illegal and a huge drama internally that wouldn't go unpunished.

We got busy calling the street and looking for sellers, but no one had any interest in the stock. So I jumped into the market and started lifting offers. Unfortunately, we didn't have algos in Norway back then so every time I bought I had to fill out a fresh order ticket and send it manually. I clicked as fast as I could and lifted everything in sight, but it was slow and cumbersome. I worried about what the locals were thinking, since all day long they'd seen my massive selling and would have assumed I was a natural seller, that is, someone who was selling shares they already owned. But now that I was ramping the market higher they might realise I wasn't a natural seller at all – I was a naked short scrambling to buy it all back by the end of the day.

A crowd gathered behind us – the operations department, the IT department, even Charlie came over to watch the action. *"Guys there's gotta be some sellers out there. Find them!"* I pleaded to Vito and Archie who were busy contacting every broker on the street. Meanwhile, I kept lifting the market as I banged away on the keyboard hard and loud, but with all the precision of a violinist. I wasn't about to let a fat-finger ruin the day. The problem was that with the order book so thin, I had to limit each order to 150k shares, worth just $600k, since anything larger might have launched the stock right into the stratosphere.

BUY.. 1.. 5.. 0.. 0.. 0.. 0.. MKT.. OK.. FILLED.
BUY.. 1.. 5.. 0.. 0.. 0.. 0.. MKT.. OK.. FILLED.
BUY.. 1.. 5.. 0.. 0.. 0.. 0.. MKT.. OK.. .. ..

"Oh shit," I heard Simon say behind me. The app I was using, Tradingscreen, was his responsibility, and it had just frozen. But then the order was filled, and we all let out a sigh of relief. There was now just five minutes remaining in the trading session.

"Damon!" Archie shouted. *"What are you up to?"*

"I'm only half way mate. I'm going as fast as I can."

"What's the balance? I got Morgan Stanley on the line. They're a size seller."

"Ah, ok! I need to buy.." but before I could finish he waved me away so he could hear Tracy on the other end of the line.

"She can offer one and a half million shares here," he said.

"Do it," I replied. *"Wait, make it one point eight."*

Everyone went silent as Archie unmuted his phone and spoke calmly to hide the enormity of the situation at our end. *"Hey Tracy, sorry about that. Yeah look that's done. I bought one point five million Marine Harvest here at 24.20. Now actually my size is a little larger. Could we make it one point eight million? Great. That's great. No, that's my full size. Ok, thanks. Gotta go, Bye."*

We held our tongues until the handset had landed firmly in its holder. We'd done it! We'd covered our naked short just in time, and everyone clapped and cheered and patted us on the back.

Later, after another mad rush to get the rest of the business completed before the close, we slumped back in our chairs exhausted. Then I tallied up the fish farm numbers and found that despite the drama Ed was up $350k in profit and remained short $4.2m worth of stock. Well, it wasn't the biggest position in the world, but it was all we could do.

The next day Vic managed to borrow another million shares, and when Ed had me dump them on the market, the stock collapsed and broke the previous day's low. We couldn't find any more borrow after that which was a shame since the $8m position looked a little small on his $250m book. Still, the stock drifted lower on no news until a week later when it broke badly on what appeared to be inside selling. The next day Ed discovered that a pool of stinky dead fish had netted him a cool $2m in profit.

22. OWL

One day Isaac called to explain that he'd built a new model called Owl. Unlike Phoenix, which was a directional futures model, Owl was an FX arbitrage model. I'd never seen a working FX arb model before and had considered it impossible because the market was too efficient. But I was wrong about that. Owl was Isaac's first foray into HFT and boy did it work. The most important thing was that it had to remain top-secret because if the brokers found out we were high frequency arbing them they'd widen our spreads. It just wasn't gentlemanly to abuse the tight markets they let us trade on. Next, it was important that Owl never traded excessively with any one of our eight FX brokers. That would limit their ability to figure out what we were doing. Finally, we had to ensure that Owl only made a small amount of money each day, for no matter how well we disguised it, they were always on the lookout for toxic flow. And Owl was the very definition of toxic flow.

Managing it turned out to be pretty simple from our end. Each morning I typed out a few lines of Python to initialise it and turn it on. Then we kept an eye on the P&L and when it got to $20k we turned it off. In the meantime, it was supposed to run on Auto. But because automated trading was still in its early years it was plagued with problems and often got into a position that it couldn't get out of. In that case, we had to manually trade out and then run some more Python code to let it know it was flat again.

To help us, Owl played these funny little tones for various events. When it opened a position, for example, by buying $2m EURUSD from Barclays, it made a sound with a rising tone, *Bing!* And when it liquidated that position, for example, by selling $2m EURUSD to Deutsche 30 milliseconds later, it made an opposite tone, *Bong!* So we had this funny little piano sitting on our screens that played this silly music all day long. But it worked really well because we came to expect the initiating and liquidating tones to follow each other, and when they didn't, we knew immediately that something was wrong.

I'd become friends with an FX sales-trader called Craig. He was a guest host on CNBC and he sure could talk a good game. He even claimed to be on the *Shadow Monetary Policy Committee* (whatever the hell that was). Well, one day he called up and started crapping on about the Fed raising rates or something. I wasn't really listening, and for no particular reason, I said, *"Mate, that's all a load of shit. The real issue is if China raised rates. Or worse, if China revalued the Yuan."*

"*What do you mean?*" he said. "*Who said that? I never heard that!*"

"*Think about it. What would happen to all the crosses if there was a revaluation of the Yuan? Would EURUSD go up or down? What about GBPUSD? Why should any particular cross move at all? But then, do you really think that the crosses wouldn't move?*"

"*Mmm. I have no idea.*"

"*Of course you don't mate. No one does. Ok look, I got to go. Bye.*"

About half an hour later Owl went completely bananas and started playing a presto agitato amidst waves of fills. We all looked at each other, wide eyed, until Vito yelled, "*Quick Damon, turn it off!*" but by the time I did, it had already made over $250k in profit. I just couldn't believe it so I ran through a system check to see if the profit was real, which it was, and whether Owl's position was flat, which it was. The thing had worked perfectly, like some sort of crazy ATM that had started spitting out free cash. Then I jumped on Bloomberg and typed EURUSD Curncy CN <GO> to bring up a scrolling news monitor. And there, right at the top of screen 3, was the headline:

11:27 CHINA COULD REVALUE YUAN SOON – Government Official

"*WTF!*" I knew instantly that Craig was responsible, that I was responsible! I typed GIP <GO> to bring up an intraday chart and saw a huge spike in volatility. Then I checked all the major crosses, and they each showed the same crazy price action. In fact, they were still jumping around all over the place with these wicked little rallies followed by mini crashes. It was as though the market just couldn't comprehend what a revaluation of the Yuan would mean for the rest of the world's currencies. It was exactly as I'd said to Craig on the phone – they couldn't find a stable level because no one knew if the event was *risk on* or *risk off*. It was neither and yet it was also a really big deal.

Later I gave Craig a call. *"Hey, that was awesome!"* he said. *"Did you see me?"*

"What do you mean 'see you'?" I replied.

"I did a live interview on CNBC. I told your story about the Yuan."

"We don't watch CNBC here mate. And I hope you didn't quote me. You know I'd be fired for that."

"No, of course not. I'd never quote you. But after we spoke I called my buddy over at the People's Bank of China, and what he told me was very interesting. Of course, I couldn't quote him either. Did you see that it made it to Bloomberg? The whole market just erupted after that. What was odd was how it hardly moved after I first said it."

"Well, I wouldn't say it's odd. I mean, only retail noobs watch CNBC."

"Ha! You're just jealous that you weren't on TV."

"Mate, if I ever went on TV it'd be on a real news channel."

"Real news? That's an oxymoron my friend."

23. ONE BAD CLICK

I feared making a trading error more than anything in the world, for depending on how bad it was, a single error could result in a trader being fired on the spot. Of course, I did screw up every now and then, and each time the awful sickness returned to my stomach, just as it had that first-time trading Roche at HSBC. It wouldn't matter if you'd traded perfectly for six hours straight with 15,000 clicks on exactly the right things at exactly the right times. When you realise you've made an error it's like *Boom!* and you almost have a heart attack. You check the last price against the filled price. It might have risen, or it might have fallen, and you hold your breath as the verdict comes in. Of course, it's infinitely worse when the error relates to a large trade. For when that happens, and the world of a perfectionist is turned upside down, a nervous breakdown was possible.

One day I returned from the bathroom to find Archie sitting in his chair white as a ghost and unable to speak. Vito had started to slacken off, and on this occasion, he was out having lunch with a broker. Archie mumbled something to me, but I couldn't understand him. I figured that if he couldn't speak then he couldn't think, so it was up to me to solve whatever mess he was in. I looked around and saw things flashing and beeping all over the place, so I jumped into action and two minutes later we were all caught up. Then I set about looking for the source of Archie's disarray.

I saw an IB chat from Jake with a size order to sell futures. I saw that Archie had replied, *"Got it,"* but not written anything in the 10 minutes since. That was bad since market orders were usually filled within 30 seconds. Then I looked at the trade blotter and saw that Archie had bought futures and then sold them a minute later – it appeared to be a simple case of mixing up buy and sell.

His eyes were glued to screen 2 where a chart showed the market printing fresh lows. I knew that screaming at him was the last thing he needed so in my calmest voice I said, *"Mate. Look at me."* He didn't want to, but finally he did. *"I'm going to help you get through this,"* I said. *"I'm going to tell you what I think just happened here, and you need to tell me if I am correct. Ok, here we go. Jake told you to sell 3500 VGZ6, but you accidentally bought them instead. That was an error. Then you reversed out of the error, which was exactly the right thing to do, but you still didn't sell the original 3500. Or did you? I can't see them on the blotter, but maybe you sold them over the phone?"*

Blank stares greeted me. *"Mate, answer me! Did you sell the original 3500 or not?"*

"No, I didn't sell them."

"*Ok then. I am doing it. I am selling 3500 VGZ6 right now.*"

I got on with it and a few minutes later I said, "*Ok that's done.*" Then I looked around to get a handle on the outstanding workload. "*I got Ed.. Jake.. Ortus.. Santa Fe.. Jamie.. Bluewave.. Phoenix.. Interweave. Is there anything else out there?*"

"*No.*"

"*Ok mate, then go downstairs, have a cigarette, and sort yourself out. Just make sure you're back here in fifteen minutes for Corn and Soybeans.*" He rose like in a dream and wandered away. Ten minutes later he was back, fully recovered, and quietly traded the Ag futures whilst I took care of everything else. Then he calculated the loss from his trading error – it was almost $200k.

"*You have to go and talk to Jake,*" I said. "*I wouldn't call him if I were you. Go around to his desk and talk to him, man to man.*"

"*Yeah, ok,*" he said.

I can only imagine what a nightmare that conversation would have been but later he returned in high spirits and told me it was all ok. I couldn't help but wonder if he'd made a deal with Jake to provide him an advanced copy of the next Sunday paper. Alas, the next day Archie didn't turn up for work, and when I asked Vito what was going on, he replied only, "*Archie doesn't work here anymore.*" And just like that, my young friend with all the potential in the world was gone.

24. KITZBÜHEL

One day Tracy called up and asked if I wanted to go skiing in Kitzbühel. *"Whatsbull?"* I replied and she laughed since a client's joke is always funny.

"Nah, I'm serious," she said, *"This weekend is de Morgan Stanley ski trip an' we're 'eadin' over ter Austria. We'd like yew ter come, yeah?"*

What followed was the most lavish affair I'd ever attended. We flew over on Friday night and after checking into the Hotel Goldener Greif, we wandered up to a nearby bar and started drinking. Colin, the head of trading, spent the first half of the night sitting or standing on the bar itself. The moment my glass of Blue Label got a little low he'd point and shout, *"Damon, 'old yer hackney marsh up for a refill!"* or *"Damon, get up 'ere wif me and tell me about Perdu."*

Later, he was so drunk that he couldn't stand on the bar anymore. I suppose I was even worse for I started banging on about how I wanted to be a portfolio manager. *"Not just a trader,"* I said, *"I wanna be a true speculator. The best that's ever lived. Like Jesse Livermore!"*

"Lawd above. For wot goods all the knowledge in the world if we can't even predict the market." He sighed heavily and shook his head as though he'd been contemplating the same his whole life. But then he perked up with a massive drunken grin. *"But dats why we the broker and yew the bloody client!"* he said punching my arm. Then he came in close and conspiratorial. *"But look, if yew wanna be a portfolio manager, den I'll tell yew wot. Yew a lucky saucepan lid workin' where yew is. Yew gonna av the best education yew can bloody 'av, alrigh' son. Just yew take it slow. Life's not a race, and neiver's speculation. Yew gotta keep learnin' and learnin'. Yew got a good five more years of loosin' in ya yet. How long your guys at Perdu work on their models for? Like 10 bloody years is wot. 20 years some 'ov 'em. Isaac's like 30 fuckin' years writing his algorithm innit!"* Then he grabbed me and together we staggered over to Tracy. *"This one's a bit mad idn't 'e!"* he said to her.

"Idn't 'e wot!" she replied handing me a bottle of Blue Label. Then she emptied her glass down her throat in one gulp. Colin and I did the same and then laughing and panting we all looked around with *Oh Shit!* expressions and wiped the tears from our eyes. Then I blurted out, *"Oh, you think I'm mad do ya? Well, you gonna see it tomorrow. We're going up the top. To the peak. And we're gonna hit that shit hard!"*

We never quite got there the next day. In fact, we woke up so late that by the time we'd rented our gear and had lunch, we could only manage an hour on the slopes before calling it a day. At dinner that night, after we'd been treated to a live performance of yodelling, I found myself seated next to Jeff. He was the one who invented sector swaps in Europe, and we loved it because sector futures didn't exist yet. Plus, even though they were the only broker with a working product, Jeff let me trade against him for just 8bps commission. We chatted about the good volume we were doing, and then he said, *"To some extent, it's easy ter make money from client flow since most funds 're 'appy ter pay me for the product. But not Perdu! Even though you're one of my biggest accounts I'm runnin' a loss ratio of nearly sixty percent! I mean, ay yo trip matey, we like to keep that below thirty."*

The loss ratio described how much commission he lost trying to get out of the position I put him in. In this case, Jeff was saying he lost $6k out of every $10k in commission I paid him. He was right to complain, and it wasn't the first time I'd been politely reprimanded by the sell-side for running up the loss ratio. But for me, I always considered a high loss ratio for the broker to mean I was doing a good job for the firm. Even so, I was well aware that the situation had to be managed carefully because he could easily just hike the commission rate to 12bps which is what he charged everyone else.

In fact, I found it quite easy to game Jeff's sector swap market. All I had to do was hit the leading stocks of a sector down a few ticks right before the clock reached 15 seconds past the minute or any 15-second increment thereafter. That's when the sector index level calculated by Eurostoxx would refresh and get printed on the tape. And it was that print that stood as a tradeable price until the next one came along 15 seconds later. So if I was buying I'd first hit (sell) a few of the heaviest stocks just before the calculation was run. Then, a few seconds later, the index would print at a lower level, and I'd get on with my real purpose which was to buy the sector in big size. Of course, I'd have to reverse out of the initial stock trades, but even with transaction costs, it saved us a lot of money. And though Jeff could see the activity on the tape, he could never be sure that it wasn't just a coincidence. For that reason, I only did it when I needed to buy in big size, or for an important portfolio manager. Ezra liked that sort of thing.

25. PHOENIX AND INTERWEAVE

Phoenix, Isaac's futures trading model, was very difficult for one person to handle when things went wrong. For though it had been automated for FIX trading just prior to me joining the firm, there were still a lot of times when we had to trade its orders manually. For example, it couldn't handle the open of the market since they were susceptible to delays and problems, so all orders for the first five minutes appeared in gold which meant they were manual orders that we had to execute ourselves.

New orders always appeared at the bottom of Phoenix's clunky old blotter, and they scrolled upward as new orders slotted in below. And when I say clunky I mean it was a real piece of shit. On average, it might have generated a new order every 20 seconds so I never really considered it an HFT model. That said, the average was a poor descriptor of its behaviour for when Phoenix was busy it could generate an order every second.

Orders came in different colours which meant different things. Gold meant it was a manual order, and when we saw one we had to mark it as working after which it would turn yellow. Then, after trading away in another app, we had to come back and mark it as done, after which it would turn white. Of course, most orders were sent via FIX, and in those cases they'd first appear in purple before turning blue and then white. Purple meant the order had been sent to the broker. Blue meant they got it. And white meant they'd completed it.

The point was that if an order stayed in purple, it meant there was a big problem because Phoenix had sent it to the broker but we didn't know if they'd received it or not. The early days of automated FIX trading were fraught with these kinds of problems, and for me, purple was synonymous with the worst days I ever had at Perdu. Purple meant game time. Purple meant one bad click in a frantic 2,000 click sequence could set off a cascade of errors from which you might never recover. Older traders from 666 spoke of waking up in the middle of the night haunted by the purple nightmare.

Though Vito had prepared me for it as best he could, there was no way I could've known how quickly things would spiral out of control. It was around 9:30 am when he stepped out to run an errand. Everything was running smoothly in a moderately busy market until suddenly a purple order appeared at the bottom of Phoenix's blotter. I stared at it. It stared back at me. I willed it to turn blue, but it didn't. Then another appeared. And another. I hit Simon's speed-dial and said, *"Bunds are purple,"* and he replied, *"On it."* Then a purple DAX appeared. I called Simon again, *"There's a DAX too. Looks like all of Eurex is down,"* and hung up. Then I looked at my TT futures app and saw that all the Eurex contracts were crossed – an impossible situation where bids were higher and offers were lower which confirmed that the market had stopped functioning. Simon was quick to get back to me, *"Eurex is officially down. All orders are being rejected. Nothing done on those purple orders."* I set up a Bloomberg tick chart and a time-and-sales monitor so I'd be alerted the moment the exchange had fixed the problem and was once again processing trades. Then I turned back to Phoenix and marked each of the purple orders as working and they turned yellow. Finally, I went to an Xterm window and ran *stopAuto EUREX* which forced all new Eurex orders to come in gold for me to do manually.

In theory, the process from there should have been fairly straightforward – each new Eurex order would appear in gold, I'd mark it as working, it would change to yellow, and I'd write it down on a piece of paper. Then I'd keep a running total for each contract and later, when the exchange reopened, I'd just trade the net size. Then I'd go back and mark all the yellow orders as done and they'd turn white. After 30 seconds, my totals were to buy 14 BUND and sell 11 DAX which was no great drama. But then, almost in response to Eurex being down, stocks started moving around in a hurry, and I received a whole bunch of orders from our fundamental portfolio managers. Taken alone they would have kept me busy. But then Avi's model, Interweave, started flashing warnings at me from its

Linux GUI in screen 4. Though it was an equity StatArb model, it hedged its net beta in the futures market. And now, with Eurex being down, it was warning me that it was out of hedge. My eyes darted to the top of its GUI where the most basic portfolio data was displayed:

LONG €737M SHORT €691M NETBETA €46M NET 6.66%

"Oh shit! What are you doing at six six six!" I yelled at screen 4. *"Bad robot!"* Its net beta was supposed to stay within +/– 2% and I could hardly believe it had gotten so long so quickly. I hit *[Auto Off]* and ran some commands in the server window to add STXE and DAX to the DoNotTrade list. Then I went back to the GUI and ran a manual cycle: *Cancel All Orders -> Compute -> Propose New Orders*. In the blotter appeared roughly 40 stock orders which were a mix of buys and sells. So I went through and deleted all the buys and then hit *[Send Wave]* to push the remaining sell orders into the market. As they were filled, I watched the net beta fall but not by much. I ran three more cycles like that but to my dismay the sell orders just weren't big enough, and the net beta only fell to +5.8%. *'This is taking too long,'* I thought. *'There has to be another way.'*

I turned back to Phoenix where I now had eight gold orders waiting for me. I marked each one as working and they changed to yellow. Then I added their sizes to the running totals on my desk. My IB chat started pinging so I jumped in and took some orders from the fundamental portfolio managers. Then I turned back to Interweave and figured it was pointless trying to manually trade it back into hedge. So I decided to sell CAC futures as a proxy for STXE and

DAX. *'What the hell else am I gonna do?'* I thought. But as I reached for my calculator I saw six new gold orders in the Phoenix blotter, and I realised activity was ramping up. Suddenly Phoenix was scrolling with new orders at a rate of one per second, and every fourth or fifth one was a gold Eurex order that I had to mark and write down. But then it sped up even more and some orders disappeared right out the top of the blotter before I could get to them. I shook it off and got on with adding those that I could to my running totals. By now it was saying: Buy 64 BUND, Buy 38 BOBL, Sell 44 DAX, Sell 92 STXE. At the same time, I took more orders from the fundamental portfolio managers, each of whom expected my full attention, but all of whom received virtually none. Then I remembered Interweave was still out of hedge, so I hit the speed-dial for Barclays and said, *"CAC futures. Sell fifty million Euros worth over ten minutes."*

"What's the exact size?" he replied.

"Figure it out buddy. Fifty million Euros worth, round down."

"Ok got it," the Barx man said and hung up. I turned back to Interweave's GUI and unchecked the *[Hedge Warning]* box and hit *[Auto On]*. Then I turned my attention back to Phoenix and the fundamental portfolio managers. Half an hour later I was still clicking for my life when Simon called with his fourth update. *"Hi Damon, no update from the exchange."*

"Great, just great! You want to help me Simon then get Vito back in here. Call him on his mobile. I don't have time." That was when Vito happened to stroll back into the office.

"Damon, what's up. You sound stressed," he said.

"Shit man! I need you. Eurex is down, and Phoenix wants to buy.. like.. like.. a billion dollars or something. I can't keep up." For all my complaints, he was superb whenever the shit hit the fan. He jumped into action and took over trading for the fundamental portfolio managers, some of whom still had unacknowledged orders in IB chat.

"Did you call Isaac?" he said.

"No, why would I call Isaac? That won't help Eurex fix the stupid exchange, and it'll just piss him off."

"Damon, you always need to call Isaac in these situations."

"Ok."

I hit Isaac's speed-dial and on the second ring in a sleepy pissed-off voice he said, *"Ahhhh eeerrr wh what whaaaat do you oo want?"*

"Isaac, it's Damon. Eurex is down."

"Ohhh ahh okay. Hooow loo lung errr long has it been down?"

Conversing in Aspergian was the last thing I wanted to do in that moment. *"It's been down for an hour,"* I said.

"An oww wa? Wwwhhy eeerrr whyyyy eeerrr.."

"Because we had no idea how long it was going to be down for. Eurex kept saying, 'soon', but, well, it's been an hour."

"Errrr da Daaa mon Daaamon yoo sh ood should have caa all led alled ready."

"Ok, I'm sorry Isaac. Look Phoenix wants to trade in big size. I don't know if you really want to do that."

"Wha wha whhhyyy?"

"Because it wants to buy almost a billion dollars' worth of futures."

"Ohhh ye es yes okay. I if if then. Jus jer jus do oo whaaaat it seh saaays tooo err dooo.

"Ok got it," I said and hung up.

"Damon!" Vito screamed. *"What the hell have you done to Interweave!"* I ignored him and marked the latest Phoenix orders as working and added them to the totals. Then I thought for a moment, *'What about Interweave?'*

"Net beta is over sixty million Euros Damon! It's long almost eight percent! What the hell have you been doing! And.. and.." He bashed away on Bloomberg and brought up a tick chart, *"the market's been falling all morning! And you've left it long eight percent! The P&Ls gonna be.."*

"It's fine," I said cutting him off." I hedged it earlier. I sold CAC with Barx over the phone."

"What? CAC?"

"Yes, CAC. Look if it says sixty million Euros then it's really ten million which is gonna be.. well seven is one percent.. so it's one and a half percent long.. Actually, can you take over the model please?"

"Sure, I'll take it. Kill your GUI."

"Damon is out. Also, make sure to call Barx and get the CAC fill."

Another hour went by, and Phoenix continued spitting out orders at a hectic pace. I kept marking and adding them to the totals. Then Simon called and said, *"Eurex is up!"* I looked at my futures app and saw at once that everything was trading again. *"Shit!"* I said to Vito, *"Call Barx and tell them to buy back the CAC and then enter them into the Interweave blotter. Then take STXE and DAX off the DoNotTrade list and let it hedge naturally."*

"Ok," he said.

I ran *startAuto EUREX* in Phoenix's xterm so all new orders would be sent via FIX and not screw up my totals. Then I madly scrolled up through the blotter looking for those lost orders that had disappeared earlier on. When I added them to the list the totals staring at me were so huge I could barely believe it. Just then Vito piped up. *"Hey with those Phoenix orders, just trade them over the rest of the day. Isaac will judge you against VWAP from now till the close".*

"Ok, my discretion then?"

"Your discretion," he confirmed.

We didn't have algos for futures back then, so I had to trade them manually. My execution strategy was pretty simple – I just assumed that Phoenix was going to be right intraday and traded according to that. For example, it was already long about €1bn worth of German government bonds, and I had to buy another €800m worth. So I bought them fairly quickly even though it meant pushing the market a little. Conversely, it was slightly short stock index futures, and I had to sell €550m worth of STXE and €400m worth of DAX. So I sold about 20% of the total fairly quickly and then spread the rest over the remainder of the session. At the end of the day I'd done ok – bonds were higher and stocks were lower. That was the first time I ever manually traded over €2bn in a single day, and I was so exhausted that I fell asleep in the taxi on the way home. I sure earned my paycheck that day.

26. BLUEWAVE

It took Ezra years to convince Nikolai to leave the Lebedev Physical Institute and join Perdu in New York. And when he agreed it was only on the condition that he'd bring with him a whole host of computer scientists, math and physics PhDs, and electrical and telecommunications engineers. They were all looking for a new life abroad after the demise of the Soviet Union. By the end of their first decade in 666 their creation had become known as Bluewave, and it was proving to be one of the best trading machines on the planet.

Bluewave wasn't just a StatArb model. It was an amalgamation of their many areas of expertise including Nikolai's principle concerns in cryptography and quantum mechanics. But the competition in the industry was fierce, and it produced an arms race for raw computing power and other resources. By the time I joined Perdu the Bluewave team had expanded to over 150 staff. As to how many CPU cores they had blazing down there in the basement, well I suspect it might have given Google a run for its money.

I soon found a few operational things that made no sense to me, and I started arguing to Simon and Harry that it was impossible for Bluewave to function the way it did. Harry bore the brunt of my endless questions about the systems and networks of the firm, and finally, when he realised I wasn't going to let it go, he took me into a meeting room for a chat.

"*Damon, take a seat. So what exactly do you want to know about Bluewave,*" he asked.

"*Well, it seems to me that we're getting fills for orders we never sent.*"

"*How do you know we never sent them?*"

"*Because I checked the FIX logs. They verify that we're getting phantom fills.*"

"*Have you told anyone else about this?*"

"*Only Vito.*"

"*And what did he say.*"

"*He said it wasn't my job to be looking through Bluewave's FIX logs, which is bullshit.*"

"*You know he can be cagey at times.*"

"*That's an understatement.*"

"*Well, I can tell you right now that they're not phantom fills. They're good, and we want them.*"

"*So where did they come from?*"

"*It's complicated.*"

"*Try me.*"

He looked out the window for a moment and then down at the table. I supposed he was trying to figure out how to explain a highly technical thing to someone who'd never studied computer science. Finally, he said, "*Ok, so you understand that our HFT servers, along* with those of competing HFT funds, are co-located (CoLo) in the stock exchange building. That gives us a speed advantage over other traders. But as a group, we insist that no HFT fund should have an advantage over any other. As such, all CoLo client servers are housed in the same rack, and use identical lengths of cabling to connect them to the stock exchange server which sits against a far wall."

"Yeah, I get that."

"Well, here's the thing. If Formula 1 racing cars are the pinnacle of automotive engineering, then what goes on in that room is the pinnacle of network engineering. Every HFT fund is battling to squeeze out every microsecond of latency. But just because we all use the same length of cabling doesn't mean we can't get a speed advantage. You have to understand that right now there are billions of dollars being poured into research on ultra-high-speed communication."

"So we figured out a way to be faster than the other guys?"

"Yes and no. Yes, because Bluewave deploys a piece of kit that no one else knows about. And no, because all our orders still have to go through the proper channels."

"I don't understand. By kit, you mean hardware?"

"Yes, it's something Nikolai developed at Lebedev. Basically, it's a tiny transmitter chip that sits on the motherboard of Bluewave's CoLo server. It's so small that nobody would even see it's there."

"Like a Wi-Fi chip?"

"Sort of but what it emits is no garden variety Wi-Fi signal. Instead, it emits twisted light – a cutting edge technology that researchers are using to increase communication bandwidth. But Nikolai's research went in an entirely different direction. He managed to combine optical vortices into waves that are invisible to third party detection."

"Wow, invisible Wi-Fi. That's awesome."

"Yeah, it's pretty amazing. In fact, we're not even sure if you can call them electromagnetic waves because that spectrum is defined by variations in wavelength. But the twisted light transmitter, what we call the TLT, emits light with infinite wavelength."

"Infinite wavelength? How can you even pick up the signal?"

"No, that's the point, you can't. It's invisible to third party detection."

"But it transfers energy?"

"We're not sure about that. I mean we're not sure that energy is the right word to describe it. The TLT can transfer information, or in the least, a change in informational state. Do you know what a NIC is?"

"A network interface controller? The bit where you plug in the Ethernet cable?"

"Yeah close enough. Well, NICs come in two types – wireless, like in a laptop, or the regular wired ones that use a physical Ethernet cable. Now obviously the exchange's matching engine server uses a wired NIC but here's the thing. Bluewave's TLT can produce a targeted interaction with components located at a distance. So if you point the TLT at the matching engine server, it can create resonance in the receive queue of the NIC."

"You've lost me mate."

"Ok, have you heard of bit-flips or bitwise operations?"

"No."

"What about deep packet inspection?"

"I know roughly what it is."

"Well, this is deep packet modification – what we call packet editing on the fly. To do it you need the full suite of circuit designs for the NIC, a copy of the firmware, and knowledge of the exchange's protocol. And of course, you need a TLT, which to the best of our knowledge, no one else has."

"Then what?"

"Then Bluewave can do things like change a buy order into a sell order, through the air, from across the room."

"So it's light speed trading?"

"Yes, we call it PFT – photon frequency trading."

"That's amazing."

"Yes, but here's the thing. You can't just insert a new order into the NIC because every order needs to have a valid order ID. You see when an order leaves an HFT fund's server and proceeds down the proper route, it first passes through a pre-trade mechanism where it gets authorised and receives a unique order ID. So if you skip that it'll cause an error, won't get filled, and probably alert the exchange."

"So you modify an old order?"

"Exactly. The TLT modifies existing orders which have already passed through pre-trade, got themselves an ID, and are travelling through the NIC right before they hit the matching engine."

"Wait a minute. How does the TLT know what order to modify? It might wind up modifying some other guy's order."

"Each HFT client gets their own dedicated receive

queue on the NIC. Plus there are often multiple NICs in operation. But each has a unique MAC address which is a physical thing that can be targeted. Look it's obviously a whole lot more complicated than I can explain, but I can tell you that these guys are world experts in NICs and protocols and bit-flipping, and they've got it so that only their orders are affected."

"Ok so how much faster is it through the air?"

"Quite a lot. There's packetisation delay, serialisation delay, plus the pre-trade mechanism slows things down a lot. I'd say the TLT can get there thirty percent faster than orders through the wire. But look, you gotta understand that it's not front-running since Bluewave has no knowledge of what other clients are doing. The only reason it modifies an order is the same reason anyone modifies an order – because new information has arrived and Bluewave has changed its mind about what it wants to do. At the end of the day what you need is a speed advantage, and this is how we get it.

"Honestly, I'd always wondered if Bluewave was quote stuffing the exchange. I mean it sends so many damn orders."

"No, we're not doing that. Quote stuffing is about sending a whole bunch of nonsense orders so that competing funds will get tied up trying to process them and thus miss opportunities. Indeed, some HFT funds, and they've been stopped now, actually sought to overwhelm the matching engine itself, or else send enough orders to surpass the bandwidth of the outgoing data feed. What Bluewave is doing is different. Yes, it sends a lot of orders, but they're all real. That they might be modified later on is the real source of our

edge."

"Wow," I said. *"I'm dumbfounded."*

"Yeah, it's a lot to take in. I felt the same way when I first heard about it."

"It's not really trading anymore is it."

"Not at all. It's physics and engineering."

"And hacking."

"Yeah, I guess you could say that."

It was time for us to get back to work but as we stood and readied to leave Harry added, *"You wanna know something really weird?"*

"Sure."

"The twisted light from the TLT is using quantum entanglement."

I stared at him for a moment trying to digest the concept. *"You mean like quantum teleportation? But you said the TLT was only thirty percent faster than Ethernet."*

"Yes, I did, but we have reason to suspect that quantum entanglement is involved. Of course, Nikolai has never acknowledged that. Look Damon, you are not to repeat this to anyone. Even Vito."

"Of course. I won't say a word. But I have to ask – do you believe it?"

"Yeah, I think I do. I mean what else can explain the incredible consistency of its P&L?"

Nikolai may have been world class in quantum entanglement and the associated concept of quantum teleportation which Albert Einstein had called *spooky action at a distance*. Yet no one had ever been able to transfer actual bits of information from one place to another in zero-time. And if it were true, then Bluewave was not an HFT or PFT machine – it was a zero-time trading machine.

That night as I lay in bed I got to wondering about whether Nikolai was the sort of man who'd ever disclose such a breakthrough should he make it. But then I recalled the firm's mantra – *those who say don't know, and those who know don't say* – and with that I had my answer. Finally, as I drifted off to sleep, the realms of possibility dawned on me. '*If Bluewave could trade in zero-time then how far was it from that murky world just beyond, where trades can go back in time..*'

27. THE GREAT QUANT MELTDOWN

It was just before three o'clock in the morning, one random weeknight, when I got a call from Harry. He explained that our offsite data centre in King's Cross had just been attacked. The bad guys had busted off the air conditioner's exhaust grill, wriggled their way through 10 meters of vent shaft, hammered off the turbo fan, and jumped down into the server room. There they removed the most expensive components, including some worth over $150,000 each, before attacking the rest of our network gear with cutting pliers. *"But don't worry,"* he said. *"We run a backup on the other side of the city. We just need to switch everything over."*

"Ok, well you've got four hours till futures open."

"Yeah, yeah, we know."

He and Simon worked through the night and by the time I got to the office the handover appeared seamless.

A few days later we learnt that it wasn't just us who was hit. Similar attacks had occurred at data centres all over the world, though I never saw any mention of it in the media. I later heard it was because the protection of financial markets was an issue of national security. *"Is this the start of hedge funds attacking the infrastructure of other hedge funds?"* I asked Harry.

"Shit, I hope not," he said. *"Did you ever hear about the Nasdaq squirrel?"*

"No, what happened?"

"The story goes that the Nasdaq once crashed because a squirrel chewed through a power line, took down the data centre, and then the backup site failed. It was down for hours."

"You know what I worry about? Hedge funds launching DDoS attacks against each other."

"Yeah, or someone setting off an EMP bomb."

The speed and volume of automated trading had risen rapidly over my first few years at Perdu, and by 2007 there was an enormous amount of capital riding on StatArb. Alas, just as I'd learnt in CBArb years earlier, I was about to discover once more that even the smartest strategies were susceptible to catastrophic failures.

It started as it always did with competition degrading returns and portfolio managers seeking out ways to maintain their past performance. The best solution was to decrease transaction costs, and to that end, Lehman were kind enough to cut our commission rates on FIX and DMA orders to just 1.5bps. But not every fund had such a tight relationship with their PB, and so it was that some started to leverage up. I even heard about one StatArb fund that had reached an average multiple of 6:1. I suppose it looked safe enough in their backtests, but in reality, it was just a fool's play since everyone knows the worst drawdown is in front of you.

Of course, being faster was the focus of much attention, and it was certainly a worthy goal considering how much capital was rushing into the same setups. That pushed traditional StatArb into HFT StatArb and eventually into ultra HFT front-running. Here, instead of buying a stock in the expectation that it would go up, you bought it in the expectation that everyone else was about to buy it. If you were the fastest you could get in first and out for a profit without ever having to worry about whether the anticipated move actually occurred. Still, it required a fully working StatArb model to get the signals of what others were about to do.

I often wondered if regulators would one day curb the unfairness of the speed advantage. Indeed, stock exchanges could have just done away with continuous trading and instead implemented a series of discrete auctions, say 10 minutes apart, or one hour apart. After all, auctions were already the trusted mechanism for the open and the close. Plus, it wouldn't have been of any detriment to the core objective of a stock market – to allocate investment capital to listed companies. An extreme view, such as Warren Buffett might have held, was that stocks didn't need intraday trading at all. They could just have an opening and closing auction each day and be done with it. Alas, it wasn't just HFT funds like ours, but the exchanges, brokers and tech companies, that derived massive benefits from high-speed trading. And no one had any intention of allowing a regulator to kill the goose that laid the golden egg.

Since there was always some kind of crisis going on, I found it hard to determine when something was a big deal or not. So in April 2007, when New Century Financial went bankrupt, I barely noticed. But then in July, two subprime CDO hedge funds managed by Bear Stearns blew up, having only just recently being valued at $20bn. That's when I remembered my dinner with Manny, two years earlier at the Hudson Hotel, where he'd told me about securitising *all sorts of dodgy shit into MBS and CDOs*. I marvelled at just how long it had taken to come out, and I wondered how much more toxic junk was out there.

Since he was our resident expert in such matters, I decided to give Jamie a call in 666. He managed a $2bn banks & financials book and was by far the biggest fundamental portfolio manager in the firm. And though I'd long since lost respect for all those guys, he was an exception to the rule. He liked my little anecdotal story about Manny, and then in no uncertain terms told me, yes, subprime debt was a big problem for the banks.

About a week later the *carry trade* blew up in what some declared was a six-standard-deviation event. I honestly never understood the carry trade. I mean how could anyone be so stupid to put on a position where the expected yearly return was equal to just a few days' worth of volatility? It seemed like the ultimate case of picking up pennies in front of a steamroller, except that the steamroller had a habit of accelerating just as you bent down to grab one. But for whatever reason, there was said to be an awful lot of money riding on it, and when it blew up it hurt a lot of people. Despite that, stocks kept pushing higher, and our strategies kept making money. So when Vito decided to take some time off for vacation, I assured him I could handle European trading by myself. He agreed, but just to be on the safe side, he organised for Bryan to help out by working the night shift from 666.

Monday, August 6, was another down day for the StatArb models. It wasn't a terrible day, but it did add to an already bad run from the previous week. I never liked it when they lost money, but I'd become accustomed to them always making it back. I had Bryan take care of the fundamental portfolio managers, and he did a pretty good job despite not knowing many European stock tickers. We kept a speakerphone line open all day between him in 666 and me in London. It didn't cost anything since the firm had leased lines and a cutting edge VOIP system. *"Hey, what's the ticker for Munich Re again?"* Bryan would ask, and I'd reply, *"M U V 2 [space] G Y mate,"* and then he'd complain that European tickers never made any sense. *"Just be glad we don't use RIC codes,"* I said. *"They're even worse."*

On Tuesday, the StatArb models got hammered again. But this time they suffered the worst losses I'd ever seen. And even though the broad market hardly moved it was an exceptionally hard day of trading. If Bryan hadn't been there to help I don't know that I could have kept up. That night I went home exhausted but proud that we'd worked well together as a team.

I arrived early on Wednesday morning. I wanted to see how the StatArb models had fared overnight in the US. So I logged into G4 (the firm's position and P&L system) and when it came up I saw Bluewave sitting at the top of the list. That was normal since the portfolios were sorted by long exposure. Unfortunately, it was immediately apparent that something had gone very wrong. I stared at the figure for Bluewave's Day P&L and shook my head in disbelief. It had lost $190m in one day. That was almost four times the size of its previous worst day ever and close to 10 times a typical day's swing. And the bad news didn't end there, for incredibly, I saw that on a percentage basis, Interweave had fared even worse. Indeed, every one of our StatArb models had been crushed.

I started up my other two servers and then logged into each of my trading apps. Then I jumped on Bloomberg, ran a query for newly announced mergers, and instructed the StatArb models not to trade those stocks anymore. Then I uploaded fresh stock borrow lists and ran through the open_shell script for Bluewave. Meanwhile, Bryan replied back to the fundamental portfolio managers that he'd received their orders and was taking care of them. Then he pounded me with questions as he struggled to get them into the market before the open. The next thing on my list was Interweave, but just as I completed logging in, Avi, the portfolio manager, called me.

"Hi Avi," I said.

"Hi Damon. Well as you might have seen it looks like the model is broken. The way it has lost money over the last week is outside my working parameters, and I do not understand why it is happening. As such, we should not be running it in these conditions."

"Ok, well you should know that all the StatArb models are getting hit."

"Yes, that is to be expected. I see that you've already started the model. Please, will you exit the GUI, then shut down the engine and the server."

"*Sure. Just a second. Ok, Damon is out. Nothing running at my end.*"

"*Thanks. Now please work to liquidate the book by the end of the day.*"

"*Today? All of it?*"

"*Yes. Just take the positions from G4. They are correct. Do you think liquidity will be a problem?*"

"*Well, I'll have to run some pre-trade analysis, but since the book is roughly..*"

"*Gross exposure is one point three billion in Europe.*"

"*One point three. All right, look if there's a problem I'll call you. Otherwise, I'm working VWAP to the close.*"

"*Good. Also, Damon, after today there will be no more trading until I give you the go-ahead. Don't start the model at all. I'll be in touch.*"

"*Ok Avi, thanks.*"

Though he'd just wiped out his entire year in five days, Avi was as friendly as ever. I sometimes wondered if it was his early onset Parkinson's Disease that contributed to him being so kind and calm. Either way, he had a near perfect personality and attitude for trading – industrious, cautious, and accepting of whatever hand he'd been dealt. And his ability to calmly enact a self-liquidation mirrored the advice Ezra had once given me. "*Never hesitate to cut risk. Never hope for a turn. If you think you're so unlucky that a stock will go up right after you sell it, then you're in the wrong business.*"

One of Ezra's golden rules was that every portfolio manager had to be able to liquidate 70% of their book in one day. On this occasion, however, Avi had asked me to liquidate 100% of it, so I anticipated there being some difficulties later in the day. But I wasn't going to let him down, and if the market couldn't provide the liquidity I needed, I'd just have to find the flow or else use my favour bank to force the sales-traders into taking the positions on risk.

Now that we had algos liquidating a book wasn't all that hard. I exported the positions from G4 into Excel, added some column headers and algo parameters, turned the longs into sells and the shorts into buys, and then saved it as a CSV. Then I imported it into Tradingscreen and after checking the list three times over I clicked *[Execute]* and let the algos do their thing. But just knowing that it was a €1.3bn basket didn't help much, for what mattered was the individual stock orders compared to the typical volumes they traded. To figure that out I uploaded the basket into our pre-trade analytics program, where I discovered about 20 orders whose size was going to be too big for the market to swallow without doing significant damage to the price. It turned out, however, that the pre-trade analysis was highly inaccurate that day, for I struggled with liquidity problems across the board. What I didn't know was that Nikolai had instructed Bluewave to liquidate 70% of its book, and that meant another €2bn worth of European StatArb stocks being dumped on the market. But even if I'd added that into the pre-trade analysis it wouldn't have helped, for unbeknownst to us, the entire StatArb world was rushing for the exit at the same time.

That day, August 8, 2007, was the start of the biggest bloodbath to ever hit the quant world. I noticed right off the bat that Phoenix was trading on stale FX quotes. I got Simon on the case and called Isaac who told me to run *StopAuto* for every FX pair and then keep track of the net sizes. *"Damn you Phoenix,"* I said to the bottom of screen 2. *"Why you gotta make trouble today?"* Thankfully, it only took Simon half an hour to fix the feed handlers, after which, I returned it to automated trading. Plus, I only had to buy around $50m worth of currency which was no great drama. Then I delved into analysing the performance of the Interweave basket, hoping desperately that liquidity would be ok. But by early afternoon it was clear that some of the mid-cap orders were having significant market impact. So I called the sales-traders looking for flow, and when they didn't have any, I strong-armed them into taking positions on risk. Of course, I always made sure to cancel the algo balance so they wouldn't be duplicated.

By 3 pm I was looking at about 10 problematic orders – the stocks I was selling were all down big, and the stocks I was buying were all up big. I really didn't want the algos to keep pushing them, but unless I could find a sales-trader to take the other side, I had no choice. So I kept calling around but even when I threatened the tags at the bottom of my list that I'd *never do business with you again!* they wouldn't budge. By now they were all aware that there was some kind of meltdown under way.

Bryan was struggling, and I soon found myself taking a lot of orders from the fundamental portfolio managers. And then a massive wave just came out of nowhere. Orders, orders and more orders. We had no time to think anything through. It was non-stop prioritising, buying, selling, calculating, initiating, liquidating, and hedging. The orders came faster and faster, and I found myself having to force my decisions for if I hesitated for even a moment, a new order might arrive and take priority. I was absolutely busting for a piss but there was no way I could leave the desk, so I wound up pissing into a coke bottle. But then, with dick in hand, Bryan started screaming through the speakerphone, *"Take that order, Damon! That's your order!"*

"What order?" I said. *"There's like twenty of them out there!"*

"IB chat! You take IB chat. I'll take Email."

Then the phone lines just lit up. It was unusual for even one line to ring since portfolio managers almost always sent their orders by email or IB chat. But during the panic they all got this crazy idea that it was safer to call in an order. And now everyone was calling. In fact, some of them didn't even have orders, they just wanted to know what the hell was going on in the market where dispersion was tearing everyone apart.

"Bryan! This is crazy! I'm gonna have to turn off the ringer on my phone. If people wanna trade then they'll just have to message them through." If I thought that would give us some respite, I was wrong. IB chat started pinging constantly and so too did email. And then I heard a sound that I'd never heard before. It was Tradingscreen, and along with an alarm that was more appropriate to a prison break, a red light started flashing to show it was suffering latency. On it dinged, over and over, until eventually the sounds blurred into one other and the system went into overload. Then it froze entirely. *"Simon! I need you over here now please."* I said after hitting his speed-dial.

"You'll have to wait. I'm in the middle of something."

"Tradingscreen is down! I have a billion dollars stuck in it."

"I'll be there in ten minutes."

"Not good enough Simon! Not good enough!!" I screamed and slammed the phone down.

"What do we do?" yelled Bryan whose own Tradingscreen instance had died too. *"How am I supposed to trade?"*

"Switch to Bloomberg EMS. Use the omnibus account. We'll post allocate after the close."

"Yes, but I don't know if it'll work. I don't think I'm set up for European permissions."

"Then call them and get set up! Tell them to copy my profile!"

"Ok! Ok!"

The stack grew relentlessly, and though we ploughed through the orders as fast as we could, we fell further and further behind. Soon we were a full 10 minutes behind our workload – an insane situation where we hadn't even acknowledged market orders 10 minutes after they'd been sent. And then, despite all my years of experience, I started to panic. *'I can't keep up! .. I have to stop! .. But I can't stop! .. What about the Interweave basket? .. It's crushing the market! .. I need to pull those orders!'* And then, just when I thought it couldn't get any worse, my eyes darted to the bottom of screen 2, where a dreaded purple order had appeared at the bottom of Phoenix's GUI. I stared at it. I prayed for it to turn blue but it didn't. And then another appeared. And another. *'Oh .. My .. God .. Phoenix .. No Phoenix .. Don't do it Phoenix .. What chaos hath thou wrought?!'*

All of a sudden my mind exploded and my vision

went crazy. It was as though someone was scrolling a mouse-wheel in my head such that everything I looked at shifted up and down repeatedly. I tried to overcome it by brute force of will, but all I could see was a turbulent sea of apps, quotes, blotters and GUIs shaking around like an earthquake in the matrix. Then darkness approached from the corners, and I was overcome by fear. I knew what it meant – I was about to black out. '*I .. can't ... let .... this ..... happen ......*'

Suddenly I thought of Charlie, and I rammed my eyes closed to take control of the situation. '*I'll get through this,*' I thought. '*Bryan is here to help me. He is relying on me. They all are. Do not black out. Do not black out.*' Alas, when I tried to reopen my eyes they refused the command, and a fresh wave of despair washed over me. Then I felt strange emotions that had no place in that moment. They were of sadness, a terrible sadness. It was as though someone had died. Someone that I loved. Had died.

'*Stop this!*' I pleaded.

'*No, don't stop!*' I answered. '*You need to save the critical systems.*'

'*But I can't save them all.*'

'*Yes, you can! Do it now!*'

'*But who has priority?*'

'*You know who has priority. Get it done. Get it done now!*'

WARNING! UNHANDLED EXCEPTION AT 0x003967f5
SYSTEM REBOOT INITIATED...

I caught my head just before it hit the keyboard, which would have been a small disaster in itself. But I felt better. Much better. My first thought was to wonder how long I'd been out for. Had it been three seconds or

30 seconds? I really had no idea. Then I went through a checklist. *'Can I see out of my eyes? Yes. Can I move my fingers? Yes. Am I of sound mind and judgement? Yes. Can I get through this day? Yes.'*

With that, I sat up bolt upright and stared ahead over the top of my screens to the far wall beyond. Then I closed my eyes and listened to the wise words that Charlie had taught me long ago, and which I'd repeated every night of my life since.

"Return to the now. Be present. Be in the moment. It is the only moment. Reach for the light switch in the emotional centre. Turn it off. Enjoy the darkness. This is the now. Float as Ezra floats. Ascend and see yourself from above. This is the now. Descend and become one. You are the now. Five.. four.. three.. two.. one.. Reset."

When I opened my eyes it was to a world of perfect calm and total control. Immediately, I looked to the bottom of screen 2 and to my surprise I saw that Phoenix was running smoothly. *'What happened to the purple orders?'* I thought. *'Was it just a purple nightmare?'* Then Simon came running around the corner. *"Damon. I'm sorry mate. We had problems with Phoenix. You might have seen some purple orders. But they're all ok now. I've switched the flow to Barclays."*

"Ok, I did see a few purple orders.."

"Yes, they were all filled. Now, what's the problem."

"Tradingscreen. Look at it. It's completely frozen."

"Ok, tell me exactly what happened."

"Well, I'm pushing over 300 VWAP orders. I just don't think it can handle it."

"Who's it for?"

"Avi. I'm liquidating his book."

"Oh, shit man, that's sad. I really liked Avi."

"Yeah, but I don't think he's been fired. He gave me the orders directly. He's liquidating himself."

"Before Ezra does I suppose."

"Yes. Now look, what are we gonna do?"

"We can try killing and restarting it, but I don't think it will help."

"Do what you need to do. In the meantime, we're using Bloomberg EMS as first backup."

Ten minutes later Simon was still trying and failing to relaunch Tradingscreen. But it was never going to work. With 300 algo orders the number of child-order fills coming back amounted to hundreds per second. And that old version of Tradingscreen just wasn't designed for that kind of flow. *"You're just gonna have to use Passport and Autobahn and EMS,"* he said.

"Yeah, that's what we're doing. But here's the thing. I need to cancel some of the orders I have working in Tradingscreen. I need to get them filled over the phone because they're killing the market."

"Then call Lehman and have them cancelled at their end."

"Will that work?"

"Yes, it's just a Tradingscreen problem. At Lehman's end, everything should be running fine."

"Ok, I will. Actually, you've just given me an idea for how to get out of these positions."

"Good luck with that. Anything else?"

"No, thanks."

I called Matt on Lehman's DMA/Algo desk and had him cancel the 10 orders that were most damaging the market. Then I called the street and again did everything I could to offload them. I got rid of six in return for substantial deposits in the favour bank. *"I owe you for this big time. I will never forget it,"* I told them. That left just four illiquid pieces of shit that no one wanted, so finally, I used my trump card and called Lehman's sales-trader. I explained that Tradingscreen had crashed and it was their fault for giving us such a shitty app in the first place and now I couldn't get out of our positions. He accepted the argument and said he'd work the orders himself. *"No, mate. I don't need you to work them. I've spent the last two hours trying to sort this out. I need them filled right now!"*

"Ok fine, I'll fill them on risk," he capitulated.

At the end of the day I collapsed in my chair and sat there for a long time doing nothing. I was totally blank. The morning felt like a distant memory from 10 years ago. And the afternoon? Well, if someone had queried something I wouldn't have had a clue what they were talking about. I suppose I was just too busy to form any new memories. It was almost 7 pm by the time we'd finished double checking every single trade of the day. Bryan said goodbye and went home, and I wrote out the end-of-day report for Ezra. I kept it short and finished with, *'Everything here is under control.'* I prayed he wouldn't call.

When I got to the elevators a few portfolio managers were hanging around, and they all but dragged me across the street to Nobu. We found a quiet little table and when the beers arrived someone set off a round of cheers. We all took a long slow swig. Then Ed turned to me and said exactly what was on everyone's mind. *"What the hell was that today dude?"* His voice was kind, but an edginess betrayed his fear. They wanted answers, and they assumed I had them, but all I said was, *"Yeah man, that was heavy."*

"Oh, come on Damon," he said. *"That wasn't just heavy. That was the craziest market I've ever seen. And look I was there. I heard it all. I know what you just went through. It's ok to admit it was a big deal. I hope you're ok."*

I didn't dare say it out loud, but to myself I thought, *'My friend you don't know the half of it. I almost had a nervous breakdown in there today.'* That's when I realised how important it was that they all believed in me, that I was solid and had it all under control. For if there were any doubts, they might well rat me out to Ezra as being a risk to the firm. They stared at me awaiting a response, and eventually, I got with the program. *"Look guys, the entire StatArb world just melted down today. It looks like someone out there blew up their shit real bad, and they dragged everyone else down with them."*

"But what about Perdu?" asked Jake.

"The firm's fine. You know we don't run excessive leverage. Look, it wasn't us that blew up. We just lost a lot of money is all. I think everyone did today."

"Well, not everyone can lose at the same time," Ed chimed in. *"Surely someone holds the other side of the trade."*

"Actually, I don't think that's true. I think in a really bad market everyone loses. I don't know how to explain it exactly – I mean I can't tell you the mechanics of how it can be – I just think there's no hedge against a bad market. Right now, I'd say you're either flat or you're losing money." No one argued since every one of them had lost despite running strategies that were totally unrelated to StatArb.

The conversation soon turned to other things, and I found that hanging out with them was the best thing that could've happened after such a horrible day. Then we ordered some food and when it arrived I stuffed my face full of black cod and lobster ceviche, left them with the bill, and went home to bed. There were no messages that night from 666. No complaints. No thank-you's. It was just the job I did and that was that. The hardest day of my life.

The chaos continued on Thursday and marked the epicentre of what became known as the *Great Quant Meltdown* (GQM). Dispersion, correlation and volatility went haywire, and factors blew out to obscene levels. Rumours abounded that a huge quant fund had gone bust, and I didn't doubt it since the footprints of capitulation were all over the market. However, it didn't hurt us too bad since we were mostly out of StatArb by then. Then on Friday, we saw a massive rebound that made no sense until it was later revealed that Goldman had injected billions of dollars into their fund, Global Equity Opportunities (GEO), to save it. At the time of the announcement, the CFO declared, *"We were seeing things that were 25-standard deviation moves several days in a row."* Ah.. *[cough]*.. what did he just say? Well, all I know is that if they hadn't saved that fund, and therefore the entire StatArb world, a whole bunch of the world's (otherwise) smartest people would have lost a shit-ton of money.

Avi called early Monday morning with an update. *"Nothing to do today Damon. Let's just wait and see."* Vito was back by now and couldn't quite believe what had happened. He spent a lot of time on the phone and found that some of our biggest competitors, including

Renaissance, AQR, PDT, Global Alpha and GEO, had lost somewhere between 9% and 30% in just two weeks. It was a testament to Perdu that our StatArb models lost less than 8%.

The Goldman injection rebound had little follow through that week, and each morning Avi called with an update. *"Not today Damon. Let's just wait a little longer."* Then, after having been flat for more than a week, he called early Friday morning and said, *"Ok Damon. Today's the day. Go ahead and start the model at your end."*

"Yes, sir!" I said with a big grin on my face. Now I'm sure it would seem like silly anthropomorphising to an outsider, but I dearly missed my friend Interweave and could hardly wait to unleash him back into the market.

```
$ startx
% start-wide
..Alive
% start-server
..Alive
% ping
..Ready
% start-gui
```

At 8:01 am I ran a command to show me a quick summary of Interweave's book, but the output didn't look right. So I forced a *[Compute]* in the GUI and then ran another quick summary. That's when I realised all the zeros were real – it was just that I'd never seen the book totally flat before. Then I ran a couple of manual cycles to satisfy myself that everything was running smoothly, and finally I hit *[Auto On]* and off it went.

Avi had no particular desire for Interweave to build up its book quickly. Per its usual operating style, it worked its orders on the passive side of the spread and provided liquidity appropriate for each stock. I expected that it might take two or three days to reach €1bn in gross exposure (the new size Ezra had authorised) but to my surprise it got there that very day. I supposed there were still a few stragglers out there liquidating, so Interweave was able to mop up the last of their positions. But as it did so it gained more and more traction, such that virtually every position was immediately profitable. For example, I had the discretion to halt trading in any stock that produced significant intraday losses. But every time I sorted the positions by intraday P&L, I saw only a couple of small losers followed by a long list of big winners.

On Monday, Interweave showed a whopping gain right out of the gate, and so too did Bluewave who'd by then also rebuilt its book. But what surprised me even more was just how long the Goldilocks period lasted after that. Within a month our StatArb funds had clawed back all their losses, and by the end of the year they were up somewhere between 10% to 15%.

28. ROBERTO

I'd gotten used to portfolio managers joining the firm, losing money, and getting fired. In fact, that's a little harsh. A lot of them actually did make money, just not in a style that Ezra felt comfortable with. So I did my best to keep them at arm's length and never get too friendly. But then Roberto came along and he was just so brilliant that I couldn't help myself. He started off with $100m to trade with, and soon enough he appointed me as his primary trader. That's when he changed desks so we could face each other directly. Roberto specialised in banks & financials and was hired by Jamie as a sub-portfolio manager to trade his European book. For six weeks, we worked brilliantly together. He made all the right calls, and I found him all the flow he needed right when he needed it. But though I'd always tried to deal fairly with the sell-side, Roberto taught me just how lucrative it could be to break their trust. Case in point was what we did to

Dresdner.

He'd had been hunched over his keyboard all morning, hiding out of view behind the screens that separated us. At one point, he got up to go to the bathroom, and as he passed he shot me a conspiratorial look. He was hatching something, but I had no idea what it was. An hour later he hit me with an IB chat.

> RO: Damon, flow in Soc Gen?
> ME: On it
> ME: Plenty of buyers, good size
> RO: Sellers?
> ME: Not really, I could call around
> RO: Pls

I searched my Bloomberg messages for anything with GLE FP or GLE.PA which were the tickers for Société Générale. Then I called those sales-traders who'd either been talking about it or had shown flow in it in the last month. Unfortunately, I found that everyone was a buyer or had nothing to do. Roberto seemed kind of desperate, so I started calling the tags at the bottom of my list. When I got to Dresdner, it was to my surprise that he said he was in touch with a seller. I told him to figure it out and get back to me asap. Then Roberto stood and said he had to make an important call and would appreciate some quiet. Vito and I nodded and went on with our work, but before sitting back down again, Roberto looked at me and said, *"sixty k"*. I called Dresdner, and the man answered on the first ring.

"Soc Gen," I said simply.

"Ah yes, I was just writing to you. I can offer thirty thousand shares here."

"Can you make it sixty?"

"I'll have to check. Hang on." At that moment Roberto leaned over the top of my screens and snapped his fingers. Then he held up his hand and motioned for me to stop. Five seconds later the voice on the other end of the line said, *"Damon, I can offer sixty thousand Soc Gen here."*

Well, the language of trading was all about brevity, but at that moment I had to stall him. So I clicked mute and said, *"Hey,"* loud enough that Roberto would hear me but wouldn't interrupt his call. Then I gave him an exaggerated nod as if to say, *"I've got it. I'm ready to deal,"* but he looked away and kept mumbling into his headset. Then, just as I was preparing to sit down, he stood tall, opened his eyes wide, and nodded. I nodded back, unclicked mute and said, *"Ok mate, that's done. I bought sixty k Soc Gen."*

"Oh, you are there. I thought you'd gone. Ok, that's fine. Shall we call it 112.25?"

"Yes. I bought sixty k GLE FP at 112.25. Thanks." Then I hung up and sent Roberto his fill.

ME: BOT 60K GLE FP @ 112.25
RO: k

A few minutes later I was busy trading for someone else when Dresdner pinged me on IB chat.

DR: Hey what the hell happened to GLE?
ME: What are you talking about?
DR: It's up 5%!

I didn't bother answering, just jumped on Bloomberg and typed GLE FP Equity GIP <GO>. He was right, almost exactly after I'd bought the block of 60k from him, the stock shot up 5% and was now pushing higher. I hit CN <GO> and saw the incredible headlines that had sparked the rally:

12:27   ATTOCREDITO SAYS MERGER WITH SOCIETE GENERALE
        MAKES "STRATEGIC SENSE"
12:27   ATTOCREDITO SAYS "RIGHT TIME FOR ACQUISITIONS"

"Roberto," I said. *"Soc Gen's up five percent."*

"And the broker?"

"Very unhappy."

"Oh well, lunch?" I turned to Vito who nodded and told me to be back in 20 minutes.

We didn't really speak until we were seated at the restaurant in Shepherd's market. *"How Roberto? How did you do that?"* I asked.

"Well, as you probably know, Attocredito just held an analyst call."

"No, actually I wasn't aware of that. Wait, earnings call?"

"No not earnings. It was just an analyst call to give the market some colour on how the business is going."

"Ok."

"Well, I was on the call and since I know some people I was invited to ask a question. So I asked the CEO about their acquisition strategy."

"And let me guess, you suggested that Soc Gen was a good takeover target."

"Yes, but it really does make a lot of sense. I mean what was he going to do – deny it? He had no choice but to confirm what I said to be true."

"Far out Roberto! Why didn't you tell me?"

"Oh, I don't know. Maybe you might have screwed it up."

"What! Me? I wouldn't have screwed it up! Oh my God. You are such a bad man!"

"Hey, that's bullshit. It's the game we play."

"I can't believe it. You totally stitched up that seller!"

"No, my friend, you stitched up that seller. I was just a guy on the phone."

"On the phone with the CEO of a major European bank with hundreds of analysts and reporters covering it in real time from around the world."

"Not exactly in real-time. It took Bloomberg 14 seconds to print the headline after he said it."

"You mean after you said it."

"No, I mean after he said it."

I laughed and shook my head. Then I checked the last price on my Blackberry. *"Shit man, Soc Gen's trading 118.65 last. You're looking at about half a million bucks profit."*

"Yeah, it's gonna be another good week."

Even though the broad market kept trading higher it was a time of massive distrust in the financial system, and in particular, the banks. For if word spread that someone held a load of subprime mortgage debt the stock was in danger of busting wide open. You see the financial crisis that developed wasn't so much about toxic debt being bad, but that no one knew who held it, or how much of it there was. As such, every bank was a suspect and when accused they'd scramble to deny it, or else, to everyone's surprise, actually admit it was true.

On one such occasion, UBI released a surprise admission that they were *having problems with their inventory of mortgage debt*. However, the statement was only released in Italian, and just five minutes before the market opened. Roberto, being Italian, was all over it, and to his surprise, the stock opened flat.

Clearly, the street hadn't heard the news.

> RO: UBI IM – How much you think you can sell here?
> ME: It's very thin, there's no flow
> ME: What's your total size?
> RO: 50k
> ME: k

A few days earlier Bloomberg had released a new function called *Blast* which allowed me to type out one message and then send it to several IB chat groups at the same time. This was my chance to try it out.

> ME: Morning mate. Where can I sell 10k UBI IM?
>   [Blast to: UBS, LB, DB, MS, ML]
> UBS: 17.50
> ME: Done, thanks
> ML: 17.50
> ME: Done, thanks
> DB: 17.46
> ME: Done, thanks
> LB: 17.44
> ME: Done, thanks
> MS: 17.38
> ME: Done, thanks
>
> ME: SLD 50K UBI IM @ 17.456
> RO: Nice!

Over the next 30 seconds the stock fell 5% in a straight line as the sell-side traders dumped it all at the same time. It was a good little trade because we didn't hurt them too bad. In fact, a $200k order was basically nothing to the big sell-side firms, and they'd have hardly noticed the small loss they each absorbed. And that was the key to using IB Blast – hit a bunch of brokers simultaneously in small size and they'd probably never even notice. That said, it wasn't often that we traded with that kind of information asymmetry, and except for the tags, I tried to treat the sell-side fairly. In fact, for the vast majority of my orders, I traded DMA on the exchange, and Roberto held the positions for several weeks. And that's exactly what I figured would happen the day he had me buy $10m worth of Northern Rock.

I read the news on my Blackberry before I'd even gotten out of bed. It wasn't the usual *difficulties in the credit market* story. This was a big one – Northern Rock had tapped emergency funding from the Bank of England because no one else would lend to them. I jumped out of bed, rushed to get ready, and was in a cab 20 minutes later. Roberto was already in the office when I arrived, and he looked up at me with a blank face. I nodded to let him know that I understood the gravity of the situation, and neither of us spoke. By 7 am I had all the quant models up and running, and when Vito arrived I asked if he could take care of them for the day. *"Of course,"* he said. *"You just concentrate on Roberto. I've got the rest of the business."*

RO: Where is NRK LN
ME: Nothing yet. It's too early
RO: Let me know asap
ME: k

By 7:30 am I still hadn't received any indications from the sales-traders as to where they saw the stock. So I blasted them on IB chat.

```
ME:   Where is NRK LN? Looking to deal pre-market
      [Blast to: LB, ML, MS, UBS, CITI, DB, JPM]
JPM:  500 – 550
UBS:  510 bid
DB:   520 – 540
CITI: 500 – 550
ML:   480 – 540
MS:   450 – 530
UBS:  460 – 520
DB:   510 – 540
LB:   450 – 550

ME:   Roberto, 520 bid, subject
ME:   What's your size
RO:   Sell it all
ME:   k, working to sell 740k NRK LN
```

If I was going to save my friend I needed to move the market higher, and I knew just the guy for the job. Ollie, my sales-trader at Citi, was the self-proclaimed greatest contrarian in London, and if ever there was a guy to spread a word quickly it was him. I hit his speed-dial and got him on the first ring.

"Ollie! It's Damon from Perdu."

"Oh, hey matey. What's going on today?"

"Talk to me about Northern Rock."

"Well, there's news out that..."

"I know the news mate. What I wanna know is if you think it's a buy down here? Actually, can you refresh your levels?"

"Same levels mate, 500 at 550. Look you're absolutely right. I think it's gotta be a buy down here."

"Couldn't agree more. It's ridiculous. The stock's down like fifty percent in six months. It's crazy. It's gotta be a screaming buy down here."

"Yeah, people are carrying on as though the interbank lending market will never function again. Of course it will. It's just temporary funding from the Bank of England. They'll probably pay it back next week."

"Hell yeah," I said doing my best to get him all worked up about it. *"The other thing is what's gonna happen to their loan book? It's not going to disappear is it. Someone's gonna buy it whether it's in its current form or some other form. So I reckon it's a takeover play too."*

"Exactly, the loan book's got value no matter how crap it is."

"Yeah, and it's not exactly crap. I mean this isn't America. It's not subprime is it! And that's gonna be a floor on the value of the company, a floor on the stock. The only question is how much it's worth? Get your analyst on it."

"Yeah, we will. I mean we are."

"Look whatever it is, with the stock down this much it's already taken a pretty damn good haircut I reckon."

"For sure. Look, let me come back to you. I'll get you our estimates."

"Mate, that would be good, but not now. I just wanna see a pre-market in a hundred thousand shares."

"A hundred k.. we are.. same mate. I am 500 at 550."

"Ok dude. Nothing done. Thanks for the chat."

I waited five minutes for Ollie to write out his contrarian masterpiece, and once he'd sent it out to half the financial world, I waited another five minutes for them to absorb it. Then, at 7:50am, it was time for the sales-traders to step up to the plate.

ME: Refresh pls, looking for NRK LN in 100k
         [Blast to: LB, ML, MS, UBS, CITI, DB, JPM]
LB: Nothing sorry
UBS: 500 – 530
ML: 520 – 540
DB: 530 bid
MS: 540 – 560

"Roberto!", I yelled, *"540 bid for a hundred k."*
"Do it!"

Alas, just as I was typing in the Morgan Stanley chat group, Tracy came back with '*Off that*' meaning she'd no longer deal there.

"Missed it, nothing done, 530 bid."
"Do it, work 520 limit."

Just then JPM refreshed with a 540 bid. I hit the speed-dial and said, *"Hey it's Damon. I sold a hundred k Northern Rock at 540."*

"Yep, that's fine. Thank you."
"Anymore?" I asked.
"No, that's it. Nothing more."
"Mate, I have more to go at the same level. I can offer another hundred k here at 540."
"Not done. We're gonna wait for the market open."
"Ok buddy, treat me subject."
"Understood."

MS: 530 – 550
ME: 100k at 530
MS   Done
ME: Tks
UBS: 500 – 530
CITI: 520 – 540
ME: 100k at 520
CITI: Done, cheers matey

ME: Refresh NRK LN please
      [Blast to: LB, UBS, DB, ML]
DB: 530 – 540
ME: 100k at 530
DB: Ok, that's done. More behind?
ME: Yes, another 100k at 530
DB: Done, you sold total 200k NRK LN @ 530
ME: Tks
LB: 520 – 540
ME: 100k at 520
LB: Done

"Update," Roberto said. It was 7:55 am.

"Sold six hundred k at 528."

"Limit off for the balance."

"Got it." I didn't sell anything in the opening auction which uncrossed at 520 and then immediately went 530 bid. That turned out to be the high of the day for half a second later I hit it with the first of seven consecutive 20k lot market orders. When I was done it was 490 bid.

"Roberto, you're out," I said.

He didn't respond, but I knew I'd done a good job in getting him out so quickly and at a loss of only 19% from the previous close. A few hours later the TV showed dramatic scenes from all across the country as thousands of customers queued up to withdraw their money from Northern Rock branches. It was the first bank run in the UK for 150 years, and by the end of the day the stock was down 30%. Roberto's loss was just under $2m which I didn't think was too bad considering he was still up $4m since joining the firm. But later in the day, after Ezra and Jamie had discussed it, I received instructions to liquidate Roberto's book. His style, they said, was just too risky and he should never have bought that stock in that size. And just like that, Roberto joined the long list of Perdu alumni who never quite made it.

I must explain that a whole lot of people were wiped out by being bearish in 2007. For despite mortgage markets melting down, money markets freezing up, and that every man and his dog could see a full-scale economic catastrophe on the horizon, stockmarkets just kept on climbing the wall of worry.

Ed had correctly resisted the urge to go net short throughout the year. But then, in early October, he suddenly changed tack and had me put on a couple of big shorts. Later, he invited me around to his desk where he showed me the macro model he was using as an overlay to his fundamental company models. It combined data on interest rates, debt levels, household spending, unemployment and the slope of the yield curve. The key, he said, was in the lag applied to each series. *"So what's the lag for the yield curve component?"* I asked. *"You know it already inverted last year, right?"*

"Yes, and inversions have preceded the last seven recessions in a row. The average lag is about a year, so right now, you could say we're slightly overdue."

Indeed, according to his model, we were looking at an imminent collapse in consumer spending and one hell of a recession. When I returned to my desk, I had a good look at his book, and he sure was putting his money where his mouth was. On top of a bunch of smaller balanced positions, he was long $110m worth of futures and sector swaps, and short $140m worth of Dixons, Next, LVMH, Inditex, and H&M.

So there he was with all the ducks lined up and the perfect book to profit from what he anticipated. But the next few weeks did a lot of damage as the retail sector rallied hard and tried to shake him out. Nonetheless, he stood firm, and by the end of November he was back in the money. All of a sudden Ed was back in the money. But then, for reasons I couldn't quite understand, he had me cover a whole bunch of shorts in early December. When I asked him about it he said he was worried about a Christmas rally, and that we could re-short everything in the new year. I supposed that such a rally was certainly possible, especially considering how many times the bears had been squeezed that year. But unfortunately, in-fact, almost immediately, the sell-off gathered steam and went on without him. Well, Ezra considered his lack of conviction to be wholly unacceptable and promptly fired him a week later. Indeed, that turned out to be the very same wave of selling that morphed into the Global Financial Crisis (GFC) and saw the retail sector down 50% from those levels. Poor Ed. He missed the whole damn move.

Now if there was one man in the firm who had no problem sticking to the game plan, it was Jamie. His $2bn global bank's book had been net short for months, but in November he turned completely bearish and put on the biggest short of his life. And it seemed nothing was going to shake his conviction that the financial world was about to fall apart.

Though I didn't mind trading for the fundamental portfolio managers, my real passion lay in running the quant models. I made every effort to be proactive and go beyond what was expected of me. It wasn't hard – I just loved those quant models. So it was that early in the new year I found myself on a conference call with the senior staff from 666. They commended me on my performance, and in particular, how I'd handled the GQM. Then Ezra revealed that despite the mid-year glitch, the firm had made a respectable 11% in 2007, and that I could be proud of my part in it. Lastly, he explained that Perdu was fitting out a new office in Singapore and asked if I wanted to move out there to trade Asia. It took me less than a second to respond in the affirmative. *"Yes* sir," I said. *"Thank you for the opportunity. I won't let you down."*

"Good," he replied. *"In that case we're going to promote you to Vice President. Good luck Damon."*

Two weeks later I said goodbye to freezing London and all that crazy shit with Karina and the Albanian mafia and HSBC locking those guys out in the cold and the bloody steak and the fake news and the glass door and the epileptic fit and the lying milk company and *you killed buster!* Yeah, I was sure glad the day I logged off from that shit-show. It was time for a new beginning.

29. ASIA

In early 2008 there were a lot of expats moving to Singapore, and the place was booming. I could see myself staying for five or ten years, so I went ahead and bought an apartment. It was the first time I'd owned anything more expensive than a surfboard. Well, one Friday night there were a bunch of trading heads visiting Singapore to see clients and run amok. As usual, we started at BQ Bar in Boat Quay. About half the group were buy-side traders like myself, and the other half were sell-side sales-traders. Of course, the sales-traders all bent over backwards to be my friend, but I resisted getting too close for I knew that one day I might have to hurt them in the market.

My friend Richie, however, was an exception since he was a sell-side trader at a retail broker. Not only did his firm never give up trades to other PBs, but almost all the client orders went straight onto his book rather than being pushed onto the market. As such, he really operated in his own little world and didn't know the rest of the street. Joe, my sales-trader at Enay Bank, didn't understand the retail trading world and quizzed him about how he made money. *"It's easy,"* said Richie. *"We give the clients enough rope to hang themselves and they always do."* I shuddered as I recalled how 100 times leverage had destroyed me during 7/7.

"What do you mean?" asked Joe.

"I can basically drive them out of any position they enter so long as the stock isn't too liquid. So let's say they buy some shitty mid-cap stock. Well, just as soon as they've finished buying I'll go ahead and hit the exchange and push the price down. And if they buy more I'll just push it down more, until eventually, they give up and take the loss. Sometimes I'll find myself with clients on both sides of the trade, and then I can put on a good old-fashioned bucket shop drive."

"A what?"

"A BSD. A bucket shop drive. It's when some of my clients are long, and some are short, so I push the stock down and stop out all the longs, and then I ramp it up and stop out all the shorts. Some clients just keep coming back and falling for the same old gag every time. You see they think they're investing in companies, or at least, that the market is random. They can't grasp the simple fact that they're gambling against the house, and the house always wins. It's like Homer Simpson when he gets an electric shock, but he keeps reaching out to touch it, over and over again."

"But don't you worry that you might be playing with fire? That they might be a whale with more firepower than you?" Budgie asked since that was why the rest of the street couldn't do it.

"I know they're not," replied Richie. *"If they had a clue then they wouldn't have opened an account with my firm in the first place. The commissions are ridiculous – fifteen basis points for stock orders and a six-pip spread on FX."*

"Six pips wide on the major crosses? Oh my God. Tell me more!" said Joe.

"We have morning meetings where we openly discuss what we're going to do that day. 'Today we got BSDs in Stock1, Stock2, Stock3,' which means we have 2-way client positions in those names and we know they'll use tight stops."

"How do you know they'll use tight stops?"

"Well, half the time they're so stupid that they enter their stops into the system, which are just big fat targets for me to aim at. But for those who don't, we have a quant team whose job is to analyse their past behaviour and predict where their pain thresholds will be. So on my charts I have these horizontal lines that show me real stops in red and predicted stops in orange. So I just wait around all day looking for clusters and when I find one I go to town on it."

"So you literally chart the client's psychological break points."

"Exactly, and it gets even better because when I run their stops our sales-traders can make these great calls to new clients where they pick the exact bottom or top of the move I'm creating. The new clients are sceptical at first, but after they see two or three good calls in a row they're hooked. And then the whole cycle repeats."

"That is insane," said Budgie shaking his head.

"Yes, but here's the thing. Even if I didn't drive

them out of their positions I know they're gonna lose all their money anyway. It's simple – they always trade with too much leverage. These days I hardly even bother to hedge my book because I know they'll lose eventually."

"Ok, so what percentage of your clients lose all their money?"

"Ninety-five percent," replied Richie, but then corrected himself. "At least ninety-five percent."

Suddenly Will arrived carrying a tray of Espresso Sambucas which we promptly slammed down our throats. Then he ordered another. And another. Soon we'd had six rounds of the good stuff and were pretty excited to get on with the night. So we piled into cabs and took off to Brix – Singapore's classiest hooker bar. Later I found myself joking around with one of the traders from Tudor. Then, out of the blue, he said, "Hey, tell me about your new boss, Tan."

"He's great," I replied. "Why?"

"Tan is a god damn legend, that's why! Did you hear about the Aussie dollar last year?"

"No, what happened?"

"Man, I only know what I heard from the guys at work. You should go have a beer with him sometime and ask him directly."

"Ok, I will."

A week later I found myself sitting with Tan in that quiet area out the back of the Fullerton. "So Tan," I said, "I heard you're a bit of a legend in the currency market."

"Oh, I wouldn't say that Damon. You know how these things get exaggerated."

"Well, I've got every FX sales-trader in Singapore

calling me, and they never fail to ask how you are. Hey, it's great for me. I'm happy to make new sell-side friends with corporate credit cards, but I really don't have much flow in FX right now. We only got one guy in London, and a few guys in 666 trading enough size to pass me worked orders. Everything else is DMA or FIX. I don't want them getting pissed off with me for not giving them any flow."

"I wouldn't worry about them," he said. "They're big boys. They get what they deserve."

"Hey, so my buddy over at Tudor said to ask you about an Aussie dollar trade from last year?"

His eyes widened at the mention of Tudor, but then he relaxed and took a sip of his beer. "Well, if you know those guys then I guess you're gonna hear some version of what happened. So let me tell you what really happened. But this is just for you ok."

"Of course."

"As you know I used to trade for GIC."

"Wait, and I'm sorry to interrupt, but how big is GIC?"

"You know I can't tell you that Damon."

"Ok, I understand, but couldn't you just give me a ballpark figure, maybe three hundred billion dollars?" I paused and stared into his eyes. They signalled that $300bn was too low so I went on quickly, "Or is it more like eight hundred billion?"

He smiled and shook his head, "Seriously I'm not saying anything!"

"Ok then, what about your FX book? Can you tell me that?"

"Nope."

"Ok, and I don't mean to harass you. It's just that

everyone knows that Singapore is one of the biggest money laundering centres in the world, and it's interesting to think about how much money might have been seized by the authorities over the last fifty years."

"Ha!" he said. *"More like a hundred and fifty years. Look, I love my country and I think you'd agree that the strength of the nation depends on no one knowing."*

"Knowing how much money was seized? Or that it's now being run as the world's most powerful currency hedge fund?"

"Do you want to hear about the Aussie dollar or not?" he asked.

"Ok, I'm just kidding."

"Well, I'd been offered a new job and was planning to leave GIC, but I had time to put on one last trade. Risk had been rallying for months, and I decided to fade it by putting out a short line in AUDJPY. Alas, the market kept pushing higher, so I responded with yards and yards of the stuff."

"Yard?" I asked.

"A yard is what we call a billion-dollar trade in the FX market. So I sold many billions of Aussie dollars against the Yen and that pushed the market down and kept it there. That afternoon, however, I received a call from Mr Macfarlane."

"You mean the governor of the Reserve Bank of Australia?"

"Former governor. He'd already left the RBA by then. But we'd been friends for years, and he knew I was one of the only people in the world who could move the Aussie dollar around at will. Well, normally he was a really polite guy, but on this occasion, he got right to the point. He said only, 'Tan, please stop hurting our

dollar,' and I said, 'Sure, no problem.' I didn't want to upset him, and anyway, I didn't like the way AUDJPY was moving. So I turned, covered, and went long.

"The next day UBS offered me some calls in big size and since they were trading cheap I went ahead and bought them. Then I spent the rest of the day buying various AUD crosses to support my position, and it felt like a good trade. But when Monday came around I was in trouble. The market was really weak, and the price action lasted all the way through until the end of the US session. It seemed like everyone was out to kill me, and for that day, I didn't fight them.

"The next morning, I got up early and got busy. I ramped the market and sent the weak shorts running for cover. Soon enough I had AUDJPY back to a fifty percent retracement but as soon as I stopped buying it turned lower again. So I bought a few yards from the street and lifted the ECNs in size. But it didn't work, and I soon found myself looking at intraday losses.

"The next day saw almost the exact same thing. I was able to move the market higher in the morning but to keep it there required buying a lot more size than I anticipated. My account certainly wasn't unlimited, as people liked to assume, so I couldn't just go on buying yards here and yards there. Plus, I discovered it was Tudor who'd sold me the calls via UBS. I really hadn't intended to pick a fight with them.

"But on Thursday my luck turned, and I kick-started a rally that put those calls well into the money during the Asian session. But I knew Tudor would fight me with all they had, and I honestly didn't sleep again until early Saturday morning. How could I when they kept raiding the market? There were periods when I sat

there with the phone line open saying, 'Ok buy another yard here. Ok buy another yard here,' and then switching to another line and saying the same thing to a different broker. Of course, I was also supporting the ECNs with iceberged limit orders. But it was tough going for it seemed like everyone on the planet was selling AUDJPY, and there's me, the only buyer, getting so long that I started to wonder if they all knew something I didn't. But still, my plan was working since though I was taking intraday losses, the market was still higher and my calls still well in the money.

"Going for days without sleep, and being under so much pressure, was really taking toll. And you know Damon, I'm over 50 years old now. I was worried that I might not make it through Friday night. Tudor, and let's be honest, there were probably a bunch of funds colluding on the other side, had fresh faced traders in every time zone waiting to do battle. But it was just me trading by myself, and if I couldn't take it, if I went to sleep for an hour or so, you could've been damn sure they'd have busted that market wide open. So I held my nerve and fought them on every raid. And in the end, it was simple. The options expired, and I won."

We sat in silence for a while, me in awe of the firepower he had at his disposal, and he with a look of reminiscence and pride. *"That was right before the carry trade blew up,"* he said. *"I suppose all I did was delay the inevitable. But anyway, I'm glad I'm out of it now. Of managing a book, I mean. There's no way I could go through that sort of thing again."*

"Yes, but Tan, that's why the boys call you a legend – because your last trade was your greatest, and you taught them all a lesson they'd never forget."

"And what's that?" he asked.

"That you don't fuck with GIC."

He laughed but didn't say anything so I went on. *"You know Tan, it's funny, but in all my years I never met a PM who could beat the FX market."*

"I'm not surprised," he said. *"I used to trade with a hundred billion dollars, and I almost never lost. Just who do you think paid for it all?"*

In February, I took a trip out to Hong Kong to meet Seb whom we'd poached from Castle Capital. He was a senior guy in the region, and it was a big hire for us. I also had a lot of people to meet from the sell-side, since outside of FX, that's where most of them were based. I flew over on Tuesday afternoon, and after checking into the Four Seasons, I headed to *Dragon-i*. It was an incredible place, and I soon found myself in the midst of a crowd of traders and sales-traders with Russian models dancing on tables all around us. Finally, I found Seb, and after chatting for a while, I was glad that he'd soon be joining me in Singapore.

Some sales-traders would do anything to start a relationship with Perdu, and I soon had one such guy getting on my nerves. I let him know it was time to piss off, and though disappointed, he took it well. *"It was good to meet you, Damon,"* he said. *"And let me just say once again, welcome to Hong Kong."* With that, he held out his hand, and as I shook it, he passed me an 8-ball of coke. I looked at him in surprise. *"Really? Is this for me?"*

"Yeah man, just make sure we go for the first line together."

"Ah, ok. Where?"

"Bathroom?"

"Sure ok," and off we went. After a line the length of a pencil we reeled our way out of the bathroom whereupon I ran into one of the other buy-side traders who grabbed me by the arm. *"Hey! Where do you think you're going?"* he said and dragged me back into the nearest cubicle. All told, that first night in Hong Kong was one of the biggest nights of my life. Unfortunately, that was an issue, since I was scheduled to spend the entire next day at Lehman Brothers.

I considered vomiting in a pot plant as I waited in the lobby of Two IFC. Finally, Raj arrived and introduced himself. He wasn't just my relationship manager at Lehman but one of the best HFT/Quant connectivity guys in Asia. He saw at once that I looked a little green, and he laughed that he'd only set up 18 meetings for me. *"18? Are you fucking kidding me?"*

"Yes," he said. *"Just kidding. You have four meetings in the conference room, and then we can just hang out on the trading floor for as long as you want."*

"Thank God."

The meetings were spaced half an hour apart, and in each one I nodded attentively as the department heads spoke. When the last meeting finally arrived, Raj spoke on behalf of the HFT/Quant teams when he explained to the room that Perdu was by far their most demanding client and how Bluewave had dragged them kicking and screaming into the future. I knew all of that already and didn't give much of a response. Instead, I just nodded and looked around for a pot-plant to vomit in. Eventually, we took off for lunch at La Pampa where I explained to Raj that I'd had an out of control night and had gotten almost no sleep. Fortunately, the KBC special I ordered perked me up, even if I could only stomach half of it. Raj, of course, was made to eat the whole thing.

After lunch, it was back to the trading floor where I met all the people I'd been talking to since coming to Asia. But after sales-trading, DMA, algos, swaps, and futures, I was tiring from so many meet-and-greets and looking forward to getting back to the hotel. Alas, Raj had organised after work drinks and then a formal sit-down dinner with his team. I pleaded with him to cancel it, but he claimed they'd been looking forward to it for weeks. So I agreed but only on the condition that I would first go back to the hotel to change the battery in my Blackberry. I dashed home, had a few lines, and was in excellent form for the rest of the night. What else could I do?

I spent the next day at Bear Stearns. Manny had been transferred to Hong Kong after his stint in the mortgage-backed bond department in New York. His new boss happened to be the owner of Privé nightclub, and by sheer coincidence, Bear was having their Chinese New Year party there that night. When Manny asked if I could come, the answer back was, *"Of course he can!"* I'd never been to a private party in a nightclub before, and boy did I get a shock. Half the firm was racking up, and no one even bothered to go do it in the bathroom. We chatted briefly about the mortgage market but he just shrugged and said, *"Look I was relatively junior when I was there. I have no idea how much toxic junk is still floating around."* Then he found us a couple of options from the EQD desk, and soon I was making out with a Cuban-Korean girl on the dance floor. What a combination. What a night.

The next morning, Friday, I really did vomit in a

pot plant. It was in the lobby of UBS, and I can only say it was their own fault for not having a bathroom nearby to reception. I spent about an hour in each of three meeting rooms before heading down to the trading floor. They had a great setup, and their program trading team really blew me away. At 1 pm I thanked everyone and took off for my next meeting at Morgan Stanley, grabbing a sandwich on the way. Again, it was a full afternoon of meetings, nodding and smiling, and wanting to vomit. Then I met up with CLSA and had drinks at Red. The turbo powder got me through till midnight, but then I finally pulled the plug and went home.

I awoke Saturday morning feeling like absolute hell. But Manny was on the phone telling me all about the amazing plans he had for us that day. *"First we'll go out on a junk boat with a bunch of girls. Then we'll go to LKF with a bunch of girls. Then.."*

"I'm sorry mate. I've got to go back to Singapore," I said.

"What? You said you've got the hotel until Sunday."

"No, there's been a mix-up. UBS said I have to check out today. I've already changed my flight. I've got to leave now for the airport."

"Man, that sucks."

"Yeah, it really sucks."

It was all lies. I did have the room until Sunday, but I was feeling so ill that I just couldn't take Hong Kong any longer. It seemed like the city was trying to kill me, and I was sure glad that Perdu had chosen to set up in Singapore instead.

Like many hedge funds, we were lured to Singapore on promises of low taxes and no red tape.

But it wasn't long before the authorities tried to make us register as a licensed brokerage and hand over $300m in regulatory capital. Upon hearing it, Ezra just laughed, said we were a private hedge fund not a broker, and that we'd simply move to Hong Kong if they kept being dicks about it.

For me, the city's honeymoon period ended after the first six months, when I realised there was something seriously amiss in the small island nation. The first clue was that the locals had virtually no interest in us expats, or indeed, in anything much at all. I read a survey that said it was the least emotional country in the world with just 2% of the workforce *engaged by their job* compared to the global average of 11%. So from taxi drivers who didn't know where Orchard Road was, to sandwich shops that couldn't make a sandwich, it was a daily occurrence for me to shake my head in disbelief at how utterly clueless and unhelpful they could be. And yet against this backdrop the younger generation were the most materialistic I'd ever come across with the local dream summed up by the *5 C's* – cash, car, condo, credit card, country club.

One day I went shopping with Richie to buy a new mobile phone. We were comparing a few models and asked about battery life. *"Dun know lah,"* said the salesman. Then we asked about memory. *"Dun know lah,"* he said again. Then we asked about screen resolution. *"Dun know oreddy lah!"* he said as though the possession of such knowledge was the most preposterous thing he'd ever conceived. We let it go and took off to find something to eat. At the restaurant Richie ordered fries with no salt, but the waiter responded, *"Cannot lah."*

"Really? Cannot? Are you sure about that?" asked Richie.

"Sure lah," the waiter responded before staring blankly at the table and awaiting the next instruction. I suppose what kept us sane was the ability to get away for weekends. Sometimes we travelled to the nearby Indonesian island of Bintan to play golf, other times we went fishing in Thailand, and just one time I went surfing in Bali.

I didn't realise I was in trouble until it was too late. And it was at that exact moment when I realised Jez was right about what he'd said all those years earlier. *"You're gonna be fat, Damon. One day you're gonna be so fat! There's no way someone can eat as much as you and not end up a porka later in life."*

"But I've got a high metabolism," I'd argued.

"Exactly! And one day that's gonna slow down."

"No way. Never!"

We'd climbed down through the cave at Uluwatu on the south-west tip of Bali, and it was so beautiful that I didn't really think about the danger. When we reached the water, we happened to hit a lull right away, so we jumped straight in and started paddling. Unlike me, Sim and Phippsy were surf-fit. In fact, Sim was a Queensland state champion swimmer, and Phippsy was a full-time surfer back home. As for me, I was just a fat trader who'd been chained to his desk for the past seven years.

After two minutes, the other guys were way ahead. It helped that they had proper boards for the conditions. All I had was a 6'2" Stuart fish – a great board – but just terrible for seven-foot Uluwatu. Nor did I bring any booties to protect my feet from the coral. I simply didn't consider anything when they'd called a few days earlier and said the surf was going off.

The other guys were scrambling like mad about 60 meters ahead when I realised there was no way I was going to make it. So I stopped paddling, figuring it was a smart move to regain some strength before going on. I watched Sim power over the first wave of the set well before it broke, but Phippsy only just made it. Only then did I realise how big it was – fucking massive. I had planned to start paddling again, straight at it, but then I decided that I couldn't duck dive a wave so big. And so I did what all respectable guys did when they were scared shitless – I threw my board aside and dove for the bottom.

Well, I'm used to surfing sand bottom point breaks, and I really didn't expect it to be so shallow. And so the most ridiculous thing happened – I dove straight into the reef. I guess it was about four-foot deep, which meant I hit it pretty hard, and then just as I was bouncing off it, along came the wave. I really didn't have a hope. It picked me up and dumped me over the falls and then over and over I went doing underwater back flips and side flips and front flips until I started kicking for the surface. But just as I reached it, and took a desperate breath, the second wave was upon me. So I did a kind of sideways dive trying not to go to deep, and it worked because I didn't hit the reef this time. Then, as the wave rolled over head, I curled up into a ball, so it wouldn't grab hold of me and drag me across the coral. After I was sure it had passed, I extended my body and kicked for the surface. Alas, I somehow kicked my foot into a crevice in the coral, and now it was stuck in there and wouldn't come out.

Now if it was a life and death situation, which I think it was, wasn't I supposed to have my whole life flash before my eyes? Well, not me. I got to thinking about Baywatch. Stupid senseless Baywatch and this idiotic episode I'd seen about 15 years earlier where Mitch saved a drowning tourist who got his foot stuck under a rock. And do you remember how fake those scenes were? So fake, just utterly ridiculous. But there was me in real life, in serious danger, and all I could think about was Mitch in a stupid fake scene from the tranquil shores of Baywatch. I mean, why didn't I think of Pamela Anderson in that red swimsuit during my last moments on earth? Because she was sitting in her tower and it was Mitch who'd saved the day in that particular scene. Damn it!

That was when the adrenalin kicked in and made me think, *'Just pull it out!'* So I jerked with all my might, the coral broke, and out came my foot. But not without first shredding it to bits. I started swimming for the surface, but then I felt a tug and realised that my board was still stuck down below. The only thing that saved me was that the leash was just long enough that I could reach the surface. After two frantic breaths I dove under a third wave before swimming down to retrieve my board from beneath its wedge. Then, finally, we both floated back up to the surface.

I looked around, and for the first time, I realised there was no beach at Uluwatu (at least not at high-tide anyway). All I could see was a cliff, and it was coming at me fast. So I started paddling away from it, back out toward the break, but I didn't make much progress. Finally, I reached a point where I thought, *'Oh shit! I'm gonna get smashed into the cliff.'* And again, my lizard brain took over. The one that didn't consider things like tired or can't. The one with direct access to emergency reserves of adrenaline. And so I paddled like a man possessed. But the water around me was frothy and lightweight, having been pounded against the cliff, and I couldn't get any traction. So I came up with a plan to use my board as a shield and then kick off the cliff and swim for my life. Thankfully, it didn't come to that for I soon found myself in a zone where the force of the water rebounding off the cliff balanced the incoming water from the broken waves.

I have no idea how long I was paddling for, but it must have been a really long time. I just kept thinking, *'Where's the beach? How is anyone supposed to get out of here?'* But then the cliffs sloped downward, and I saw the Balangan Resort jutting out above me. And below that was a solitary 40-meter-wide stretch of sand. When I got myself safely up the beach, I lay there for a long time thinking about why the ocean had tried to kill me. But then I got to thinking about how lucky I was to be alive, and I vowed to buy a new board and attack the surf again the next day. That's when a holidaymaker came down to check on me. I must have looked a real sight with all that blood pouring out of my foot and reddening the sand. *"Hey man, are you ok?"* he said.

"Yeah, I'm ok," I said breathing heavily.

"Shit, did you get carried all the way down here from Dreamland?"

"No, from Uluwatu."

"Oh my God. That's like four miles away. Do you want a lift back there? I got a motorbike."

"Sure man, thanks."

I might have almost died, and I sure took a beating, but true to my word I followed the boys out for another crack the following day. This time I had booties and a brand new 6'10" DHD. But the swell was even bigger now, and though I made it out the back, I struggled to commit to my first wave. Suddenly, a storm was brewing, and some of the guys started heading back in. *'Just one wave,'* I thought to myself. *'Just catch a small one so I can escape this madness.'*

That's when I heard Sim shout, *"Your wave Damon! Go go go!"* I paddled hard and it picked me up, but my take-off was awkward and I lost my balance. So straight down the face I fell, and then over the falls I went, hoping for the best, but fearing the worst. When I resurfaced I found myself alone in the whitewash, my board nowhere to be seen, just half a snapped leg rope dangling from my ankle. Then I saw it way up ahead, but it was all I could do to watch it get smashed into the cliff. With no intention of suffering the same fate, I changed direction and headed for the opening of the cave. Somehow, I managed to make it back in one piece.

We sat for hours that day watching the seas rage in fury. A few pros took up the challenge; a few daredevils went home in ambulances; and all were struck by the tremendous power of mother nature to destroy what she had built.

30. THE GLOBAL FINANCIAL CRISIS

All of a sudden Bear Stearns imploded - another good old-fashioned run on the bank but this time by institutional lenders. Jamie had bought some Bear CDS at around 250bps, and when it spiked to 700bps, it looked like he'd nailed it. But then the Fed refused to let Bear go bankrupt for fear it would trigger a CDS credit event and tear the financial system to pieces. Instead, they had JP Morgan buy Bear in what was the largest Fed-backed financing deal in history. Poor old Jamie wound up selling his CDS for 180bps.

Well, on the back of this credit non-event the stockmarket took off on a two-month rally. As they say, bear market rallies are vicious. But it was in the oil market where the most ridiculous fraud was taking place, and perhaps never in history had a market been so divorced from economic reality. You wouldn't have believed it possible, but oil rallied all the way through till June. Why? Because of an army of cheerleading analysts who stood ready with a bag of bullshit sandwiches to counter anyone with common sense. That's when I heard about pension funds buying oil to diversify away from equities and bonds. *'Uh-oh,'* I thought. *'The retail mom-and-pop investors are about to get wiped out.'* And right on queue Goldman put out one last piece of bullish bullshit asserting that oil could go to $200 per barrel. In fact, it soon peaked at $147 before collapsing all the way to $40 in just six months.

It was around that time that I noticed there were all these TV shows about *Deadly Weather* or *When Weather Attacks!* It was because the whole world had gone off its rocker about global warming. It started in 2006 when meteorologists predicted a record hurricane season with nine expected to make landfall. That was when Amaranth put on an 8:1 leveraged natural gas position. Alas, that hurricane season produced a real whopper – zero – and with that Amaranth imploded into a $6bn loss and took the latest title for the worst hedge fund blow-up in history. But ever since the media had continued to preach their dire warnings that bad weather would tear apart oil rigs, rip up pipelines, and swamp entire cities with giant waves. Why did the media always want to make people unhappy? Was it all just to benefit some guy betting on the oil market?

With Bear Stearns gone Jamie kept adding to his shorts as financial stocks fell. That was around the time when all the asset classes became correlated, banks stopped trusting each other, and Libor became the most important financial figure in the world. I set up a bunch of Libor charts on Bloomberg, and I saw them spike whenever someone was accused of holding the bag of toxic debt. This correctly signalled an increase in credit risk so it appeared that Libor was working properly. But then I read an article about *Lying Libor* that claimed banks were manipulating the rate because if they actually showed real demand for cash people would turn on them and say, *"Hey look! Those guys are in trouble! Big trouble!"* Now if real Libor rates were substantially higher, then it was the mother-load of all mispricings since Libor pegged interest rates on trillions of dollars of debt and derivatives. To gauge the extent of the fear I called up my old friend Gherkin who was now working in the treasury department of Goldman's London office. *"The Furry Gherkin!"* I said. *"How are you?"*

"Good mate, what's going on?'

"Same shit, different day. Did you hear about Lying Libor?"

"I did. It's kind of a big deal over here."

"That's why I called you."

"Ok look, right now I won't lend money to anyone, even overnight money, even to HSBC."

"What?" I asked incredulously. *"Do you seriously think that if you lend HSBC five hundred million dollars overnight, you might not get it back?"*

"Yep," he said. *"I don't care who it is. The whole financial system is bankrupt, and we all know it. It's just a matter of how well banks can lie and cheat and pretend they're solvent. Level three accounting helps but you have to wait until reporting time to run that scam."*

"Ok buddy, that's all I need to know. I'll let you get back to it." Then I hung up and called Jamie to pass on the word.

In June, Lehman announced a net loss of almost

$3bn for Q2 – not bad considering they'd been the largest underwriter of subprime MBS. That was when Ezra started diversifying our PB base by moving some of our cash and positions to other prime brokers. The deal was that they had to match Lehman's ability to handle our Bluewave flow, and I can tell you, that was a real struggle. In any case, we kept the vast bulk of Perdu's capital at Lehman up until the final days.

It was 1 am on Tuesday, September 9, when for some crazy reason my Blackberry started ringing. I wanted to kill the idiot but when I picked it up I saw it was Simon. *"Hey mate, how's the weather over there in shitty London,"* I asked but he cut me off quickly.

"Damon, listen carefully. Tomorrow don't trade at all with Lehman. Trade everything at Enay Bank PB. No Lehman."

"Ok, got it. No trading with Lehman. I'll use Tradingscreen Enay, phone orders to settle at Enay, and futures and FX at Barx."

"Good. Now go back to sleep. It's gonna be a big week."

Until then I'd never thought about the possibility of Lehman going bust because from where I sat they were so damn good at what they did. But then I never traded mortgage derivatives and knew very little about that world. I suppose very few did. Even so, it was clear to me that if we moved our cash and positions away from them, it could threaten the liquidity they needed to survive, especially if other funds did the same thing. And then what? Could a bank failure of that magnitude trigger a system meltdown? Could ATMs run out of money? Could teacher's paychecks stop coming in the mail? Well, you can be damn sure that's what the media said would happen.

When I got to work a few hours later everything had changed. News was out that the Korea Development Bank had pulled out of talks to buy them, and it was such bad news that the stock later fell 45% in the US session. In the meantime, I was ordered to liquidate everything at Lehman and initiate the same positions at Enay. That didn't make any sense to me because a simple position transfer would have saved hundreds of thousands in commission and slippage. *'Wait a second,'* I thought. *'Most of our positions are on swap, so we don't really own the positions, Lehman does, and we can't transfer swaps from one PB to another.'* I wasn't sure if my logic was correct, but the back office was in no mood to explain it to me. Then I realised that if we enacted a full position transfer the whole street would know by lunchtime, and then Lehman would collapse faster than the positions could settle.

It was heavy trading and 666 handed down instructions as we went. Though we were used to liquidating the books of portfolio managers who'd been fired, it was unusual for us to handle more than two in a day. But now we found ourselves liquidating and initiating up to six at a time. It was the ultimate fat-tailed workload but we'd been training for it our whole lives and weren't going to let the firm down.

Basket 1:   Export, launch, copy, paste-special, sort, long -> sell, short -> buy, weigh, save-as, load, check, recheck.
[Execute: LB]

Basket 2:   Open, invert, save-as, load, check, recheck.
[Execute: EB]

The first pair of inverted baskets waded out into the river of capital. One swam us away from Lehman, the other netted us back into the safety of Enay. I figured HFTs would be swarming all over our market impact, like sharks sensing the electrical signals of their prey. So to confuse them I switched algos every half hour or so from VWAP to ¼-Vol to Implementation-Shortfall and back again.

Of course, the most important portfolio in the firm was Bluewave, but Nikolai had programmed it to liquidate and reinitiate itself programmatically. Even so, not everything could be done in the market, so he passed me around 30 problematic positions and said to liquidate them. *"Wait, liquidate only?"* I asked.

"Yes," he said. *"We can't reinitiate these positions at Enay because the spike in volume would be too obvious and we'd get in trouble for wash trading."*

A wash trade was when you simultaneously bought and sold the same stock to yourself. But because it created fictitious volume it could be considered market manipulation if that volume was too high a percentage of the ADV. *"Ok Nikolai, but this is gonna be difficult. Can I take until the end of the week?"*

"We want to be out as soon as possible. But yes, you have until Friday."

I loaded the illiquid stocks into pre-trade analytics and then sorted them by liquidity in one window and by value in another. Then I got on the phone and called every sales-trader in Asia who'd been active in those names. I asked if they had the other side and some said they did. Easy. But when they didn't I harassed them and belittled them and demanded that they take them on risk. Some guys told me to get fucked and,

"*This isn't how it works in Asia*", but others were amenable and stepped up. Then I moved onto the next stock and the next sales-trader and over and over again.

We kept going for the rest of the week with 666 passing down the priority portfolios to be moved. At the same time, I kept working my way through Bluewave's illiquid positions. Finally, for those remaining stocks I couldn't get rid of, I turned to playing on their greed. A year earlier Jamie had taught me a concept called *feeding the fish*, and I used it that week to feed many stocks to many fish. Though the sizes varied, and the names varied, they all went down something like this.

On Tuesday, I had an order to sell 500k AGL. The market was thin, and if I tried to sell even 50k I'd have probably knocked the price down 5%. So I got on the phone and called a tag at the bottom of my list. "*Hey Pal, I got a block of fifty k AGL to go. You want it?*"

"*No, I'm good,*" the tag replied.

"*Come on man. I know you have heaps of flow in this stock.*"

"*Had flow, my friend. That buyer finished weeks ago. I got nothing to do now sorry.*"

"*Ok look, you know it's illiquid. You just take fifty k here at 7.50 and then I won't sell another thing. All you have to do is buy another ten thousand shares in the market, and this thing will totally rip. You know it will!*"

Silence. Perfect. So I pushed harder. "*It's just a pissy little position. Why are we even discussing it? Just take fifty k shares from me ok?*"

"*Yeah ok. I bought fifty thousand AGL at 7.50.*"

"*Yes, you did. Thanks.*"

Then I called another tag and did the same thing.

Then, right on cue, both of them went into the market, bought more stock, and easily pushed it up to 7.75. At the close their positions showed them a profit, so they were happy. And I got rid of 100k shares, so I was happy.

On Wednesday, I called two more tags and repeated the process. They each bought 50k shares from me at 7.80 and then bought more in the market pushing it up to 8.10. Everyone was happy. On Thursday, I still had 300k shares to go but when I called around that morning no one was interested in buying *up here*. The original tags, however, were happy to see the rally and sent me kind messages. One even thanked me for putting him into such a *great stock*. I immediately called that idiot. *"Hey mate, yeah it's a great little company with a really bright future. Actually, I had no idea why the portfolio manager wanted to sell it, but I just learnt that he's been fired. Yep, just this morning. So I'm sitting here with a liquidation order, and I've got a few small positions left. One of them is AGL. You want another hundred thousand shares?"*

"No man, a hundred thousand is a too big for me."

"Oh, come on it's tiny. Plus, you already made like eight percent on this trade – a trade that I put you in remember."

"Ok look, I could buy another fifty k here."

"Done. You bought fifty thousand AGL at.. ahh.. 8.15. See what I mean? There are other buyers out there. This thing goes up every day! You're lucky you get to buy it from me instead of on the damn market."

"Yeah, ok 8.15. Done."

"Fine but just remember if I don't find another buyer to take this last fifty k I'm gonna have to sell it

on the market. You had your chance. It's still yours if you want it."

"No, I don't want anymore."

"Ok fine, bye."

The next tag wouldn't bite and kept saying the stock was too high. I explained that nothing was ever too high to buy, but he wouldn't budge. I thought of what Andy might say. '*My friend, this is just between you and me ok. I'm hearing about an impending takeover battle for the company. You're gonna kick yourself if you miss out on the hottest merger rally of the year!*' But then I decided that being on the phone was a waste of time, so I went into the market and sold 50k over two hours which promptly knocked it down to 7.80. Then, to my surprise, it rallied back to 8.10. '*Ha!*' I thought. '*They're trying to fight me!*' So I set some iceberged limit orders at 8.15 and every five cents up to 8.30, and they showed a bit of strength by lifting everything up to and including my offer at 8.25. But no one would touch the 8.30 offer so I pulled it and waited for five minutes to see if they'd attempt an upside breakout on low volume. Alas, nothing happened, so with 170k still to go, I quit being cute and started selling aggressively. I got rid of another 50k by the end of the day but it was tough work, and I had to take the price down to 7.60. The good thing was that I appeared to be the only real seller, which meant all the tags I'd given blocks to were sitting tight.

On Friday, they marked the stock up as best they could in the opening auction, and I let them have their way with it for 15 minutes. By then it was trading 8.05 – 8.10 and if only I had the time I would have let them push it higher. That might have brought in some new money and saved their sorry asses. But it was Friday, and I had to finish up. When I started selling it was a one-way market. No new money came in, and suddenly everyone else was selling too. I got busy smashing it down five or six ticks at a go, but I'd only sold 50k by the time it had fallen all the way to 7.20. Then no rally. So I kept at it, and by mid-afternoon, I'd knocked it down to 6.30 with only 20k left to sell. *'Most of these guys are going to capitulate today,'* I thought. *'Therefore, it's gonna close on its lows no matter what I do.'* So I offered an iceberg for the balance way down at 5.90, and an hour later it was all gone. But upon seeing such a low print, the poor old tags capitulated, and they puked that stock all the way through to the end of the session where it closed at 5.50. My average for the whole 500k was 7.62 – very close to where it had started – whereas every one of those greedy tags lost money. So why did I feed the fish and then make them puke? Because they should have taken the full size from me in the first place. Then I wouldn't have had to hit the market, and they could have marked it up wherever they wanted.

What was funny was that every day in every one of those stocks the media just had to give their expert opinion on why it had moved. But they knew nothing of me and my liquidation order which meant they knew nothing at all. So they'd make up some bullshit headline just to pretend that stock prices were related to company fundamentals and keep the readers coming back for more. That way, their egos could be satisfied that they were now informed:

16:27 AGL PLUNGES IN HEAVY TRADING - Investors weigh a possible cut in guidance

Of course, you could weigh anything you liked in the imaginary mind of an imaginary investor. But back in the real world it was just me and a few sales-traders playing a game of positions. We were the ones who moved the market, not financial theories, or speculations about the future. It was trading, pure and simple. And though I destroyed a lot of relationships that week, it was well worth it to have gotten out of those tough positions. Especially considering what came next.

31. LEHMAN BUST

TECTONIC SHIFT ON WALL STREET AS LEHMAN
FAILS WITH RECORD $613 BILLION DEBT

On Monday, Lehman Brothers exploded into the biggest bankruptcy in world history. And it wasn't just the biggest – it was six times the size of the previous record. There started the epicentre of the GFC in which financial markets became a wrecking yard of capitulation and chaos unlike anything I'd ever seen. Every day a crash either happened, or was imminent, but the danger in being short was that government or central bank intervention could quite easily produce a massive rally, or *reverse crash,* as I called them. That's the thing about extreme uncertainty – it divides two states that are polar opposites, yet exist only a knife edge apart. Indeed, both crashes and reverse crashes occurred several times over the following months.

It wasn't long before the politicians and the presstitutes started blamestorming for a scapegoat. Of course, they could never admit the truth – that it was the highly regulated banks, insurance companies, and ratings agencies that were at the root of the problem. In fudging their ratings of mortgage-related debt, S&P, Moody's and Fitch did something infinity worse than Arthur Anderson had done when it cheated on Enron's accounting. And yet whereas Arthur Anderson was shut down forever, the ratings agencies got away with it scot-free and went on with their quid pro quo business as usual. That those people weren't put in jail was a travesty of justice. Well, soon enough they had Joe Public believing that the crisis was the result of *evil short sellers* and that a short sell ban would stop *the crisis on Wall Street turning into a crisis on Main Street*.

In truth, short selling had nothing to do with anything, and such accusations had been bandied about in every crash since the first stock exchange opened in 1602. Even so, they got their way, and bans were implemented around the world. Initially, I could see the misguided logic of their thinking – that a short sell ban could precipitate a massive short-cover rally – but in fact, that never happened. There were just so many long sellers out there that whatever short-cover buying it produced had little effect on the market. In fact, during the short sell ban the S&P 500 fell 18% and financial stocks fell 26%, which is to say that markets did exactly what they were always going to do except that hedge funds were banned from making money out of it.

Well, that wasn't entirely true for the ban only applied to stocks while all the other asset classes continued to trade freely. Plus, I found a way around the ban. You see before the crisis Enay Bank had been the only broker who let us short stocks in mainland China. Officially, that was illegal, but they let us long sell someone else's stock so long as we kept our mouths shut. Well not long after the short sell ban was introduced I got a call from their sales-trader. *"Hey Damon, wanna short some HSBC?"*

"Short sell ban bro. Anyway, there's no borrow out there. Believe me, I looked."

"No man, I got a way around it."

"How's that?"

"We can put on a synthetic short for you."

"On any stock?"

"Yep, in any major market."

"Ok, but how are you offering this to me? Am I long selling someone else's stock?"

"No, this is different."

"So what are the mechanics going on in the background?"

"Easy. We buy every stock in the index except the one you want to short. Then we sell futures against the basket."

"Mmm. That's actually quite brilliant. You'll have to.."

"Yeah, we know, we already built the perfect swap. But look there's going to be some tracking error, and it could be quite big, and you're going to have to swallow that."

"Sounds like a pretty complicated swap."

"Yes, but we'll make it completely transparent for you. Your confirm will have all the individual fills on it."

"How's the basis?"

"It's tracking pretty tight."

"For now, yeah, but who knows what will happen."

"Sure, and that's your risk."

"Ok, so how much are you charging for this."

"Fifteen basis points on the stock and five on the futures."

"Sounds expensive."

"It is, but as far as I'm aware we're the only broker on the street offering it."

"True. I never heard of it before."

"And let's keep it that way."

"You have my word."

I immediately called Jamie and explained the deal. Of course, he'd been net short banks for more than a year, but he'd had me cover his position in HSBC because the borrow had been pulled. You see the short selling ban didn't mean you actually had to cover. It just meant you weren't allowed to short any more stock. But what happened was that after the ban was introduced a lot of long-only funds stopped lending their stock. And in some stocks, like HSBC, you couldn't get any borrow from anywhere. So when I told Jamie I could put on a new synthetic short he didn't even hesitate. *"Ok Damon, do it,"* he said.

"How much?"

"Twenty million dollars' worth."

"Will do."

To my surprise, cash and futures tracked pretty tight, and Jamie made $7m out of that synthetic short over the next three months.

With so much volatility, Phoenix was a total nightmare. That's because every time an Asian futures contract moved +/- 10% the exchange halted trading. But unlike when it happened due to a software error, these halts necessarily occurred just when the market was hysterical. And that meant Phoenix was trading at its highest frequency and in the largest size I'd ever seen. Of course, it didn't understand when an exchange had halted trading, so it kept right on spitting out orders – dreaded purple orders to be sure:

BUY 8 KMZ8 .. BUY 12 KMZ8 .. BUY 16 NIZ8 .. BUY 11 KMZ8 .. BUY 8 NKZ8 .. BUY 9 KMZ8 .. BUY 16 NIZ8 .. BUY 12 NKZ8

Orders, orders and more orders, all coming a split second apart until *Boom!* The GUI crashed and disappeared from screen 2. *"Bad robot!"* I yelled and jumped into an xterm to run the command to relaunch it. Alas, just as it came back up, it crashed again. *"Damn you Phoenix. What have you done this time!"* Then I hit Isaac's speed-dial hoping desperately that he was in a good mood. *"Hi Isaac, it's Damon."*

"Herrr heerrr herrr," he stammered.

'*No. That's not it,*' I thought.

"Heee heee.."

'*No Isaac, this is no laughing matter.*'

"Hhh hiii Daaaa mon." He actually sounded pretty happy. I assumed his P&L was up.

"Isaac, we've just had a reverse crash in Asia. There's talk of an intervention, Fed bailout, or something. Futures are up ten percent. Nikkei and Kospi are locked limit up in. We don't know when they'll reopen."

"Ahh ahh well errr jer jus juuust do oooo arrr doo what the mo mod el wer on wants to loop er dooo emmm yes."

"I don't think so, Isaac. The size is going to be massive. It's a ten percent up day, and the model is long and getting longer. The market has only been closed for ten minutes, and you already want to buy

two billion dollars' worth of futures. Imagine what it might want to do if the market doesn't reopen for an hour."

"Aarrhh mmm ahh yeesss. I sir see. The state mmm statement is jus do oo ha ha half of what it wants. Just doo oo half."

"Understood. I will do half of what it says. But there's something else. The GUI crashed, and I can't get it back up again."

"Errr if then emm ok. I will log en in an fix it. Jus call me whh en when the market oo pens."

Soon enough he'd logged in, cancelled a bunch of orders, and fixed the GUI. And by the time the market reopened I only had to buy half a billion dollars' worth of futures. Later I checked his P&L, and yes, he was happy because he was making money. In fact, despite the chaotic markets that year, or perhaps because of them, Isaac/Phoenix pulled in a cool $800m profit in 2008. I suppose what looked like chaos to the rest of us fit perfectly into his nonparametric models.

That's when I first heard about the *Troubled Asshole Relief Program* (TARP). At first, I thought it was a joke because it alluded to throwing a tarpaulin over the dead body of capitalism. But the banksters were serious and insisted that a bailout was the only way to halt the crisis. That really upset a lot of people for it was the overwhelming public opinion that any bankers who profited from creating and selling toxic debt should go to jail, and the firm they worked for be left to fail.

Soon the day came when the House of Representatives were called to a vote, but most people assumed that since the system was rigged, the bankers would get their money. But then, to the astonishment of the whole world, the House actually rejected the bailout. It was almost like, dare I say it, like a real democracy. Alas, that wasn't what the market expected so the S&P 500 had a hissy fit and fell 8% the next day. I could almost hear it scream out loud, *"Listen up Congress! If you don't give us a bailout we're gonna put on the biggest crash in history!"* Terrified of what would happen if they didn't comply, the Senate rushed through a few token changes and sent it straight back to the house. This time, there was no time for debate. They simply did what they were told and that was that. The will of the people was rejected, the banksters extorted $700bn from the government, and democracy went back to being a joke.

Of course, a whole raft of other crazy shit happened including AIG and WaMu, but they all became a blur to me. Except for one event that I'd never forget. By now Jamie was sitting on a $450m profit from his $2bn banks book. As I explained, he was the rare exception of a man who could successfully trade stocks the old-fashioned way. But all that was tested when Wachovia, in which he held a $200m short line, rallied 57% in one day on merger rumours. I just couldn't believe it. I kept thinking it had to be a bad tick or something. How on earth could a bank, in the midst of a banking panic, be up 57% in one day? But it was true, and no amount of disbelief could change the fact that poor old Jamie lost $114m in one stock in one day. Now any normal person would have thought, *'This is bullshit. It's just a short squeeze. It'll go straight back down again tomorrow.'* But that was just the opposite of Jamie's reaction. Emotion and reason, right and wrong, fair and unfair – it all went right out the window, and in its place he forced upon himself a total acceptance of the card he'd been dealt with no caveats. And so he locked in that loss, the most horrific loss of his career, by covering the entire short that very day. And that was what saved him, for in the days that followed the stock continued to rally hard. Then, far from acting out of fear or doing something rash, he calmly held onto his other shorts, and the broad market started sliding again. With that, his P&L recovered, and he finished out the year with $380m in profit. Still to this day I shake my head in disbelief at his courage to close that short and remain steadfast, while everyone else was losing their minds in the midst of the worst stockmarket smash-up for 70 years.

It didn't surprise me that by the end of 2008 the vast majority of portfolio managers in the firm had lost money. Of course, what really mattered was how the big guys did. But though Jamie and Isaac did well, Nikolai and Avi showed only moderate gains, and unfortunately, they weren't quite enough to offset the losses in the rest of the firm. And so it was that after an incredible 18-year run, Ezra suffered his first down year with a 4% loss. It pained me to concede that even a vampire ghost couldn't trump a black swan.

32. LEFT PERDU

Early in the new year, Bryan was fired from 666. Since he'd been one of the golden boys of the firm, I took it to mean that Ezra was on the warpath to clean house, and no one was safe. By then, most of the final 2008 performance numbers for the hedge fund industry had leaked out. And with the CS/Tremont Index down 19%, the multi-strat sub-index down 24%, and some of our competitors doing even worse (Highbridge -27%, Citadel -55%), the media started highlighting our outperformance. First, it was just an odd mention in some lesser known publications, but then Bloomberg named us in a few articles. It looked to me like someone in the firm was leaking information. But then, to my utter astonishment, an article entitled *Inside Ezra's World* started doing the rounds. In it I read about Perdu having been hit by *massive client withdrawals,* and worse, it referred to us as a *once-secretive firm*. *"Once-secretive!"* I yelled at screen 3. *"What the hell are you talking about?"* So it was that the next day I was happy to receive a firm-wide email explaining the situation.

From: , Ezra

As you may have seen, there is a detailed and for the most part favourable article about us in the current issue of Alpha Reversal magazine. You can never control these things and where they added some drama to the story was to exaggerate our recent redemption calls. So please allow me to set the record straight (but only for internal consumption please):

If you have any questions, please stop by.

Regards,
Ezra

He explained that our redemptions were in fact relatively small and totally manageable, and his message left me feeling comfortable that nothing had changed. Then, without thinking, I forwarded it to my Gmail account so I could read it again when I got home. Why I didn't think of just reading it off of my Blackberry, I can't say, but that seemingly innocuous action led to the end of my career as a hedge fund trader.

It started a few days later when a guy called me from CNBC. He said he was a friend of Craig's – the same Craig who'd once parroted my suggestion live on air that China could revalue the yuan. I thought for a moment and then, finally, I remembered meeting him once before. We caught up that night for drinks at *Le Noir* and after about an hour he invited me to come on his news program. He said if I did a good job then I could be guest host the next time around. I was a bit star-struck, but nonetheless, I shook my head and said, *"No way mate. Strict policy at Perdu. No way in the world I can do that."* He was friendly enough but kept pushing, and the more he did, the more I thought about it. Finally, he mentioned that I'd get to meet Amanda, the blonde Aussie anchor whom everyone in Asia had a crush on. And that she was single. And that she loved traders. I laughed, and we had a good time, and I told him I'd think about it.

A week later I was busy drawing charts on screen 3 when I saw that the S&P 500 had printed a new overnight low of 666. *"Bad market!"* I yelled at the screen. *"What are you doing at six six six!"* Now I'm all but certain that a younger version of me would have jumped right out of my chair at the great coincidence of seeing the market at 666, whilst working for a billionaire vampire ghost whose phone number was 666, and whose firm occupied the top three levels of a Manhattan skyscraper with a giant red 666 on the top of it. Indeed, that turned out to be the exact low of the financial crisis and has since propelled one of, if not the, greatest bull markets in history. If only I'd heeded the omen, then I would've loaded up my personal account with triple leveraged ETFs and been rich forever. Alas, I'd long since committed to believing that the numbers didn't mean anything. Besides, 666 had more malevolent plans for me that day.

The phone rang. It was Edgar, the global head of compliance. I picked up on the second ring, but before I could even say hello he started screaming at me like a mad man. *"Just what are you playing at Damon? Did you really think we wouldn't know if you talked to the press?!"*

"Press?" I asked. *"What are you talking about?"*

"Did you, or did you, not forward Ezra's email to an outside server?" He screamed such that it wasn't really a question anymore.

"I.. I.. it.." Suddenly I found myself emulating Isaac-speak. *"I just sent it to my Gmail account. To MY Gmail account."*

"Yes, we have the evidence. Evidence that you leaked confidential information originating from Ezra that specifically said it was for internal use only! You have abused the firm's technology and effected a major breach of security."

My reaction was one of utter non-belief. *"Edgar, what are you talking about? I sent an email from me to me. No one else has seen that email, and I didn't forward it to anyone, and I can prove it."*

"Prove it? Prove it! Just who do you think you are!" He shrieked as if from the depths of hell, and a searing 666 whirled through my mind. *"You can't prove anything! Once it hits those Google servers you are not in control! NOT IN CONTROL!"* That's when I realised my Gmail account had been hacked and Ezra's email sold to the press. No wonder CNBC tried to put me on

air. They weren't going to ask me about subprime or some other stupid shit. They were going to ask me about Perdu. I could hear Edgar breathing heavily into the phone, and I dared not speak. Then he drew the sword. *"Get Seb on the line."*

"Seb, can you pick up. It's Edgar from 666."

"Ok," said Seb.

"Seb, you there?"

"Hi Edgar, yes I'm here. We're both on the line. Go ahead."

"Damon. Get up from your desk and go to the lobby. Then wait for instructions from Natalie. Seb, stay on the line."

A minute later I stood in bewilderment by the elevators. I didn't understand if I'd just been fired or suspended. But then Natalie got off the phone, walked over, and gave me a big hug. *"Good luck Damon,"* she said.

"What do you mean?" I asked dearly holding on to the last shred of hope.

"Oh, I thought you knew already," she replied in an embarrassed tone.

"Knew what?"

"Well.. umm.. you don't work here anymore. The accounting guys are working on the final numbers for your Singapore tax. I'll need you to hand in your Blackberry, passport, and work permit. You'll have 30 days to leave the country." She looked sad and dropped her eyes to the floor. Then she turned on her heel and headed back to the reception desk.

By the time the elevator had hit the ground floor I'd acknowledged what I'd known all along – at Perdu it was just a matter of time until your number was up. My

10,725 hours at the firm was something to be proud of, no matter how unpalatable was the final hour. And besides, I wasn't the only one with a sad story about losing their job in the GFC. When I got home, I figured I'd resign before they could officially fire me. I mean, Natalie spilling the beans wasn't an official firing as far as I was concerned. So I sat down and wrote out my resignation letter. It was the hardest thing I ever wrote.

Dear Ezra,

After almost four years with the firm I am very disappointed with how I've been treated over the matter of the forwarded email. I have explained the situation and can provide full access to my Gmail account that shows no work emails were ever forwarded to anyone outside the firm.

I feel the firm has behaved inappropriately over what is at worst a technicality. I do not believe I have breached firm policy in a material way, and in the circumstances, I have no alternative but to tender my resignation.

Without an Employment Pass I am facing ejection from the country and severe financial hardships with my apartment. I trust the firm will be prepared to compensate me for the losses I have incurred as a result of my employment.

Regards,
Damon

Of course, it wasn't in Ezra's nature to feel sorry for anyone or think he owed anyone. And so it was an enormous surprise when a few hours later I received a call from 666.

"Hello?" I said cautiously.

"Hi, is that Damon?"

"Yes, it is."

"Please hold for Ezra."

A moment later a click connected us. *"Damon,"* he said in a friendly tone.

"Hi Ezra. I'm surprised to hear from you."

"Well, I wanted to wish you well and say thanks for all your hard work."

"Ah ok, but you know I didn't want to leave."

"Yes, I know, but it's time for you to move on."

Silence.

"Look Damon, things are changin' in the firm, okay? We're gonna take institutional money and that means a huge reorganisation."

"You mean middle management, HR?"

"Yes, all those things. It won't be the same firm in six months' time, and I know that's gonna bother you."

"Yeah well, I just don't believe in that stuff."

"I know, but the world changes and we change with it. Besides, that's not the only reason for you to move on. How old are you now?"

"I just turned thirty."

"And how's your financial situation?"

"Terrible."

"How so?"

"Well, I bought an apartment here last year and now it's fallen thirty percent."

"How much did you pay for it?"

"One point two five million."

"Ok, then I'll buy it off you for one point three. That should cover costs, okay?"

"Ah, yes. It would."

"Right then, good, it saves us havin' to pay them

extortionate Singapore hotel rates."

"Thank you, Ezra. I'm not sure what else to say."

"You wanna be a portfolio manager, don't you?"

"Yes."

"That's why we had to letcha go. It's time for you to get on with your purpose. You with me?"

"Yes, but I don't think I'm ready."

"No one ever is. But wouldn't you say you're more ready then most?"

"I guess so."

"So whaddayuh learn at Perdu? Whaddayuh learn about tradin'?"

"I suppose the most basic lesson is that only a handful of people can actually beat the market."

"Yes, and who are they?"

"Well, I suppose some of them disguise themselves as fundamental portfolio managers.."

"Disguise?"

"Yes, like Jamie. He touts and pretends that stock prices are correlated to a company's audited financial statements. He can talk all day about P/E, EBITDA, FCF/Sales, but he knows they make no sense when it's so easy for them to mislead the outside world."

"So how does he make money?"

"I'm not exactly sure. Maybe you can tell me?"

"Ok. Well in essence, Jamie doesn't drink the cool-aid, okay? He's well aware of the widespread manipulation that defines the system, and he waits patiently for pure tradin' opportunities to present themselves. So unlike your friend Roberto, okay, Jamie doesn't need to invent or disseminate information to help his positions. Instead, he seeks only to be a third-party beneficiary of the manipulation of others."

"And he's as tough as nails," I added.

"Indeed, but so too are the other portfolio managers who thrive at Perdu."

"The quant portfolio managers?"

"Yes. Now Damon, you're in a unique position to take what you learnt and build your own model. And assumin' that's what you do, I'd be happy to consider you for a portfolio manager mandate in the future."

"Wow. That would be incredible."

"Well don't get too excited. You got a long hard road ahead of you. Just come back in five years with a pitch book and a track record and we'll take a look, okay? You know the drill – we might or might not take you on. You might or might not survive. But with your apartment taken care of you should have enough to make a start."

"I.. I.."

"You're welcome."

"Thank you, Ezra."

"Good luck Damon."

Click.

33. GOODBYE SOCIETY

"I must create my own system or be enslaved by another man's."
- William Blake

"Most inventors and engineers I've met are like me – they're shy, and they live in their heads. They're almost like artists. And artists work best alone where they can control an invention's design."
- Steve Wozniak

"It presented me with a window into the infinite. It allowed me to create order out of chaos."
- Stephen King

I wasn't sure where to go next, but it had to be somewhere cheap and where I wouldn't be subject to any outside influences. So I decided on Thailand and became one of the first digital nomads to settle on the island of Koh Samui. For almost two years I stayed in a charming little resort on Chaweng Beach, and it sure was an idyllic life. Next door was a place called *Ark Bar*, and Pat let me leach their Wi-Fi for free. But the signal was weak and every time it rained it stopped working, so I maintained a ready supply of sim cards that I could insert into a dongle and then into the USB port of my laptop. The 2G Internet they delivered might have been slow but at least it was stable. And anyway, it was fast enough for my purposes.

Though I appeared to be the only trader on the island, there were a lot of other expats hanging around, and each had their story about how and why they'd left the first world during the GFC. It seemed that from the vantage of our island sanctuary, many of the problems of first world capitalism became apparent, not least the relentless pursuit of *making it* and the futility of trying to keep up with the Joneses. It was never enough to have a good job and a good car. First world people inevitably wanted a better job and a better car. But we'd moved on from that now. Most of us owned nothing and owed nothing, and that gave us peace of mind.

As a hedge fund trader, the entire fibre of my being had been about being the fastest, since I was the bottleneck between the firm and the market. And over the years I'd gotten so used to the excessive secretion of hormones and neurotransmitters that the roller coaster of stress, fear, aversion, regret, elation, and back again, had seemed normal. But away from the stress of the past, I noticed a massive change in my body. For instance, one day I lost my keys, and in the moment of realisation I looked down at my stomach and waited for it to twitch and flutter like it used to. But nothing happened, and I was left thinking, '*That's so weird. I don't have a physical reaction to stress anymore.*' And without being on the clock, I got to sleeping in for as long as I wanted. So after eight years of six hours per night, I got to sleeping 10 to 12 hours per night. And then all I had to do was stroll 50 meters to the beach and dive into the tranquil warm waters, before grabbing some fruit and a coconut and heading back to my bungalow to work on the model. When I needed a break I went snorkelling, sailing or running on the beach, and at night I ate Thai food, drank San Miguel beer, and made new friends. It was a great life, and I was happy there.

Though I'd have preferred a few more years under my belt, I'd always intended to build my own trading model, and now it was time to do just that. I started by distilling all of the lessons I'd learnt into a broad list of do's and don'ts. Then I taught myself the programming skills necessary to encode it. Then I set about building something that was completely unique.

One of the most common misconceptions people had about financial markets was a belief that if only they had more information, or better information, then they'd stop losing money. Some even harboured a deep-seated jealousy of *the hedge fund guys* or *the insiders* or *the smart money*. So they'd subscribe to all kinds of analysis and reports, and they'd kill themselves with study. But in procuring ever more of it they'd wind up like a dog chasing his tail.. woof woof.. around he goes and back again.. woof woof. Why? Because they couldn't see that we'd long ago moved on from the information age to the age of misinformation. Or worse, they were too egoic to respect epistemology and the limits of human knowledge.

I can't tell you how many times I heard people say, *"Oh I know the media tells lies. But I'm really good at filtering them out."* Little did they know it was nearly impossible to remain objective in the face of the media's targeted exploitation of human biases. For while it was evident that misinformation was manipulation, what was less understood was that even real information was just a poor substitute for knowledge. Financial markets didn't care about whether information was true or not. They only cared about moving in the exact manner that caused the most people to lose the most money. I never figured out what that mechanism was exactly. Perhaps it was some sort of grand conspiracy where the manipulators sent out electromagnetic waves to brainwash everyone into *wanting to buy* or *wanting to sell* at certain times. More likely, it was an elaborate play on the limitations of the human mind.

It was hard to give up on the idea that Information -> Knowledge -> Predictive Power. So how did I do it? Well I stopped asking *why?* for that little word was the problem all along. Instead, I focussed on *what*. Because even though *what* required information, it could never be confused with knowledge. And without *why?* ruling my mind, it was easy to stop searching for the mythical *truth* and *understanding* of financial markets. Instead, I simply agreed to just let the math figure out what to do, and then let the math control the money. Of course, I wasn't the first to let go of the real world and focus purely on quant techniques. Over the years I must have seen twenty or thirty quant portfolio managers fail to build something that worked. But I think where they failed was in never having the chance to fully devote themselves to their own philosophy. That's the thing about people – they always thought they could filter out distractions and brainwashing and propaganda. But no one could, and that's why I chose to live on a secluded island because I knew it couldn't reach me there.

As I ploughed on with the task, I continued to watch the markets. The prices I mean. I never read any text or listened to voices on the TV. That's when I happened upon a nice little arbitrage between Eiger Index and Sema Markets that worked great for a long time. Alas, after I'd taken them for $80k, they got wise and changed their methodology for calculating cash index bets, and with that, the arb disappeared.

Eventually, I reached the final leg of the model building process – brute force optimisation. My little laptop had nowhere near the power to get it done, so I bought an old travel agency, fit it out with 10 PCs, and turned it into an Internet Cafe. It was a good little business, but more importantly, I could optimise the model by running all the computers at night when the shop was closed. Alas, I soon found that even all that power just wasn't enough. That's when I heard about AWS – Amazon's cloud server business – and with that I realised I didn't need rows of physical PCs anymore. How I loved technology. How it always surprised me.

It was almost two years after leaving Perdu that I completed the model. Of course, I had no guarantee that it would work. There was always that worry, deep down inside, that all I'd done was waste a decade of my life on the silly notion of being able to predict the market. And so it was, that with a little bit of fear, and a little bit of hope, I finally clicked my mouse and went live.

34. NOMAD TRADER

I lived a perfect little life in Koh Samui, but eventually, my resort fell into the hands of the worst of capitalism. My bungalow was demolished and replaced by a grossly extended Ark Bar, and what had been a cool little place, became a five block mega-club. Why did profit always have to destroy beauty? Now if it were only about escaping that terrible music, I could have simply moved further down the beach. But the truth was that I was getting restless in paradise. So I bought one of those small suitcases that pass for cabin baggage, and I filled it with clothes and toiletries. Then I crammed my laptop along with a whole range of charges, converters, batteries, and cables into a backpack.

I flew to Phnom Penh and checked into the *FCC Hotel*. I continued up to Siem Reap to *Hotel d'Angkor*, across to *La Residence* in Hue, up to *The Metropole* in Hanoi, across to the *Maison Souvannaphoum* in Luang Prabang, to *The Strand* in Rangoon, then down to the

Eastern & Oriental in Penang. The Wi-Fi might have been sporadic, but no matter where I went I could always buy a 2G sim from 7 Eleven. The one issue I had was that with no fixed address I found it impossible to open a trading account with a real broker. As such I had to keep on trading through my old accounts with the bucket shops in the UK.

Well, one day my alarm went off at the close of Japan, so I pulled out my laptop and logged in just like I did every day at the open and the close. I launched the model, started the feed, ran a calculate-initiate-liquidate cycle, and got the net order size. The model told me to sell 40 lots so I sold 20 and waited for the bucket shop bounce. That was the smart thing to do since they always moved the market against me after I traded. I found that if I split the order into two, I could gain a few ticks of positive slippage on the second order. However, on this occasion, the market fell 1% in a straight line. *"Cheeky bucket shop!"* I said to the screen. Then I hit them for the remaining 20 and logged off.

It was about two hours later when I first heard that a massive Tsunami had hit the east coast of Japan. In fact, the earthquake that triggered it had occurred 15 minutes before the stockmarket had closed, but for whatever reason, stocks hardly moved over the remainder of the session. On the other hand, the futures market figured it out a few minutes after the cash close which happened to be right in the middle of my selling. That was why the market had gapped lower. I suppose the information was slow to disseminate, or else people just didn't think it was a big deal. But they were wrong, for it turned out to be the worst earthquake in Japanese history – a magnitude 9.0 monster that triggered a 40m high tsunami and killed almost 16,000 people.

That was Friday afternoon, and over the weekend that followed, the media showed horrifying images of cars going around in whirlpools as though they were toys in a bathtub. Then it was revealed that the Fukushima Daiichi nuclear power plant had been damaged, though the media were quick to assert that everything was under control. I didn't believe that for a second since I knew the media only said what they were paid to say. Plus, I knew it was the Japanese way to allow people to save face.

On Monday, the Nikkei closed -6.5% and brought me a substantial profit. But then the model told me to double my short and take the book up to maximum exposure. I wasn't influenced by the media's assertion that everything was under control. I didn't think about not wanting to short the market *down here*. I simply hit the bucket shops for another 40 and felt totally comfortable doing what everyone else would have thought was madness. The next morning was a bloodbath. The nuclear power plant had indeed melted down, and the Nikkei dumped -15% at the open. It was the most amount of money I'd ever made in my life. "*Good robot,*" I said with a smile.

The model had me cover the full short that morning, and at the close it had me stay flat again. But a little while later I noticed that the bucket shops had diverged from the real Nikkei futures. Straight away I knew what they were doing – it was a good old-fashioned bucket shop drive. You see the cash index bets they offered were really just OTC derivatives that referenced the real Nikkei futures. But they never had any legal obligation to match them exactly. In fact, they weren't even allowed to use the name Nikkei 225 for trademark reasons, so they used to call them JAPAN225 or JPN225. Years earlier I'd called up and asked about tracking error. *"You don't need to worry,"* the man said. *"We track almost exactly to the underlying. You can check yourself by looking at the charts."* I did just that and agreed that they were damn near perfect. But not on this occasion, for all of a sudden Eiger had moved their market down 75bps – their clients must have been net long – while Sema had ramped their market up by 50bps – their clients must have been net short.

So there I was, with a mountain of winnings bloating my accounts, when a 125bps arb started screaming at me for quick action. Of course, I felt obliged to put on a huge position and make the most of it. But I'd learnt over the years that arbs can go wider than you can imagine, so I spent a good deal of time doing the math and formulating a game plan. Then, as calm as you'd like, I hit Sema and lifted Eiger in the same size at the same time.

For three long days they tried to shake me out. But every time I came close to a margin call I added fresh cash to keep my accounts safe from attack. If they were really clever (or really crooked) they would have rejected my card transactions citing some fake payment problem. Then they could have stopped me out and stolen all my money. However, it all proceeded to plan, when on Friday the two markets converged, I closed out the arb, and I secured my second enormous profit for the week. And with that I had my start.

35. EPILOGUE

Imagine for a moment that central bankers were something other than a self-serving pack of unelected string-pullers. Well, in that case, their primary directive would be that when you invent free money (quantitative easing) you distribute it fairly across society. No need for fancy theories here – you simply deposit it into real people's bank accounts. Then, not only would it be a fair distribution, it would be an economically efficient one too. That's because people, not corporations or conflicted central-planners, would be the ones to decide what to spend it on. After all, that's the essence of capitalism, isn't it? Alas, in less than a decade of prejudicial distribution, central banks have managed to undo decades of progress on income inequality. It's sickening to think about what could have been achieved with all those trillions that went instead to being skimmed by the financial sector or hoarded by the corporations in a sociopathic circle-jerk of the rich.

As for trading, well there are mistakes of causality and mistakes of overconfidence that lead most people astray. Take, for example, the basic assumption that a good economy causes higher stock prices. Or that a lot of uncertainty causes higher volatility. In truth, it might be just the opposite – agents of the state could push stock prices up in order to improve the economy. Or they could push VIX down to reduce market volatility without any regard to actual levels of uncertainly.

And it gets worse for there's no reason to assume causality resides at either extreme. It might, or it might not, and all the logical reasoning in the world won't help you find the answer. This leads to a second more deadly error that people make in financial markets – trading with too much confidence, and therefore, too much leverage. As Robert Rubin said, *"Some people are more sure of everything than I am of anything,"* though I'd suggest changing the first word of that statement to *Most*.

It is only through the pain that comes from having skin in the game that traders learn to overcome their egos and accept the epistemological limits of their knowledge. Unfortunately, such recognition is precisely the opposite of what the media are paid to express. In times of haziness, they profess clarity. In times of uncertainty, they've got all the answers. It doesn't matter if they're right, wrong, or just making it up, because the only skin in the game they have is whether an article reads good and gets the nod of approval from the editor.

Whether it's a result of deliberate deception or just failing at an impossible task, the media has proven itself quite untrustworthy as a disseminator of objective truth. More often than not the fear they peddle is just fabricated to keep up with that silly part of the human brain that seeks it out. War, for example, is a ridiculous charade in which more soldiers kill themselves than get killed by the so-called enemy. And though the world has never been a more peaceful place, the message gets lost in the stream of media neurosis that characterises the modern world. I wish I could explain to the warmongers and the weapons manufacturers that there's another way to appease their bloodlust outside of bombing and murdering. It is to pit themselves against the market where the financial war forever rages on.

I'm just a nomad trader out here on my own, fighting the good fight, and trying to survive. I can't teach you how to trade and neither can anyone else. For though market knowledge and methods might be prerequisite, beyond that lie hurdles few can cross – overcoming your own nature and psychology, and that the entire media and financial worlds are rigged against you. Just remember what Mark Twain said, *"If you don't read the newspaper, you're uninformed. If you read the newspaper, you're misinformed."* And what we said at Perdu, *"Those who say don't know, and those who know don't say."*

Printed in Great Britain
by Amazon